MEMOIRS OF THE OPERA

VOLUME I

Da Capo Press Music Reprint Series

GENERAL EDITOR

FREDERICK FREEDMAN

VASSAR COLLEGE

MEMOIRS OF THE OPERA IN ITALY, FRANCE, GERMANY, AND ENGLAND

By George Hogarth

VOLUME I

DA CAPO PRESS • NEW YORK • 1972

Library of Congress Cataloging in Publication Data

Hogarth, George, 1783-1870.
  Memoirs of the opera in Italy, France, Germany,
and England.
  (Da Capo Press music reprint series)
  Reprint of the 1851 ed.
  First ed., 1838, has title: Memoirs of the
musical drama.
  1. Opera—History and criticism. I. Title.
ML1700.H72 1972   782.1'094   71-166101
ISBN 0-306-70256-8

This Da Capo Press edition of
Memoirs of the Opera
is an unabridged republication of the
1851 edition published in London.

Published by Da Capo Press, Inc.
A Subsidiary of Plenum Publishing Corporation
227 West 17th Street, New York, New York 10011
All Rights Reserved

Manufactured in the United States of America

MEMOIRS OF THE OPERA

VOLUME I

MADAME MARA.

as Armida.

London Published by Richard Bentley, 1851.

MEMOIRS

OF THE OPERA

IN ITALY, FRANCE, GERMANY, AND ENGLAND.

BY GEORGE HOGARTH,

SECRETARY OF THE PHILHARMONIC SOCIETY OF LONDON,
AND HONORARY MEMBER OF THE PHILHARMONIC
SOCIETY OF PARIS.

A NEW EDITION OF THE "MUSICAL DRAMA."

IN TWO VOLUMES.

VOL. I.

LONDON:

RICHARD BENTLEY, NEW BURLINGTON STREET,
Publisher in Ordinary to Her Majesty.
1851.

LONDON:
Printed by Samuel Bentley & Co.,
Bangor House, Shoe Lane.

PREFACE.

The author of the following pages has called them
Memoirs, not a *History*, of the Opera; because,
though he has endeavoured to give a connected,
and (he hopes) tolerably comprehensive view of
the progress of the musical stage, yet he has not
deemed it advisable to treat the subject with that
degree of severity, in regard to form and substance,
which "the dignity of History" might have required.

While he has attempted to trace the origin of
the combination of music with theatrical exhibitions in those countries of Europe which possess a
national opera; to show how the progress of the
opera in one of these countries acted on its progress
in the others; to give an account of the principal
works, belonging to this branch of the drama, which
have appeared in these various countries, and of the
manner in which the production of these works
contributed to the advancement of the art; and
to take a critical view of the qualities and merits
of the most distinguished poets, musicians, and
performers belonging to the lyrical stage; he has
interwoven these particulars with many details,
anecdotes, and circumstances connected with the
opera, calculated to throw light on the lives and
characters of eminent individuals, as well as to

afford glimpses of the state of society and manners in different ages and countries.

The arrangement of such a work as the present must to a certain extent be arbitrary. Where history descends in parallel streams, the narrative must of course follow them in succession, passing from the one to the other, in such a manner as to keep contemporary occurrences as near to each other as possible. Particular points frequently present themselves at which the narrative may be conveniently broken off; but in many instances this must be done, simply because one branch of the history seems to be getting too much in advance of the others. In such instances no two writers would proceed in the same way ; and no way that can be adopted will prevent a certain degree of inconvenience which must arise from the nature of the subject.

In the present Edition the prevailing demand for cheap publication has been consulted in the smaller and less expensive form in which the volumes are printed, and likewise in the condensation of some portions of the text, and the omission of various details, chiefly connected with the earlier history of the Opera, which are not essential in a popular work, having lost much of their interest to the general reader of the present day. The more remarkable events connected with the progress of the Opera, since the publication of these Memoirs, have been included in this new Edition.

CONTENTS

OF

THE FIRST VOLUME.

CHAPTER I.

PAGE

Origin of the Musical Drama—Mysteries, Moralities, and Masques—Allegorical and Mythological Entertainments in Italy during the Fifteenth Century—Intermezzi —Invention of Recitative — Earliest Italian Operas — Monteverde's use of Instruments—First Public Performances at Rome—At Venice—Scroll-pieces—Italian Singers of the Seventeenth Century 1

CHAPTER II.

The Musical Drama in France—Mysteries—Queen of Navarre—Italian Opera brought into France—Italian Companies in Paris—Isabella Andreini—Lulli—Opera-ballets— Quinault—Fontenelle — La Fontaine—Lulli's Music—French Singers—French Musical Drama till the time of Rameau 19

CHAPTER III.

The Musical Drama in England—Music in old English Plays—Masques in the Reigns of Henry VIII. and Queen Elizabeth — Plays performed by the Singing Boys of the Churches — Masques by the Gentlemen of the Inns of Court — Ben Jonson's Masques for the Court of James I. —Manners of that Court — Alfonso Ferabosco — Nicolo Laniere 37

CHAPTER IV.

PAGE

Time of Charles I.—Shirley's Masque, *The Triumph of Peace* — Prynne's *Histrio-mastix* — Milton's *Comus* — Henry Lawes 55

CHAPTER V.

The Commonwealth — Sir William Davenant's Entertainments—His Musical Pieces—First Female Performers—Theatre established after the Restoration—Matthew Lock—*Psyche*—*Macbeth*—Duchess of Mazarin . . 72

CHAPTER VI.

Dryden— *The State of Innocence*—*Albion and Albanius* —Purcell — *Dido and Æneas* — Purcell's Instrumental Music— *The Tempest* 83

CHAPTER VII.

King Arthur—*The Indian Queen*—*Tyrannic Love* . 104

CHAPTER VIII.

The Prophetess — *Bonduca* — *Don Quixote*—Purcell's Songs in various Plays—His Death and Character—Principal Dramatic Singers in his Time — Dryden's *Secular Masque*—Eccles—Jeremy Collier's Attack on the Stage 125

CHAPTER IX.

Degeneracy of the Italian Opera at the commencement of the last century — Marcello's Satire, *Il Teatro alla moda*—Principal Composers of that Period — Scarlatti — Caldara — Lotti — Vivaldi — Improvements effected by them — Dramatic Poets — Apostolo Zeno—Metastasio — His Appearance an Era in the Italian Opera . . 156

CHAPTER X.

PAGE

The early Musical Drama in Germany—German Operas—Introduction of the Italian Opera—German Composers of the Seventeenth Century—Mattheson—Keiser—Arrival of Metastasio 175

CHAPTER XI.

The Italian Opera introduced into England—Battista Draghi—Arrival of Italian Singers—Margherita de l'Epine—Mrs. Tofts—Musical Factions — Opera of *Arsinoe*—*Camilla*—*Rosamond*—Addison and Clayton—Nicolini—*Pyrrhus and Demetrius*—The *Tatler*—Leveridge—*Almahide*—*Hydaspes*—The *Spectator* 181

CHAPTER XII.

Arrival of Handel in England—*Rinaldo*—Addison's Opinions respecting the Italian Opera, and Observations on them 207

CHAPTER XIII.

Life of Metastasio 225

CHAPTER XIV.

Writings of Metastasio—Minor Italian Poets . . 254

CHAPTER XV.

State of the Italian Opera in the earlier part of the Eighteenth Century—Great Composers—Leo—Vinci—Sarro—Porpora—Rinaldo di Capua—Pergolesi—Hasse—Domenico — Scarlatti — Feo — Galuppi — Terradellas — Perez—Logroscino 271

CHAPTER XVI.

PAGE

Great Italian Singers during the above period—Tesi—
Faustina—Cuzzoni—Farinelli—Senesino   .   . 295

CHAPTER XVII.

Caffarelli —Gizziello —Carestini —Guarducci — Durastanti—Guadagni—Mingotti—Gabrielli—Want of Tenor
and Bass Singers 315

CHAPTER XVIII.

The Italian Opera established in England—Handel's
Rinaldo—Calypso and Telemachus—Galliard—Anastasia
Robinson—*Amadigi—The Contrivances*—The Royal Aca-
demy of Music—Its first Composers and Singers—*Rada-
misto—Astarto— Muzio Scevola*—Opera Subscriptions—
Griselda — Bononcini—Ariosti —Neglect of the Italian
Opera—*Tolomeo Ré d' Egitto*—Close of the Royal Academy of Music—Opera conducted by Heidegger and
Handel—New Singers engaged—*Parthenope*—The Nobility's Opera—Opposition to Handel—Ruinous Consequences to Him—He Abandons Dramatic Composition—
Chronological List of his Italian Operas—His Published
Operas—Observations on Handel's Italian Music—Operas
of Contemporary Composers—Decline of the Italian Opera
about the middle of the Eighteenth Century   .   . 343

MEMOIRS

OF THE OPERA

IN ITALY, FRANCE, GERMANY, AND ENGLAND.

CHAPTER I.

ORIGIN OF THE MUSICAL DRAMA—MYSTERIES, MORALITIES, AND
MASQUES—ALLEGORICAL AND MYTHOLOGICAL ENTERTAINMENTS
—IN ITALY DURING THE FIFTEENTH CENTURY— INTERMEZZI—
INVENTION OF RECITATIVE — EARLIEST ITALIAN OPERAS —
MONTEVERDE'S USE OF INSTRUMENTS—FIRST PUBLIC PERFORM-
ANCES AT ROME — AT VENICE — SCROLL-PIECES — ITALIAN
SINGERS OF THE SEVENTEENTH CENTURY.

WE shall not attempt, as many writers have done,
to go back to the days of the Greeks and Romans
in search of the origin of the Musical Drama.
In the ancient tragedy, it appears, the declamation
of the actor was accompanied by certain musical
instruments which regulated the tones of his voice ;
and the stage was occupied by a *Chorus* consisting
of a number of persons, who, though not actually

engaged in the action of the piece, were interested in it, and mingled their reflections or exclamations with the dialogue of the drama. In the modern opera the characters speak in recitative, and there is a chorus; and hence it is inferred that the modern opera has sprung from the ancient tragedy. It is probable that the idea of Recitative was suggested to its inventors by what they had read of the musical declamation of the ancient tragedies; and the chorus of an Italian opera is very analogous, in its functions and connexion with the drama, to the chorus of the Greeks. But the one cannot be said to have been derived from the other : for, before the invention of the opera, the knowledge of the mode of performing the ancient tragedy had been irrecoverably lost by the lapse of a long series of ages.

The modern theatre, of every description, may be traced to those dramatic entertainments which seem to have been common in the darkest periods of the middle ages. Mankind has a natural propensity to mimicry and the representation of feigned characters. Children begin to act as soon as they can speak ; and there is hardly any tribe that is without some notion of inventing and performing plays. When Europe was immersed in ignorance, those fictitious representations called *Mysteries* and *Moralities* were the favourite pastime of all sorts of people. As learning and civilization advanced, those uncouth entertainments gained some degree of refinement and regularity, and acquired something of the form of those ancient dramatic pieces which now came to be known and studied. In this way the modern drama, though originating in the middle ages, may be considered as having received its polish and cultivation from the models of classical antiquity.

It was thus that the opera, as well as the other branches of the drama, took its rise. Songs, choruses, and dances were introduced into the rude exhibitions we have mentioned; and, indeed, continued to form a part of all dramatic representations down to a comparatively recent period. The union of dialogue and action with music, dancing, and pageantry, produced that species of entertainment known by the name of the *Masque*, which enjoyed its greatest favour in the sixteenth and seventeenth centuries, and was the immediate forerunner of the Opera.

This has been the progress of the Musical Drama in all those countries where it now flourishes; but it was in Italy, that it first assumed a distinct form. In that country, the *Mystery*, or religious tragedy, gradually assumed the shape of the *Oratorio*, or sacred musical drama; and the *Masque*, or secular play, intermixed with music and *spectacle*, was converted into the regular opera. The oratorio, as well as the opera, of other countries, was derived from those of Italy.

When the religious dramas, divested of their profanities and grossness, were introduced into the church, and distinguished by the name of oratorios, they were no longer acted, as they had formerly been. The poem was generally in a dramatic form, and, in the performance, each part was allotted to a different singer : but the piece was merely sung and recited, without action, or any of the adjuncts of theatrical representation. Such is the shape which the oratorio has ever since retained. Many oratorios have not a vestige of the dramatic form, even in the structure of the poem, or the composition of the music. The greatest of Handel's oratorios, for instance, *The Messiah* and *Israel in Egypt*, with many others which might be mentioned, are not dramatic in any sense of the word. The oratorio, therefore, is improperly classed under the head of the Musical Drama. It belongs to the Church, not to the theatre ; and a musical drama, on a sacred subject, adapted for theatrical representation (such as Rossini's well-known *Mosè in Egitto*) is not an oratorio, but an opera.

The very term, oratorio, applied to these performances of sacred music, shows that they were connected with the service of the church. The word, derived from the Latin "oratorium" means a chapel containing an altar, where the devout can offer up their prayers. The Italian writers agree in ascribing the origin of the oratorio to SAN FILIPPO NERI, who founded the Congregation of the Oratory at Rome, in the year 1540. This was an order, or establishment of priests, which gradually spread itself all over Italy. It was their practice to render the service of the church as agreeable as possible, in order to attract young people thither, and draw them away from stage-plays and other profane amusements. For this purpose they began by the introduction of canticles, and spiritual songs and choruses ; and afterwards, to increase the attraction, scripture stories and incidents were formed into dramatic poems, written in dialogue, and set to music by the best composers of the time. These productions were recited and sung, with the accompaniment of instruments, before and after the sermon ; so that the attention of the congregation was thus (it was presumed) secured to the religious instructions of the preacher. These pieces were founded on the story of the good Samaritan, the trials of Job, the prodigal son, the annunciation of the Blessed Virgin, and other subjects calculated to excite the feelings or the imagination of the auditory.* They

* An English traveller gives the following account of these performances at Bologna, in 1720. " They have in their churches a diverting piece of devotion, which they call an oratorio. It is a musical drama of two acts, after the manner of the stage operas, with *recitativo* between the songs. The subject is either a scripture story, or a story of some of their saints; generally the last. Between the acts there is a sermon; so timed (I suppose) to secure such of the audience as might be apt to leave the preacher in the lurch, if they were not to have some music to sweeten their mouths with at last. The whole is introduced with a performance somewhat unusual, a *Discorso* (as they term it) spoken by a little boy. We heard two of them. The first was about six years old, who mounted the rostrum with a stately gravity, and, after having saluted the audience, cocked his hat (for they are covered upon such occasions in the churches), and, with a solemn wave of the hand, pronounced, *silenzio !* before he began his discourse.

speedily acquired great popularity; and oratorios became common in the principal churches through-out Italy, where indeed they are regularly per-formed to this day. In Italy the performance of oratorios is still confined to the churches. In this and other countries, they are also performed in public halls, concert rooms, and even theatres: but in no case, not even when the poem is in a dramatic form, is there the slightest approach to dramatic representation.

In the sketch, therefore, which we are about to give of the progress of the Musical Drama, we shall not include the oratorio; considering it as being neither comprehended in our subject nor at all connected with it.

The oldest of those entertainments which ri-pened into the Italian Opera, belong to the fif-teenth contury. They were not performed in public theatres, but in the halls of the great, by whom they were given for the amusement of

The latter could not be above four years old, both by his size and speech, for he could but just speak plain ; him they dressed up in the habit of a priest, and the little creature per-formed to a miracle. The subject of the discourse is taken from the occasion of their meeting. The former was upon the eve of All Souls: charity to our friends in purgatory was the topic. The latter was on the night of the grand procession on account of the plague, which was then at Marseilles : of that, repentance and humiliation was the subject. They teach these little orators, not only the emphasis and accent, but the proper action likewise, which they perform extremely well." — *Wright's Observations in travelling through France, Italy, &c.*

distinguished guests. Their subjects were generally classical, and very like those of a much
later period. Perhaps the *Orfeo* of the celebrated poet and scholar Politian, may be regarded as the lineal progenitor of the Italian
opera. It is to be found in the *Parnaso Italiano ;*
and is a drama in five acts, founded on the ancient
tale of Orpheus and Eurydice. The subject of
the first act is the love of Aristæus, a Thracian
shepherd, for Eurydice, the wife of Orpheus, who,
endeavouring to escape from him, is stung by a
serpent, and dies. The shepherd sings his love
and her cruelty, in a pastoral strain of great
beauty. The second act consists of the lamenta-
tions of Aristæus, accompanied by a chorus of
Dryads, for the death of Eurydice. In the third
act, Orpheus appears, singing in *Latin* heroic
verse the exploits of Hercules. A Dryad tells
him the sorrowful tale of Eurydice's death; and a
satyr follows him to see whether the mountains
are moved by his song. The fourth act contains
the descent of Orpheus into the infernal regions,
his recovery of Eurydice, and her final loss. In
the fifth act, the Thracian women, enraged at his
inconsolable grief and resolution never to love
another, fall upon him and tear him to pieces.
This drama, which is very short, seems intended
to have been wholly sung, the poetry being of a
lyrical kind and finely adapted to the purposes of
music. It must have been written towards the end
of the fifteenth century, as Politian, who is cele-

brated as one of the revivers of learning, died in 1494, at the age of forty.

During the sixteenth century, the Italian drama became gradually more and more regular in its form. In the infancy of the Italian stage, music seems to have been employed in all dramatic pieces. When the dialogue was declaimed, or spoken, choruses were introduced, who sang the prologue and epilogue, and also verses between the acts. By degrees, the musical drama came to be separated from tragedy and comedy: the prologues and epilogues being no longer sung, but merely declaimed, as well as the dialogue; and, in these pieces, the choruses began to be laid aside. But musical *Intermezzi*, or Interludes, were introduced between the acts; and these, though interrupted by the action of the principal piece, were frequently regular dramas themselves; so that a tragedy or comedy, and its interludes, were in truth, two distinct pieces performed in alternate acts. At last, these intermezzi, which were really independent of the pieces to which they were originally joined, were performed by themselves, and received the name of *Operas;* though operas of a light and comic character continued long afterwards to go by the name of *Intermezzi.*

The invention of *Recitative,* from which the existence of the Italian opera may properly be dated, took place in the end of the sixteenth century. The honour of this invention is ascribed to two persons; Jacopo Peri, of Florence, and Emilio

DEL CAVALIERE, of Rome. In the same year, 1597, Peri produced the opera of *Dafne*, and Emilio del Cavaliere the oratorio, *Dell' Anima e del Corpo;* and both of these pieces, too, were published in the same year, 1600. The invention is claimed by both composers, and it seems impossible now to determine which of them has the preferable claim. They both speak of it as an attempt to revive what was imagined to be the musical declamation of the Greeks and Romans. It is next to impossible that two persons should have separately constructed, on so slight a foundation, a musical language so entirely new. One of them must have borrowed it from the other; and it is to be regretted that it cannot be known to whom we are indebted for an invention which forms so remarkable an era in the history of music.*

Peri's opera of *Dafne* was performed in the house of Signor Corsi, a distinguished Florentine *dilet-*

* Burney, with some hesitation, decides in favour of Cavaliere, but on grounds which appear insufficient. He says (vol. iv. p. 87), that " Cavaliere seems better entitled to the invention of narrative music than the Florentine composer, by the very dates of the two dramas, which form an era in the history of the opera or oratorio ; *L'Anima e il Corpo*, the first sacred drama or oratorio, in which recitative was used, having been performed in the oratory of the church of Santa Maria della Vallicella, at Rome, in February, 1600 ; and *Euridice*, the first secular drama, or opera, at Florence, in December of the same year." But the first opera performed at Florence was not *Euridice*, but *Dafne*, which, as we have mentioned above, was performed in 1597 ; and this fact is stated by Burney himself, vol. iv. p. 18. *Euridice* was produced by Peri, after *Dafne*.

tante. The applause which it received induced
RINUCCINI, the poet and the composer, to bring
out in succession two other operas, *Euridice* and
Ariadne. *Euridice* was the first opera which was
performed in public. It formed part of the entertainments given at Florence, on the occasion of
the marriage of Mary of Medicis to Henry IV. of
France, in the year 1600 ; and the poem and music
were published separately the same year. Dr.
Burney found a copy of the music in the library of
the Marchese Rinuccini (a descendant of the author
of the poem), at Florence. He says that the music
was printed in score, and barred, two very uncommon circumstances at the time of its publication ;
that the recitative seemed to have been not only the
model of subsequent composers of early Italian
operas, but of the French operas of Lulli ; but that
though the word *aria* sometimes occurred, it was
difficult to distinguish air from recitative. The
orchestra was placed behind the scenes, and consisted of the stringed instruments known in that
day,—the harpsichord, guitar, and viol da gamba.

CLAUDIO MONTEVERDE, whose name is celebrated
in musical history as one of the greatest discoverers
in the then unknown regions of harmony, composed the opera of *Orfeo,* for the court of Mantua,
in 1607. It was printed at Venice in 1615. The
boldness of this composer's genius is observable in
the great improvement of the orchestra. The number and variety of instruments are greatly increased,
and the voices are not indiscriminately accompanied

by the whole band; but the music performed by
the several singers is accompanied by instruments
of various kinds, specially assigned to each character. Thus, the Genius of Music, who speaks the
prologue, is accompanied by two *gravicembani*, probably misprinted for *clavicembali*, or harpsichords;
Orpheus by two *contrabassi di viola*, or bass-viols;
Eurydice by ten *viole di brazzo*, or tenor viols; a
chorus of nymphs and shepherds by an *arpa doppia*,
or harp with double strings; Hope by two *violini
piccoli alla Francese*, a phrase which supports the
claim of the French to the invention of the violin;
Proserpina by three *bassi da gamba*, an instrument
which has given place to the violoncello; and Pluto
by four trombones. The overture is a very short
prelude in harmony of five parts, for a trumpet
and other instruments, which is directed to be
played three times before the rising of the curtain.
Then the prologue is delivered in recitative; its
purport being to explain the argument of the piece
and bespeak the attention of the audience. The
opera begins by a speech in recitative by a shepherd, followed by a chorus in five parts, accompanied by all the instruments. Other choruses are
directed to be accompanied in different ways—by
guitars, violins, and flutes. There are no airs for a
single voice, but recitatives, choruses, trios, and
duets make up the piece, which concludes with a
dance to a tune called a *moresca*, probably an
original Moorish air. It is a lively strain, with a
well-marked but peculiar rhythm, four times re-

peated, and ingeniously carried into different major and minor keys.*

Monteverde's management of his orchestra, in the very infancy of this branch of the art, is worthy of particular notice; as he appears to have anticipated the principle of instrumentation which has been since adopted by the greatest dramatic composers, though it is now too much disregarded. In an Italian opera of the modern school, every instrument in the band is kept constantly at work, from the overture to the finale. The most tender and pathetic air or duet is accompanied, as well as a joyous or martial chorus, by violins, tenors, violoncellos, double-basses, flutes, oboes, clarinets, bassoons, horns, trumpets, trombones, and drums. What can be more absurd than this? The variety and effect of the orchestra are destroyed by such an indiscriminate and unmeaning use of all its resources. It was not thus that Gluck and Mozart, the models of dramatic instrumentation, employed the powers of the orchestra. Look into the opera scores of these great masters, and we shall hardly find two scenas, or two movements, accompanied in the same manner. The different kinds of instruments are used in every variety of combination, so as to produce an endless diversity of effect, and to allow the united strength of the orchestra, when called into action, to produce its full impression on the audience. That system required learn-

* For specimens of the music of this and other primitive Italian operas, see the Histories of Burney and Hawkins.

ing, skill, and delicacy ; the method now in vogue
is a mere cloak for ignorance.

The first public performance of musical pieces
in a regular theatre, took place at Venice, in 1637,
when the opera of *Andromeda*, written by BENE-
DETTO FERRARI, and composed by FRANCESCO
MANELLO, was brought upon the stage, in the
theatre of Santo Cassiano, in a splendid manner,
at the expense of the poet, who, for that purpose,
collected a company of the best singers in Italy ;
a remarkable instance of spirit and enterprise.   In
the following year, *La Maga Fulminata*, by the
same poet and composer, was performed in the
same manner, and at the expense of the former.
Between 1641 and 1649, there were upwards of
thirty different operas performed in the several
theatres of Venice, the composers of which were
Monteverde, Manello, Cavalli, Sacrati, Ferrari,
Fonte, Marazzoli, and Rovetta.

The most celebrated opera of that period was
the *Orontea* of MARC' ANTONIO CESTI, which was
first performed at Venice in 1649, and appears to
have kept possession of the stage, in various cities,
for nearly forty years.   The music of these early
operas is almost all lost, as very few of them were
printed ; but Dr. Burney gives a scene from this
opera of *Orontea*, which was found in the music-
book of the celebrated painter, Salvator Rosa, in
his own handwriting.   This scene, when compared with the specimens of Peri or Monteverde,
exhibits a striking improvement in dramatic music.

The air, which is in E minor, and in the time of three minims, is flowing, expressive, and modern in its effect, from the free use of the diminished seventh both in the melody and harmony. The recitative is *parlante*, and divested of the formal closes used by the older composers : indeed it differs very little from the recitative of the present day. And the concluding air, in D major, is bold and spirited, with a firm moving bass very much in the manner of Handel. Of Cesti little more is known, than that he was admitted into the Pope's chapel as a tenor singer in 1660, and produced several other operas, which had great success. He composed a great number of cantatas, many of which are still extant. Cavalli was at this period a prolific composer of operas, the most celebrated of which are *Giasone* and *Erismena*. From what remains of his music, it seems to have been inferior to that of Cesti.

Venice appears to have taken the lead among all the cities of Italy, in respect to the musical drama. Between 1637, when *Andromeda* was produced, and 1700, we are told by Riccoboni, that three hundred and fifty operas were performed there. Operas were generally represented daily, and in six different theatres, all open at once. There was no public opera-house at Rome until 1671, nor at Bologna till 1680. In that year we have an account of the performance of the opera of *Berenice*, composed by Domenico Freschi, at Padua, in a style of splendour which reduces to insignificance the utmost achievements of scenic display, even in the present age of *spectacle*. In this opera (of the poetical or musical qualities of which there is no record) there were choruses of a hundred virgins and a hundred soldiers; a hundred horsemen in steel armour, a hundred performers on trumpets, cornets, sackbuts, drums, flutes, and other instruments, on horseback and on foot; two lions led by two Turks, and two elephants led by two others; Berenice's triumphal car drawn by four horses, and six other cars with spoils and prisoners drawn by twelve horses. Among the *scenes* in the first act, was a vast plain with two triumphal arches; another with pavilions and tents; a square, prepared for the entrance of the triumphal procession, and a forest for the chase. In the second act there were the royal apartments of Berenice's temple of vengeance; a spacious court, with a view of the prison, and a covered way, along which passed a train of carriages. In the third act there were, the royal dressing-room, magnificently furnished; stables containing a hundred live horses; a portico adorned with tapestry; and a superb palace seen in perspective. In the course of the piece there were representations of hunting the boar, the stag, and the bear. And to conclude the whole, an enormous globe descended from the sky, which divided itself into lesser globes, suspended in the air, on which were seen allegorical figures of Fame, Honour, Nobility, Virtue, and Glory. We find many descriptions of exhibitions of this kind, chiefly at Venice, but none of them seem to have rivalled the splendour of *Berenice.*

Our countryman Evelyn, in his *Diary,* gives some notices of the state of music at Venice in the middle of the seventeenth century. In 1645, he says, " This night, having with my Lord Bruce taken our places before we went to the opera, where comedies and other plays are represented in recitative musiq by the most excellent musicians, vocal and instrumental, with variety of sceanes painted and contrived with no lesse art of perspective, and machines for flying in the aire, and other wonderful motions ; taken together it is one of the most magnificent and expensive diversions the wit of man can invent. The history was Hercules in Lydia ; the sceanes changed thirteen times. The famous voices, Anna Rencia, a Roman, and reputed the best treble of women ; but there was an eunuch who in my opinion surpassed her; also a Genoese that sung an incomparable bass. They held us by the eyes and eares till two in the morning." After giving a description of the pastimes during the carnival of 1646, he says, " The comedians have liberty, and the operas are open ; witty pasquils are thrown about, and the mountebanks have their stages at every corner. The diversion which chiefly took me up was three noble operas, where were excellent voices and musiq, the most celebrated of which was the famous Anna Rencia, whom we invited to a fish dinner after four daies in Lent, when they had given over at the

theatre. Accompanied with an eunuch whom she
brought with her, she entertained us with rare
musiq, both of them singing to an harpsichord. It
growing late, a gentleman of Venice came for her
to show her the galleys now ready to sayle for
Candia. This entertainment produced a second,
given us by the English consul of the merchants,
inviting us to his house, when he had the Genoeze,
the most celebrated base in Italy, who was one of
the late opera band. This diversion held us so
late at night that, conveying a gentlewoman who
had supped with us to her gondola at the usual
place of landing, we were shot at by two carbines
from out another gondola, in which was a noble
Venetian and his courtezan unwilling to be disturbed, which made us run and fetch other weapons,
not knowing what the matter was, till we were
informed of the danger we might run by pursuing
it further."

The Italian singers, from the very infancy of
the musical drama, attained that superiority over
those of other countries which they have always
preserved. Della Valle, who wrote in 1640, com-
memorates a number of vocal performers, of both
sexes, who flourished during his time. LEONORA
BARONI, of Mantua, was the most celebrated
singer of that period. She is not only spoken of
in enthusiastic language by Della Valle, but is described by Bayle, in his Dictionary, as having been
one of the finest singers in the world. A whole
volume of poems was published in her praise with

this title, "Applausi poetici alle glorie della Signora Leonora Baroni;" and, among the Latin
poems of Milton, there are no fewer than three
entitled, "Ad Leonoram Romæ canentem." Milton frequented the musical entertainments of the
Cardinal Barberini; and it was there, no doubt,
that he heard this lady sing.

CHAPTER II.

THE MUSICAL DRAMA IN FRANCE—MYSTERIES—QUEEN OF NA-
VARRE — ITALIAN OPERA BROUGHT INTO FRANCE — ITALIAN
COMPANIES IN PARIS—ISABELLA ANDREINI—LULLI—OPERA-
BALLETS—QUINAULT—FONTENELLE—LA FONTAINE—LULLI'S
MUSIC—FRENCH SINGERS—FRENCH MUSICAL DRAMA TILL THE
TIME OF RAMEAU.

In France, as in Italy, the regular musical drama was preceded by mysteries, masques, and other exhibitions, performed in the churches on solemn religious festivals, or in the palaces of princes, for the amusement of their visitors and guests. Many of these are described by French writers; but they are so similar to those which have been already mentioned as prevailing in Italy, that it is unnecessary to enter into any details respecting them. Music generally made a part of them, as well as action, machinery, and dancing.

The celebrated Marguerite de Valois, queen of Navarre, composed mysteries and moralities, which were represented by the ladies of her court. Several of her dramatic pieces are contained in the collection of her works, published in 1547, under the punning title of *Marguerites de la Marguerite des Princesses, très-illustre Reyne de Navarre.*

They consist of four mysteries, a comedy, and a farce.

The French writers admit that they owe the establishment of the opera to the Italians. Rinuccini, who went to France in the suite of Mary of Medicis, on her marriage with Henry IV., first introduced Italian music into that country. The first Italian company of performers appeared in Paris, in 1577. They attracted such multitudes (says an old writer), that the four best preachers in Paris had not such numerous assemblies when they preached. Another Italian company was brought to Paris, by Cardinal Mazarin, during the minority of Louis XIV., in the year 1645. But Italian operas seem to have been little encouraged at that time. French pieces called *ballets*, though they appear to have had words, as well as dancing and music, were the favourite amusement of the court; and it was in composing the music of these pieces, that LULLI first brought his talents into notice.

This celebrated musician, the son of a Tuscan peasant, was born in 1633. Having shown a disposition for music, he received some instructions in the rudiments of the art, from a priest. The Chevalier de Guise, when on his travels in Italy, had been requested by Mademoiselle de Montpensier, a niece of Louis XIV., to procure for her a handsome Italian boy, as a page; and, happening to see young Lulli, at Florence, he chose him for that purpose, on account of his wit and vivacity, and his skill in playing on the guitar. The lady, however, not liking his appearance, for he was far from handsome, sent him into her kitchen, where he was made a *sous-marmiton,* or under-scullion. At this time he was ten years old.

In his leisure hours, he used to be constantly scraping on a wretched violin which he had contrived to pick up; and some person of taste, who happened to hear him, having told the princess that he had a great talent for music, she had him regularly taught to play upon the violin. He was soon admitted into the king's band, and so much distinguished himself as a musician, that he was placed at its head, and employed to compose the music of the court ballets, in which the king and other great personages used to dance. One of these pieces was *Alcidiane,* performed in 1658, in which his majesty himself was one of the dancers. The performance not being ready to begin at the proper time, the king sent message after message to Lulli, to tell him to make haste. At last he sent to say he was weary of waiting, and desired that the piece should begin immediately. The messenger told Lulli that the king was out of all patience and in a violent passion : but the musician, wholly intent on his preparations, said coolly, " His majesty can wait." The king laughed at the answer, and quietly waited till Lulli was ready. The composer preserved during his life this plain and blunt humour, and used a freedom of speech which frequently annoyed the courtiers, but never seems to have offended the king himself, whose favour for Lulli was uninterrupted.

These opera-ballets continued to be the entertainment of the court for a few years longer, till the regular French opera derived its being from the celebrated Quinault.

PHILIP QUINAULT was born at Paris in 1636; but we have no account of his family. His genius for poetry displayed itself at an early age; and, before he was twenty years old, he had written several comedies, which were performed with success. His friends, however, having wisely advised him not to trust to poetry for a livelihood, he placed himself under an eminent advocate, and made himself capable, in a few years, of exercising that profession. But he still continued to produce a series of dramatic pieces, chiefly tragedies, which were well received by the public; though some of them were severely attacked by the critics, especially Boileau, who for some unexplained reason, seems to have taken a violent dislike to him. Boileau was much censured, even in his own time, for this conduct; and it is now universally admitted that he did Quinault great injustice. His famous couplet,

> " Si je pense exprimer un auteur sans defaut,
>   La raison dit Virgile, et la rime Quinault,"

as well as his

> " L'or de Virgile, et le clinquant du Tasse."

are quoted now only as instances of the sacrifice of truth to point and antithesis.

It was not, however, till Quinault became associated with Lulli in the composition of operas that he produced those pieces which have rendered his name illustrious.

Quinault, notwithstanding his reputation as a poet, did not abandon the profession of the law. He married the rich widow of a merchant, and afterwards purchased the office of an auditor of the chamber of accounts, the duties of which he performed till his death. He died on 29th November 1688. It is said that, during his last illness, he was extremely penitent, on account of the voluptuous tendency of various parts of his writings.

Quinault's dramatic works are well known to the readers of French poetry. All his lyrical dramas are full of beauties; but *Atys*, *Phaëton*, *Isis*, and *Armide*, have been considered as the best. *Atys*, which was produced in 1676, was the finest opera that had yet appeared, and had an astonishing success. On the day of its first performance, the doors were forced, at ten o'clock in the morning, by persons who wished to secure places, and, before mid-day, the theatre was completely crowded. It did not disappoint the expectations of the public; though it affords several specimens of that " morale lubrique " so justly censured by Boileau;* as in these lines of a duet,

---

* " Et tous ces lieux communs de morale lubrique,
   Que Lulli rechauffa des sons de sa musique."

" Il faut souvent, pour être heureux,
   Qu'il en coûte un peu d'innocence."

The king having asked Madame de Maintenon which was her favourite opera, she said it was *Atys.* " Ah," said the gallant monarch, " Atys is a happy man." It was at a performance of this opera that Boileau said to the boxkeeper, " Put me in a place where I shall not be able to hear the words ; I like Lulli's music very much, but have a sovereign contempt for Quinault's verses." Notwithstanding the dislike of the Aristarchus of the age, however, *Atys* continued to please the public, and for a long time kept possession of the theatre.

Armide was produced in 1686, and was the last of Quinault's works. It is said that Lulli insisted on his writing the last act five times over ; and that for this reason he conceived a dislike to writing for the stage. Others ascribe to devotion his resolution to abandon dramatic composition. This opera was at first coldly received, the music not having pleased so much as usual. Lulli, who was so passionately fond of his own compositions, that (as he himself confessed) he would have killed any one who said they were bad, had it performed for his own gratification, he himself forming the whole audience. This odd circumstance having been reported to the king, he thought that the opera could not be bad if Lulli himself had so good an opinion of it. Having, therefore, ordered it to be performed before him, he was charmed with it ; and then both the court and the public

changed their opinion of its merits. Nothing can
be finer than the subject of this opera, affording,
as it does, ample scope for impassioned poetry,
striking situations, and the accessories of beautiful
scenery and stage decorations. On this account it has
often been chosen by dramatists, but none of them
appear to have treated it so happily as Quinault.
The last scene in the second act, consisting of the
soliloquy of Armida, when she is about to stab
Rinaldo in his sleep, and is prevented by the
sudden influence of a passion of which she is as yet
unconscious, is exquisitely beautiful. The fourth
act is comparatively feeble ; but the fifth, which
(unlike the operas of the present day) is terminated
by a soliloquy of the heroine, is full of magnificent
poetry. It was by this noble production that
Quinault terminated his brilliant career; and he
had the uncommon felicity of making his last work
his masterpiece. *Armide* was afterwards reset by
Rameau; and, more recently, by Gluck, with
whose music it is still performed in France and
Germany.

During the time that Lulli was employed in
composing the music of Quinault's operas, he
appears to have set only two others, *Psyche* and
Bellerophon, both by Fontenelle, the first of which
was performed in 1678, and the second in 1679.
They are both to be found in the works of that
author. Lulli's last opera was *Acis et Galatée*,
written by a forgotten poet of the name of Cam-
pistron. It was performed in 1687.

Lulli, in the course of his musical career, had become so great a favourite of the king, that his majesty had granted him letters of nobility : a sort of distinction somewhat similar to that of being knighted in this country. Somebody, by way of mortifying Lulli, told him that it was lucky for him that the king had exempted him from the necessity of obtaining his nobility in the common way, by having first been appointed one of his majesty's secretaries—an appointment which he could not have got, as the king's secretaries would not have received him into their body. Lulli was piqued at this, but said nothing for some time. In 1681, Molière's *Bourgeois Gentilhomme*, containing a burlesque Turkish interlude, with music composed by Lulli, was performed before the court at St. Germain. Lulli himself played the part of the Mufti, which he acted and sang to the admiration and delight of the audience. The king, who had been excessively amused, paid Lulli many compliments on his performance. Lulli seized the opportunity : " Please your majesty," he said, " I have been anxious for the honour of being one of your secretaries, but I understand they would not receive me." " Not receive you ? " said Louis ; " upon my word it would be doing them a great deal of honour. Go and talk to the chancellor about it." Lulli went immediately to M. le Tellier ; and the report spread that the musician was going to be made a royal secretary. There was a great commotion, and loud complaints among the people in office that a player and buffoon should be admitted into their honourable fraternity. Even M. Louvois, the minister, taxed Lulli with his impudence, which, he said, by no means became a man who had no other recommendation but that of making people laugh. " Why, what the devil," cried Lulli, " you would do as much, if you were able ! " The king's will, however, was expressed in a way which silenced all opposition, and Lulli got the appointment. On the day of his reception, he gave a grand dinner to the official gentlemen whom he had joined. In the evening his guests went to the theatre, when his *Triomphe de l'Amour* was performed, and it was amusing to see, seated on the benches nearest the stage, two or three rows of grave personages, in black cloaks and big wigs, listening, with serious faces, to the minuets and gavots of their new colleague the musician. M. de Louvois himself soon laid aside his ill-humour; and next time he met Lulli in the midst of a crowd of courtiers at Versailles, he called out to him laughingly, " Good day, brother ! " Lulli, besides being a distinguished artist, was wealthy, and of irreproachable character : and, as the post was one which it was customary to give as a sinecure, and a mere mark of honour, it is impossible to think that, in his case, it was improperly bestowed.

The king having had a dangerous illness in 1686, Lulli composed a *Te Deum* on his recovery, which was performed in the church of the Feuillans, on the 8th of January, 1687. In beating the time with a cane, he struck his toe so severely that the hurt, probably from a bad habit of body, caused a mortification. In place of having the part amputated, which might have saved him, he listened to the promises of some quacks who undertook to cure him without this expedient; and the Princes de Vendôme, who had a great regard for him, offered them four thousand pistoles if they cured him, and lodged the money in the hands of a banker. But all their attempts were vain; and his case became evidently hopeless. His confessor refused to give him absolution, unless he burned his opera of *Achille et Polixene*, which he was then preparing for the stage. He consented, and the manuscript was committed to the flames. Some days afterwards, when he had seemed a little better, one of the young princes came to see him. " What, Baptiste," cried the prince, " have you been such a fool as to burn your opera?"—" Hush, my lord," whispered Lulli, " I have got a copy of it." It is said, however, that in his last moments he showed sincere penitence and a strong sense of religion. He died on the 22nd March, 1687, in the 54th year of his age. He was plain in his appearance and rough in his manners, but honest and good-natured. His greatest failing was his fondness for wine and money. He left a fortune of 630,000 livres, an enormous sum in those days. He married the daughter of Michael Lambert, an eminent musician, by whom he had three sons and three daughters, whom he left in possession of sufficient wealth and powerful friends. Two of his sons were also musicians. They composed, in conjunction, the music to the opera of *Zephyr et Flore*, performed in 1688; also, two other operas, called *Orphée et Alcide*.

Between the death of Lulli and the end of the century, several operas were composed by Colasse, a musician of small reputation. One of these was *Thetis et Pelée*, written by Fontenelle, and performed in 1690 with little success. Colasse also composed the music of *Astrée*, a tragic opera, written by La Fontaine, and produced in 1691. A characteristic anecdote is related of this celebrated poet. At the first performance of this piece, he was sitting in a box behind some ladies who did not know him. They heard him constantly saying to himself, "wretched! detestable! trash!" until at length one of them, weary of his repeated murmurs, said to him, "O, sir, the piece is by no means bad—the author is a man of genius, the famous M. de la Fontaine."—"Well, ladies," said he, very coolly, "the piece is not worth a farthing, and this M. de la Fontaine whom you talk of is a blockhead—he tells you so himself." At the end of the first act he went away, and, going into an adjoining coffee-house, sat down in a corner and fell fast asleep. A gentleman of his acquaintance coming in, and seeing him, exclaimed, "What, M. de la Fontaine here! should he not be at the first representation of his opera?"—"I am just come from it," said La Fontaine, rousing himself and yawning. " I sat out the first act, but was so completely sick of it that I could not stay any longer. Really, the Parisians have a wonderful stock of patience!"

About this time was performed an opera ballet, called *Arethusa*, written by Danchet, and composed by Campra, one of Lulli's imitators. It had not much success: and as the author and composer, seeing it likely to fail, were considering how they could support it by rendering it more attractive, " I know but one way," said a friend who heard their conversation, — " you must lengthen the dances and shorten the ladies' petticoats."

Lulli was the only French dramatic composer of any reputation, prior to the end of the seventeenth century. He may properly be called a French dramatic composer, notwithstanding his Italian birth: for, having spent his life in France, from the time he was ten years old, it is impossible to imagine that his taste or style could have been affected by the fleeting musical impressions he had received in his childhood. Voltaire, who wrote with equal confidence, if not with equal knowledge, upon all subjects, has some criticisms on Lulli's music, which may be considered not so much his own opinions as those which he was accustomed to hear. " It may be observed," he says, " that when Lulli, the true father of French music, came into France, the dramatic music of Italy was of the same grave, noble, and simple kind as that which we still admire in the recitatives of Lulli. And

nothing can more resemble these recitatives than
Luigi's famous *motet*, composed and universally
admired in Italy about the same time ; *Sunt breves
mundi rosæ.* However, the poetry of Quinault
animated the musis, more than the music of Lulli
animated the words. The genius of two such
men, with great acting, was necessary to form such
an exhibition, in some parts of *Atys, Armide,* and
Roland, as neither antiquity nor any contemporary
people ever knew. The airs are not equal to the
recitatives of these great scenes. They are short
simple tunes, more in the style of our Noëls
(Christmas Carols) and Venetian ballads, than
opera songs. But such was the taste of the times.
And the more artless the music, the more easily it
was remembered." These remarks set out with
the evident absurdity that Lulli had formed his
style of French recitative on the dramatic music of
Italy when he left that country at ten years old.
Voltaire finds a resemblance between Lulli's recitatives and a *motet* of an Italian composer of that
day : but the motet was a hymn, or anthem, for
the church, in harmony of many parts, and had no
sort of affinity to dramatic music. It is true that
Lulli's recitative, which is a sort of drawling
psalmody, tolerable to no ears but those of French-
men, may have some resemblance to church music;
but it certainly is as unlike as possible to the
speaking recitative of Cavalli or Cesti. As to
Lulli's airs, so much undervalued in comparison
with his recitatives, any musician of the present

day, who makes this comparison, will form an opposite opinion. They are short and simple, but we have found some of them exceedingly smooth, flowing, natural, and more agreeable to modern taste than the airs of Rameau, the idol of the French at the time when Voltaire wrote these strictures.

Lulli contributed greatly to the improvement of instrumental music. He appears to have been the inventor of the overture to dramatic pieces, and was so successful in this species of composition, that even Handel, in his opera-overtures, took him for his model. He also increased the power of the orchestra by making use of kettle-drums and side-drums in the accompaniments of his choruses.

Our opinion of Lulli's genius must be enhanced by considering the wretched state of vocal and instrumental performance in his time. When he was placed at the head of the king's band, they could play nothing but what they had learned by heart; and it must have been by great exertion that he made them capable of executing the overtures and accompaniments of his operas. His vocal performers were equally uninformed and ignorant; and he not only taught them to sing and to act, but was even obliged to give lessons to the dancers. He was the only instructor of the celebrated La Rochois, who was the *prima donna* in most of his pieces; and his other singers must have been equally ignorant, as they could have received no previous education in an art which he may be said, in so far as regards France, to have called into existence.

Among the singers of that period, who are mentioned by French writers, there are none whose names are worthy of being preserved on account of their talents. One of them, however, La Maupin, the successor of La Rochois, may be noticed on account of her wild and lawless character, and the strangeness of her adventures. She was born in 1673, and married at a very early age, but soon ran away with a fencing master, from whom she learned the use of the small sword. After remaining for some time at Marseilles, where she narrowly escaped the punishment of being burnt alive for setting fire to a convent, she went to Paris, appeared on the opera stage at the age of two-and-twenty, and was for a considerable time the reigning favourite of the day. Having on some occasion been affronted by Dumeni, a singer, she put on male attire, watched for him in the Place des Victoires, insisted on his drawing his sword and fighting her, and, on his refusing, caned him and took his watch and snuff-box. Next day, Dumeni having boasted in the opera-house that he had defended himself against three men who had attempted to rob him, she told the whole story, and produced his watch and snuff-box in proof of her having chastised him as a coward. Thevenard, another singer of note, was nearly treated in the same manner, and had no other way of escaping, but by publicly begging her pardon, after hiding

himself in the Palais Royal for three weeks. At a
ball given by Monsieur, the brother of Louis XIV.,
she appeared in men's clothes, and, having behaved
impertinently to a lady, was called out by three of
her friends. Instead of avoiding the combat, by
discovering her sex, she drew her sword and killed
all the three; and then, returning very coolly to
the ball-room, told the story to Monsieur, who
obtained her pardon. After some other adventures,
she went to Brussels, where she became mistress
of the Elector of Bavaria. This prince, having
quitted her for the countess of Arcos, sent her by
that lady's husband a purse of 4,000 livres, with an
order to quit Brussels. But this singular heroine
threw the purse at the count's head, telling him it
was a recompense worthy of such a contemptible
scoundrel as himself. She afterwards returned to
the Parisian stage, which she left in 1705. The
conclusion of such a life is not the least extraordinary part of it. She became at last very devout;
and, having recalled her husband, from whom
she had been long separated, lived with him in
a pious manner till her death, in 1707, at the
age of thirty-four. Such is the history of this
woman, given by Laborde and other writers;
and, strange as it is, there seems no reason for
doubting its truth.

Addison gives a lively description of the French
opera at the beginning of the eighteenth century.
" The music of the French," he says,* " is indeed

* Spectator, No. 29.

very properly adapted to their pronunciation and accent, as their whole opera wonderfully favours the genius of such a gay airy people. The chorus in which that opera abounds, gives the parterre frequent opportunities of joining in concert with the stage. This inclination of the audience to sing along with the actors, so prevails with them, that I have sometimes known the performer on the stage do no more, in a celebrated song, than the clerk of a parish church, who serves only to raise the psalm, and is afterwards drowned in the music of the congregation. Every actor that comes on the stage is a beau. The queens and heroines are so painted that they appear as ruddy and cherry-cheeked as milkmaids. The shepherds are all embroidered, and acquit themselves in a ball better than our English dancing-masters. I have seen a couple of rivers appear in red stockings; and Alpheus, instead of having his head covered with sedge and bulrushes, making love in a fair full-bottomed periwig and a plume of feathers; but with a voice so full of shakes and quavers, that I should have thought the murmurs of a country brook the much more agreeable music. I remember the last opera I saw in that merry nation was the *Rape of Proserpine*, where Pluto, to make the more tempting figure, puts himself in a French equipage, and brings Ascalaphus along with him as his *valet de chambre*. This is what we call folly and impertinence; but what the French look upon as gay and polite."

The French musical drama continued in the state which has now been described till nearly the middle of the last century. The stage was supplied with the productions of Lulli, and his imitators, Colasse, Campra, Destouches, and others; till a new era was created by the appearance of the operas of RAMEAU.

CHAPTER III.

THE MUSICAL DRAMA IN ENGLAND — MUSIC IN OLD ENGLISH PLAYS—MASQUES IN THE REIGNS OF HENRY VIII. AND QUEEN ELIZABETH—PLAYS PERFORMED BY THE SINGING-BOYS OF THE CHURCHES — MASQUES BY THE GENTLEMEN OF THE INNS OF COURT—BEN JONSON'S MASQUES FOR THE COURT OF JAMES I. —MANNERS OF THAT COURT—ALFONSO FERABOSCO — NICOLO LANIERE.

THE modern drama, in England, as in other countries, may be traced to the Mysteries, or spiritual representations, of the middle ages. The history of these pastimes of our forefathers, in which they combined devotion with amusement, is exceedingly curious and interesting, and has occupied the pens of many eminent writers: but the most comprehensive and entertaining account which has been given of them, is contained in Mr. Collier's valuable *History of the English Theatre.* Mr. Collier objects to the appellation *Mysteries,* as applied to these old English religious shows, on the ground that it was not given to them in their own times; and he, therefore, substitutes the term *Miracle-plays.* But we are not convinced of the necessity of disusing a name which they have long received, in common with those of Italy, France, Germany,

Spain, and by every writer who has had occasion to speak of them.

Music, which was always a part of those ancient exhibitions, continued to be introduced into the more regular dramas which succeeded them. Down to the seventeenth century, and including a considerable portion of it, there are few of our tragedies and comedies in which there is not vocal or instrumental music. In *Gammer Gurton's Needle*, the first English regular comedy, written in the year 1551, there is a song (the well-known Bacchanalian ditty, " I cannot eat but little meate,") and an instance of the use of music between the acts ; for, at the end of the second act, one of the characters, leaving the stage, says to the musicians,

> " Into the town will I, my friendes to visit there,
>   And hither straight again to see th' end of this gere.
>   In the meantime, fellowes, pype up your fidles.
>   I say, take them,
>   And let your friendes hear such mirth as ye can make
>   them."

In the tragedy of *Gorboduc*, or, *Ferrex and Porrex*, written by Lord Buckhurst, in 1561, there are directions for exhibitions of dumb-show before each act; the first being accompanied by the music of violins, the second by the music of cornets, the third by the music of flutes, the fourth by the music of hautboys, and the last by drums and fifes.

In addition to the above, Dr. Burney mentions the tragi-comedy of *King Cambyses*, in which music was performed at a banquet, and the tragedy of *Jocasta*, in which each act was concluded by a chorus (though it is by no means clear that these choruses were sung), as instances of the introduction of music in old English plays. But he has overlooked a much more remarkable instance, namely, the comedy of *Damon and Pythias*, by Richard Edwards. This may almost be called a musical drama, in the modern sense of the phrase. The author was not only a poet, but a musician; and, in the beginning of Queen Elizabeth's reign, was appointed one of the gentlemen, and master of the children, of the Chapel Royal. The play is really amusing, from its rudeness of construction, ludicrous absurdities, and the exceeding homeliness of the language in which all the characters express themselves. The scene, of course, lies at the court of Dionysius, the tyrant of Syracuse, where Damon and Pythias, two Grecian gentlemen, make their appearance, with each a servant, Will and Jack. There is Snap, a tipstaff; Gronno, the hangman; and a sort of clown, called Grimme. Carisophus, a parasite, accuses Damon to the tyrant; and, by way of completing the happy *denouement*, receives poetical justice by being kicked off the stage by the king's privy councillor. The famous debate before the tyrant, in which each of the friends contends that he ought to die for the other, is conducted after this fashion:

" *Pythias.* Let me have no wronge, as now standes the case, Damon ought not to die, but Pythias :

By misadventure, not by his wyll, his houre is past ; therefore I,
Because he came not at his just time, ought justly to die:
So was my promise, so was thy promise, O kynge ;
All this courte can bear witness of the thinge.

   Damon.   Not so, O mightie kynge, to justice it is contrarie,
That for another man's fault the innocent should die :
Ne yet is my time playnly expired, it is not fully noone
Of this my day appointed, by all the clockes in the towne.

    Pythias.   Believe no clocke, the houre is past by the sonne."

Damon closes the debate, by addressing the
hangman ;—

" Come, Gronno, do thine office now ; why is thy colour so
    dead ?
My neck is so short, thou wylt never have honestie in striking
    off this head."

Honestie here means honour, or credit. The
author borrowed this speech from Hall's account
of Sir Thomas More's execution. "Also the hangman kneeled down to him, asking him forgiveness
of his death, (as the manner is,) to whom he said,
I forgive thee, but I promise thee thou shalt never
have honestie of the stryking off my head, my
neck is so short."

This hangman is a merry fellow, and, like
Scott's *Petit André*, very kind to his patients.

" *Dionisius.*   Gronno, despoyle hym, and eke dispach him
    quickly.
   Gronno.   It shall be done : since you came into this place,
I might have stroken off seven heads in this space.
By'r lady, here are good garments ; these are myne by the
    roode,
It is an evyll winde that bloweth no man good.

Now, Pythias, kneele down, ask me blessing like a pretty boy,
And, with a trice, thy head from thy shoulders I will convoy."

In this piece,* unlike any other plays of such
antiquity, the actors are also singers. When
Damon is carried to prison, his friend laments
his fate in the following *scena.*

" *Pythias.* Ah ! wofull Pythias ! sithe now I am alone
What way shall I first begin to make my mone ?
What words shall I finde apt for my complaynte ?
Damon, my friend, my joy, my life is in peril, of force I must
    now faint.
But, oh musicke ! as in joyful tunes thy merry notes I did
    borrow,
So now lend mee thy yernful tunes, to utter my sorrow.

    Here Pythias sings, and the regalles† play

        Awake, ye woful wightes,
          That long have wept in woe :
        Resign to me your plaintes and teares,
          My haplesse hap to show.

* Among other pieces of pedantry, the characters are much
given to quoting Latin : and, in one place, Jack addresses
Grimme, in French, " *Je bois à vous, mon compagnon ;*" to
which Grimme replies, " *J'ai vous pleigé, petit Zawne.*" The
annotator of the second edition of Dodsley's Old Plays, says,
" I know not what is meant by *Zawne.*" The meaning is quite
plain ; Grimme calls Jack " *petit Jean.*"

† The regals was an instrument in common use in England,
in the sixteenth century. It seems to have been a small organ,
though its nature and powers are not distinctly known. Altieri,
in his Italian and English dictionary, says, " *Regale,* sorta di
stromento simile all' organo, ma minore."

My woe no tongue can tell,
Ne pen can well descrie :
  O what a death is this to heare !
  Damon my friend must die !

The loss of worldly wealth
  Manne's wisdom may restore,
And physike hath provided, too,
  A salve for every sore :
But my true friend once lost
No arte can well supplie ;
  Then, what a death is this to heare !
  Damon my friend must die !

My mouthe refuse the foode
  That should my limbes sustayne !
Let sorrow sinke into my brest,
  And ransacke every veine :
You furies all at once
On me your torments trie :
  Why should I live, since that I heare
  Damon my friend must die !

Gripe me, ye greedy griefs,
  And present plagues of death ;
You sisters three, with cruel hands,
  With speed come stop my breath :
Shrine me in clay alive,
Some good man stop mine eye ;
  O death, come now, seeing I heare
  Damon my friend must die."

When Pythias, as Damon's hostage, is carried to prison, "the regalles play a mourning song." When, on Damon's failure to return at the appointed time, his friend is about to suffer death, Eubulus, the benevolent councillor, enters and sings a song of lamentation for his fate, each stanza of which has a burden sung by "the Muses," in chorus; though we are not informed how the Muses came there. There is also a comic trio, sung by Jacke, Will, and Grimme; and the whole concludes with a regular *finale*, or song in honour of the queen, (before whom the play was performed by the children of her chapel,) ending thus;

" Long may she governe in honour and wealth,
Voyde of all sicknesse, in most perfect health ;
Which health to prolonge, as true friends require,
God graunt she may have her own hearte's desire :
Which friends will defend with most stedfast faith,
The Lord graunt her such friends, most noble queene Elizabeth."

The author of this play was, no doubt, also the composer of the music. He died according to Sir John Hawkins, on the 31st of October, 1566.

Shakspeare, who was evidently a passionate lover of music, has introduced it in a number of his plays. *The Tempest*, even in its original form, may almost be considered a musical drama. Besides " Come unto these yellow sands," " Full fathom five thy father lies," " Where the bee sucks," and other songs, it contains a Masque with music, presented by the spirits of the enchanted island. The same is the case with *As you like it*, in which there are the fine sylvan glees, " Under the green-wood tree," " What shall he have that kill'd the deer," and " It was a lover and his lass ;" the exquisite song, " Blow, blow thou winter wind ;" and the music in the last scene.

Many of his other plays contain beautiful lyrical pieces ; and the passages descriptive of the charms of music, and its effects, are innumerable. This admixture of music is to be found in the plays of Jonson, Beaumont and Fletcher, Shirley, Dryden, and other dramatists of the sixteenth and seventeenth centuries, and did not cease till the musical drama acquired a separate and independent existence. The masques, which became the favourite amusements of the court in the sixteenth century, were the precursors of the opera in England; and (in the words of Burney) belong to the chain of dramas which completed the union of poetry and music on our stage. It was by a gradual progress that the masque ripened into the musical drama; and there are several steps between the pageants exhibited before Henry the Eighth and Queen Elizabeth (and in which these sovereigns themselves were frequently actors), and the *Comus* of Milton.

The masques, which formed the favourite amusement of the court during the reigns of James and Charles the First, were almost all composed by Ben Jonson, and are a delightful portion of his works. They have suffered much less from the injuries of time than his regular dramas, especially his comedies, which are founded, not so much on the permanent varieties of human character, as on the obsolete manners and peculiarities or *humours* of his own age, and are full, moreover, of allusions which all the labours of antiquarian research have not succeeded in rendering intelligible. Jonson's lyrical productions seem to belong to another and a later age. The style differs from that of the present day in little more than its richness of classical imagery; a richness which has exposed the poet, though unjustly, to the charge of pedantry. His garb is magnificent, but not cumbrous; its gorgeous ornaments are tasteful and well disposed; and he wears it lightly and gracefully. Nothing can be more flowing and harmonious than the poetry of these pieces, both in the spoken dialogues and the songs; and their lofty sentiments, and purity of thought, although written for the entertainment of a court, the manners of which were anything but pure, give an exalted idea of the character of their author.

These masques were professed imitations of the newly-created Italian opera of that day. In some of them the dialogue is directed to be delivered "in *stilo recitativo*:" and the music, being the production of Italian composers, was of course in the Italian style. They resembled the Italian opera, too, in being founded on mythological subjects, and in being performed with great splendour of scenery and decoration. At this time all attempts to heighten the illusion of the stage by scenic display were confined to the expensive entertainments of the court. Queen Anne, the consort of James the First, took great delight in these performances, in which she herself, with her children, and the nobles and ladies of the court, took a part, figuring

in the pageants, and dancing in the ballets.
Modern writers have characterized these court
pastimes as pedantic and tasteless, pompous and
operose. Surely, however, so permanent a relish
for a kind of entertainment which employed the
highest powers of one of our greatest poets, indicated considerable refinement of taste, if not of
manners; and the opinion of Gifford* is at least
as near the truth, notwithstanding the characteristic asperity with which it is expressed. " It
must have been a very graceful and splendid
entertainment: and, with due respect be it spoken,
nearly as worthy of the nobility as the private
masquerades, &c., which, with such advantage to
good manners, have been substituted for it. It is
with peculiar modesty that we, who cannot eke
out an evening's entertainment without the introduction of gamblers, hired buffoons, and voluntary
jack-puddings, declaim on the ' pedantry and
wretched taste' of James and his court."

But whatever may be said in defence of the
taste of a court which was addicted to this species
of amusement, nothing can be said in favour of its
manners. Sir John Harrington, in his *Nugæ
Antiquæ*, gives an account of a scene which took
place at the performance of one of these masques,
during the visit of Christian IV. of Denmark to
this country, so extraordinary as to be almost incredible, were it not for the character of the relater.

* See note on the masque, "Pleasure reconciled to Virtue,"
in Gifford's edition of Jonson.

"One day," he says, "a great feast was held, and after dinner, the representation of Solomon his Temple, and the coming of the Queen of Sheba, was made, or, (as I may better say) was meant to have been made before their majesties, by device of the Earl of Salisbury and others. But, alas! as all earthly things do fail to poor mortals in enjoyment, so did prove our presentment hereof. The ladie, who did play the Qeeen's part, did carry most precious gifts to both their majesties: but, forgetting the steps arising to the canopy, overset her caskets into his Danish majestie's lap, and fell at his feet, though I rather think it was in his face. Much was the hurry and confusion; clothes and napkins were at hand to make all clean. His majesty then got up, and would dance with the queen of Sheba, but he fell down, and humbled himself before her, and was carried to an inner chamber, and laid upon a bed of state, which was not a little defiled with the presents of the Queen, which had been bestowed on his garments; such as wine, cream, jelly, beverage, cakes, spices, and other good matters. The entertainment and show *went forward*, and most of the presenters *went backward*, or fell down; wine did so occupy their upper chambers. Now did appear in rich dresses, Hope, Faith, and Charity: Hope did essay to speak, but wine rendered her endeavours so feeble that she withdrew, and *hoped* the king would excuse her brevity: Faith was then left all alone, for I am certain she was not joined

with good works, and left the court in a stagger-
ing condition.   Charity came to the king's feet,
and seemed to cover the multitude of sins her
sisters had committed; in some sort she made
obeisance, and brought gifts, but said she would
return home again, as there was no gift which
Heaven had not already given his majesty.   She
then returned to Hope and Faith, who were both
sick in the lower hall.   Next came Victory, in
bright armour, and presented a rich sword to the
king, (who did not accept it, but put it by with
his hand,) and by a strange medley of versification
did endeavour to make suit to the king.   But
Victory did not triumph long; for, after much
lamentable utterance, she was led away like a
silly captive, and laid to sleep on the outer steps
of the ante-chamber.   Now did Peace make entry,
and strove to get foremost to the king; but I
grieve to tell how great wrath she did discover
unto those of her attendants, and, much contrary
to her semblance, most rudely made war with her
olive-branch, and laid on the pates of those who
did oppose her coming.   I have much marvelled
at these strange pageantries; and they do bring to
my remembrance what part of this sort in our
queen's days, of which I was sometime a humble
presenter and assistant, but I ne'er did see such
lack of good order, discretion, and sobriety, as I
have now done.   I have passed much time in seeing the royal sports of hunting and hawking, where
the manners were such as made me devise the

beasts were pursuing the sober creation, and not man in quest of exercise and food. I will now, in good sooth, declare to you, who will not blab, that the gunpowder fright is got out of all our heads, and we are going on hereabout as if the devil was contriving every man should blow up himself by wild riot, excess, and devastation of time and temperance."

Jonson's masques, extending over a period of thirty years, are numerous. One of the prettiest of them, called *The Masque of Hymen*, was performed at the ill-starred nuptials of Robert Earl of Essex, and the lady Frances Howard, daughter of the Earl of Suffolk. This couple were mere children; the bridegroom in his fourteenth, and the bride in her thirteenth year. Essex was sent abroad on his travels; and his wife, in his absence, entered into a guilty intrigue with Robert Carr, Viscount Rochester, the celebrated favourite of James. After Essex's return, she found means to obtain a scandalous divorce, and immediately married her paramour, who was at the same time made Earl of Somerset. Sir Thomas Overbury, who had endeavoured to prevent this union, was poisoned in the Tower by creatures of the Earl and Countess; and though they, as well as their agents, were tried and condemned for this atrocious deed, yet the lives of the principal criminals for some unaccountable reason, were spared by the king. They lived for many years shunned by every one, and adding to the wretchedness of

their existence the bitterness of a mutual hatred,
so intense and implacable, that, though dwelling
in the same house, they were never seen to exchange
a single word.   Before her disgraceful second marriage, this lady appears to have been a frequent
performer in the court entertainments.   This second
marriage was favoured by James, still under the influence of his minion, and a splendid masque was
performed in celebration of it ; but this masque was
not written by Jonson.

   The Hue and Cry after Cupid was performed at
the Lord Viscount Haddington's marriage at court,
on the Shrove-Tuesday, at night, 1608.   This Lord
Haddington was the Sir John Ramsay who had
saved the king's life, by stabbing the Earl of Gowrie,
when he and his brother made their memorable as-
sault on the king, at Perth, in the year 1600.   This
piece contains some fine lyrics.   The following
song, sung by the three Graces, may be taken
as a specimen of Jonson's musical numbers.

" 1*st Grace.*   Beauties, have you seen this toy,
                Called Love, a little boy,
                Almost naked, wanton, blind ;
                Cruel now, and then as kind ?
                If he be among ye, say ;
                He is Venus' runaway.

   2*nd Grace.*   She that will but now discover
                Where the winged wag doth hover,
                Shall to-night receive a kiss,
                How, or where, herself would wish :
                But, who brings him to his mother,
                Shall have that kiss, and another.

3rd Grace. He hath marks about him, plenty ;
You shall know him among twenty.
All his body is a fire,
And his breath a flame entire,
That being shot, like lightning, in,
Wounds the heart, but not the skin.

1st Grace. At his sight, the sun hath turn'd,
Neptune in the waters burn'd ;
Hell hath felt a greater heat ;
Jove himself forsook his seat :
From the centre of the sky
Are his trophies rear'd on high.

2nd Grace. Wings he hath, which though ye clip,
He will leap from lip to lip,
Over liver, lights, and heart,
But not stay in any part ;
And if chance his arrow misses,
He will shoot himself, in kisses.

3rd Grace. He doth bear a golden bow, '
And a quiver, hanging low,
Full of arrows that outbrave
Dian's shafts ; where, if he have
Any head more sharp than other,
With that first he strikes his mother.

1st Grace. Still the fairest are his fuel,
When his days are to be cruel,
Lovers' hearts are all his food,
And his baths their warmest blood.
Nought but wounds his hand doth season
And he hates none like to Reason.

2nd Grace. Trust him not ; his words, though sweet,
Seldom with his heart do meet.
All his practice is deceit ;
Every gift it is a bait ;
Not a kiss but poison bears ;
And most treason in his tears.

3rd Grace. Idle minutes are his reign ;
     Then, the struggler makes his gain,
     By presenting maids with toys,
     And would have ye think them joys ;
     'Tis the ambition of the elf,
     To have all childish as himself.

1st Grace. If by these ye please to know him,
     Beauties, be not nice, but show him.

2nd Grace. Though ye had a will to hide him ;
     Now, we hope, ye 'll not abide him.

3rd Grace. Since you hear his falser play ;
     And that he 's Venus' runaway."

ALFONSO FERABOSCO, the composer of the music
in the greater number of Jonson's masques, was
English by birth, but Italian by parentage and
education.   His father, of the same name, was an
eminent madrigalist, and appears to have been a
superior musician.   Ferabosco the younger, however, was for a long time the most fashionable
composer of his day, for the stage and the chamber.   The encomiastic verses, by Ben Jonson and
others, prefixed to a book of *Ayres*, published by
him in 1609, show the opinion entertained of his
merits — an opinion of which he himself largely
partook ; as appears from his dedication to Prince
Henry, written in a quaint style of self-satisfac-
tion.   " I could now," he says, " with solemn in-
dustry of many in *epistles*, enforce all that hath
been said in praise of the *faculty* of musique, and
make that commend the work : but I desire more,
the work should commend the *faculty :* and therefore suffer these few *ayres* to owe their grace

rather to your *Highnesse* judgment, than any other
testimonies.   I am not made of much speech ;
only I know them worthy of my name ; and therein I took paines to make them worthy of yours."
The modern ear, however, will take no pleasure in
these *ayres*, or in any other specimens of this
composer's music which are still extant.   They
are sufficiently regular in modulation and harmony; but the airs are stiff, laboured, and unmeaning; and the accent and rhythm of the poetry
are quite disregarded.   We cannot imagine Jonson's beautiful and flowing measures united with
such dull and insipid sounds, and listened to with
delight by a courtly and elegant audience.   But no
better melody was then known in England ; and
the most refined taste will rarely transcend the
highest standard of existing excellence.

Another of Jonson's musical coadjutors was
NICOLO LANIERE, also an Italian.   He was a
painter and engraver, as well as a musician; but
his greatest excellence was in music.   He etched
a considerable number of plates for a drawing-
book; was an able connoisseur in pictures; and
possessed the picture-dealing art of giving modern
pictures an air of antiquity, and passing off copies
for originals.   From the directions given in the
printed copies, in Jonson's works, as to the manner
of performing some of the masques which Laniere
set to music, it is evident that, having newly
arrived from Italy, he followed the Italian mode of
the day; setting the dialogues *in stilo recitativo,*

and intermingling them with airs for single voices, and choruses. Indeed, the masques of Ben Jonson, as set by Ferabosco and Laniere, bore a much closer resemblance to the regular Italian opera than the pieces called operas which prevailed on the English stage during the greater part of the last century.

Specimens of Laniere's music are to be found in Playford's collections. As might be expected, his recitatives are better than his airs; and are superior to those of any English composer of that day.

CHAPTER IV.

TIME OF CHARLES I. — SHIRLEY'S MASQUE — THE TRIUMPH OF PEACE—PRYNNE'S HISTRIO-MASTIX—MILTON'S COMUS—HENRY LAWES.

IN the early part of the reign of Charles the First, masques remained in undiminished favour at court. They suited the gay disposition of his Queen, Henrietta Maria, and the love of dramatic amusements which she brought with her from the court of France. She was frequently a principal performer in the masques, which continued to be written chiefly by Ben Jonson. A great number of masques are mentioned as having been represented at court during the first years of Charles's reign, some of which were performed by the queen, and others by the gentlemen of the Inns of Court.

The most remarkable of the masques given by these gentlemen was one which was performed in 1633, before Charles and his court, as a testimony of loyalty to the king on his return from Scotland, after terminating for the time the discontents of that kingdom. It was written by Shirley, and entitled *The Triumph of Peace*. The circumstances connected with its performance are minutely detailed by Lord Commissioner Whitelock,

in a manuscript autobiography, written by him
for the use of his children. *   This masque had
another object beside that of being an expression
of love and duty to their majesties.   " Some,"
says Whitelock, " held it the more seasonable,
because this action would manifest the difference
of their opinion from Mr. Prynne's new learning,
and serve to confute his *Histrio-mastix* against
interludes."   Of this celebrated book, which had
been published the preceding year, we shall presently give some account.

A committee of members of the four societies
was appointed to manage the business : and Whitelock himself, being an amateur, was intrusted with
the charge of the musical department.   He made
choice of Simon Ives, a musician of considerable
merit, and the celebrated Henry Lawes, to compose the music of the masque, and to conduct its
performance, under himself.   " I also made choice,"
he says, " of four of the most excellent of the
queen's chapel, M. La Ware, M. Duval, M. Robert, and M. Mari, with divers others of foreign
nations, who were most eminent in their art, not
in the least neglecting my own countrymen whose
knowledge of music rendered them useful in this
action, to bear their parts in the musicke, which I
resolved, if I could, to have so performed, as might
excell any that ever before this time had been in
England.   Herein I kept my purpose, causing the

* This account, here abridged, is quoted at full length by
Burney, vol. iii. p. 369.

meetings of all the musitians to be frequent at my house in Salisbury Court; and there I have had together att one time, of English, French, Italian, German, and other masters of musicke, fourty lutes, besides other instruments, and voyces of the most excellent kind in consort."

The masque was performed on Candlemas night, the persons engaged in it having proceeded, in procession, from Ely-house in Holborn, to White-hall. This procession is minutely described, and must have been a magnificent affair. The actors in the masque were sixteen in number, four gentle-men of each Inn, who were drawn in four chariots and six. There were "one hundred gentlemen of the Innes of Court in very rich cloathes, five and twenty chosen out of each house, of the most pro-per and handsome young gentlemen of the socie-ties. Every one of them was gallantly mounted, on the best horses, and with the best furniture that the king's stable and the stables of all the nobility in towne could afforde, and they were forward on this occasion to lend them. The richness of the apparel and furniture, glittering by the light of the multitude of torches attending them, with the mo-tion and stirring of the mettled horses, and the many and various gay liveries of their servants, butt especially the personal beauty and gallantry of the handsome young gentlemen, made the most glorious and splendid show that ever was beheld in England."

This gallant array was followed by a series of

anti-masques, or burlesque processions of beggars mounted on the most sorry jades that could be procured, men on horseback imitating the notes of birds, and disguised in the shapes of animals, with other devices of a ludicrous and satirical kind. In one of them " rode a fellow upon a little horse with a great bit in his mouth, and upon the man's head was a bit with headstall and reins, fastened, and signified a projector, that none in the king-dome might ride their horses but with such bits as they should buy of him. Another projector, who begged a patent of monopoly to feed capons with carrots; and several other projectors, were in like manner personated, which pleased the spectators the more, because by it an information was covertly given to the king of the unfitness and ridiculous-ness of these projects, against the law; and the attorney Noy, who had most knowledge of them, had a great hand in this anti-masque of the projectors."

When the procession arrived at Whitehall, through streets crowded with spectators, " the king and queen stood at a window, looking straight for-ward into the street, to see the masque come by, and being delighted with the noble bravery of it, they sent to the marshall to desire that the whole show might fetch a turne about the Tilt-yard, that their majesties might have a double view of them, which was done accordingly, and then they alighted at Whitehall-gate, and were conducted to severall roomes and places prepared for them.

" The king and queen and all their noble train
being come in, the masque began, and was incom-
parably performed, in the dancing, speeches,
musicke, and scenes; the dances, figures, properties, the voices, instruments, songs, aiers, com-
posures, the words and actions, were all of them
exact, none fayled in their parts, and the scenes
were most curious and costly. The queen did the
honour to some of the masquers to dance with
them herselfe, and to judge them as good dancers
as ever she saw, and the great ladyes were very
free and civill in dancing with all the masquers as
they were taken out by them. Thus, they continued in their sports until it was almost morning,
and then, the king and queen retiring, the masquers
and Innes of Court gentlemen were brought to
a stately banquett, and after that was dispersed,
every one departed to his own quarters."

The queen was so delighted with this show, that
it was repeated at Merchant Tailors' hall, where a
banquet was given to their majesties by the lord
mayor. " This," says Whitelock, " gave great
contentment to their majestyes, and no less to the
citizens, especially those of the younger sort, and
of the female sexe, and it was to the great honour
and no less charge of the lord mayor and freemen."

" After these dreames past," he continues, " and
these pompes vanished, all men were satisfied by
the committee justly and bountifully. For the
musicke, which was particularly committed to my
charge, I gave to Mr. Ives and to Mr. Lawes 100*l.*

apiece for their rewards; for the four French gentlemen, the Queen's servants, I thought that a
handsome and liberall gratifying of them would be
made known to the Queen, their mistress, and well
taken by her. I therefore invited them one morning to a collation att St. Dunstan's taverne, in the
great room, the oracle of Apollo, where each of
them had his plate layd for him, covered, and the
napkin by it; and when they opened their plates
they found in each of them forty pieces of gold, of
their master's coyne, for the first dish, and they
had cause to be much pleased with this surprisall.
The rest of the musitians had rewards answerable
to their parts and qualities; and the whole charge
of the musicke came to about one thousand pounds.
The clothes of the horsemen, reckoned one with
another at 100*l.* a suit, att the least, amounted to
10,000*l.* The charges of all the rest of the masque,
which were borne by the societies, were accounted
to be above twenty thousand pounds."*

* In Whitelock's account there is a trait of simple vanity
too characteristic to be omitted. "I was conversant with the
musitians, and so willing to gain their favour, especially at this
time, that I composed an aire myself, *with the assistance of Mr.
Ives,* and called it *Whitelock's Coranto ;* which being cried up,
was first played publiquely, by the Blackfryar's musicke, who
were then esteemed the best of common musitians in London.
Whenever I came to that house (as I sometimes did in those
days, though not often) to see a play, the musitians would
presently play *Whitelock's Coranto,* and it was so often called
for that they would have it played twice or three times in an
afternoon.   The queen hearing it, would not be persuaded that

The book by William Prynne, which is alluded
to by Whitelock, and the effects of which were
attempted to be counteracted by the exhibition of
the above masque, had been published in the preceding year, 1632. It is entitled "Histrio-mastix,
the Player's Scourge, or Actor's Tragedie, in which
it is pretended to be evidenced that stage-playes
(the very pompes of the divell, which we renounced
in baptisme, if we believe the fathers) are sinfull,
heathenish, lewde, ungodly spectacles, and most
pernicious corruptions; condemned in all ages as
intolerable mischiefs to churches, to republickes,
to the manners, minds, and soules of men. And
that the profession of play-poets, of stage-players,
together with the penning, acting, and frequenting
of stage-plays, are unlawful, infamous, and mis-
becoming Christians. All pretences to the contrarie are here likewise fully answered, and the
unlawfulness of acting or beholding academicall
interludes briefly discussed, besides sundry other
particulars concerning dancing, dicing, health-
drinking, &c." This ample title gives a very
good summary of the contents of the book, which

it was made by an Englishman, because she said it was fuller
of life and spirit than the English airs use to be; butt she
honored the *Coranto* and the maker of it with her majestye's
royall commendation. It grew to that request, that all the
common musitians in this towne, and all over the kingdome,
gott the composition of it, and played it publiquely in all
places, for above thirtie years after." *Whitelock's Coranto*
has been preserved from oblivion by being inserted in the histories of both Hawkins and Burney.

is directed not only against plays performed in public theatres, but also against "academicall interludes," or the masques and other entertainments, then so much in fashion, presented by the students of the Inns of Court.

This book, however absurd and ridiculous its contents may now appear, was, at the time of its publication, looked upon in a very different light. It spoke the sentiments of the Puritans, a great and increasing body, who held in abomination all those amusements against which it was levelled. By them, therefore, it was received with great approbation, while it excited the indignation and alarm of the court party, who held it to be a satire against their Majesties themselves, as being fond of these pastimes. The Queen was supposed to be especially aimed at, because she frequently acted a part in the masques which were performed at court; and the phrase in the table of contents, "Women actors notorious whores," was considered an innuendo against her Majesty. Prynne, therefore, who was a barrister of Lincoln's Inn, was indicted in the court of Star Chamber, that memorable instrument of arbitrary power, for a libel, found guilty, and sentenced to be put on the pillory in two places, Westminster and Cheapside; to lose both his ears, one in each place ; to pay 5,000*l.* fine to the King, and to be imprisoned during life; and this barbarous sentence was executed.

Milton's Masque of *Comus,* one of the brightest gems of English poetry, was written for the Earl of

Bridgewater, at whose mansion it was first performed in 1634. The story of the piece was founded
on an incident which had occurred to the Earl's
children. When he resided at Ludlow Castle, in
Shropshire, his two sons, Lord Brackley and Mr.
Egerton, and his daughter Lady Alice Egerton,
were benighted in passing through a neighbouring
forest, and the young lady for some time could not
be found. This adventure excited Milton's imagination, and gave rise to the masque, which was represented on Michaelmas-eve for the amusement of
the family and the nobility and gentry of the neighbourhood. The two brothers were performed by the
Earl's sons, and his daughter was the *Lady*. Lady
Alice Egerton, who was then a girl of thirteen,
afterwards became lady Vaughan and Carbury,
and was distinguished for her talents and accomplishments.

Henry Lawes, the celebrated composer of the
music in this masque, taught music in the family of
Lord Bridgewater, and Lady Alice Egerton was his
pupil. His first book of "Ayres and Dialogues,"
published in 1653, is dedicated to her, and Lady
Herbert of Cherbury, her sister. Lawes himself
acted the part of the attendant spirit. In 1637
Lawes published the *poem* of *Comus ;* but the music
does not appear to have ever been printed. It appears, however, from a manuscript in Lawes' own
handwriting, mentioned by Hawkins and Burney,
that the two songs, " Sweet Echo," and " Sabrina
fair," together with three other passages in the

poem—" Back, shepherds, back," "To the ocean now I fly," and " Now my task is smoothly done," were probably the whole of the original music; and that the rest of the poetry was simply declaimed.

If we were to judge of the genius of Henry Lawes from the specimen given of it by Hawkins and Burney, the song, "Sweet Echo," in this masque, our opinion certainly would be very unfavourable. The lyrical beauty of the words does not seem to have inspired the composer. His music has neither the accent and emphasis of *recitative*, nor the rhythmical flow of *air*. It is a sort of stiff and constrained chant, destitute of melody, and, except in the passage—

> " Where the love-lorn nightingale
>   Nightly to thee her sad song mourneth well,"

where there is a glimmering of feeling at the words " sad song,"—it is equally destitute of expression.

Though we agree with Burney in his strictures on this composition, yet we think he has led the world to entertain an erroneous opinion of Lawes' character as a musician. " I have examined," he says, "with care and candour all the works I can find of this composer, which are still very numerous, and am obliged to own myself unable, by their excellence, to account for the great reputation he acquired, and the numerous panegyrics bestowed on him by the greatest poets and musicians of his time." " But *bad* as the music of Lawes appears to us," he says in another place, " it seems to have been sincerely admired by his contemporaries in general." And he adds, that " most of the productions of this celebrated musician are languid and insipid, and equally devoid of learning and genius."

If such was Lawes' musical character, the fact, that no musician ever enjoyed, in a greater degree, the admiration of his contemporaries, is singular and unaccountable. Burney says, " his temper and conversation must certainly have endeared him to his acquaintance, and rendered them partial to his productions." This is true—Lawes was both esteemed and beloved; but this was not sufficient to render his music the admiration of the most accomplished, refined, and distinguished people of his time; and, in particular, to draw the most enthusiastic eulogies from Milton, whose exquisite taste had been cultivated by a residence among the poets and musicians of Italy. In *Comus* there are several beautiful allusions to Lawes. The attendant spirit, a character represented by Lawes himself, says,

" ———— But I must put off
These my sky robes, spun out of Iris' woof,
And take the weeds and likeness of a swain
That to the service of this house belongs,
Who, with his soft pipe and smooth-dittied song,
Well knows to still the wild winds when they roar,
And hush the waving woods."

He is thus alluded to by the *Elder Brother*—

> " Thyrsis, whose artful strains have oft delay'd
> The huddling brook to hear his madrigal,
> And sweeten'd every musk-rose of the dale."

And also in this passage—

> " He lov'd me well, and oft would beg me sing,
> Which, when I did, he on the tender grass
> Would sit and hearken e'en to extasy."

Such warmth of expression must surely have been inspired by strains different from such as are described by Burney.

Lawes has also been praised by Waller. The first book of his *Ayres and Dialogues* contains encomiastic verses by that poet, by Edward and John Phillips, the nephews of Milton, and others. Fenton, the editor of Waller's works, says, that " the best poets of Lawes' time were ambitious of having their verses set to music by this admirable artist." Indeed, he not only composed music for the verses of almost every eminent poet of his time, but of many young noblemen and gentlemen, who appear to have become song-writers from the pleasure of having him to clothe their verses in a musical garb. In his different collections there are songs written by Thomas Earl of Winchelsea, William Earl of Pembroke, John Earl of Bristol, Lord Broghill, Thomas Carey, son of the Earl of Monmouth, Henry Noel, son of Lord Camden, Sir Charles Lucas, and Carew Raleigh, son of Sir Walter Raleigh. Many of the songs of these amateur poets possess great merit: and Lawes' three books of *Ayres and Dialogues* contain a body

of elegant and spirited lyric poetry which deserves
to be better known.

This, too, in some degree, is the case with the
music contained in these, and other collections,
in which Lawes' compositions are to be found.
Burney says he has examined these collections
with care and candour. If so, his sweeping con-
demnation of the author is surprising; for we will
venture to say that few musicians will examine
them carefully without finding the task a very
agreeable one. The trifling specimens he has
given (vol. iii. p. 397) are by no means fair ones;
and the songs of which he has mentioned the titles,
are far from being the best he could have pointed
out. We have not only found many airs which
appear to be at least equal to any that had as yet
been produced by English composers, but some,
which are in themselves so graceful and flowing,
and so happily united to elegant poetry, that they
would require only the addition of a modern
accompaniment, and the assistance of modern singing, to gratify the public, even at the present day.
Among these we may mention "Careless of love
and free from fears," and "Why shouldst thou
swear I am forsworn?" both which are as smooth
and melodious as if they had been composed yesterday. " Gaze not on swans in whose soft
breast," would be a very pleasing song, but for a
defect in the rhythm of the air; which, however,
arises from an evident oversight, and is easily cor-
rected. "Dearest, do not delay me," and " Lovely

Chloris, though thine eyes," are exceedingly pretty :
the latter is very like Arne's " Water parted from
the sea."—" Little love serves my turn," in six-
four time, is in a gay, dancing measure, and quite
modern in its effect. " Chloris, yourself you so
excel," a song by Waller, is a fine specimen of the
concetti so fashionable in the amorous poetry of
that age. It is addressed to a lady, on her singing
some of the author's verses.

> " Chloris, yourself you so excel,
>   When you vouchsafe to breathe my thought,
> That, like a spirit, with this spell
> Of mine own teaching I am caught.
>
> The eagle's fate and mine is one,
> That, on the shaft that made him die,
> Espy'd a feather of his own,
> Wherewith he wont to soar so high.
>
> Had Echo with so sweet a grace
> Narcissus' loud complaints return'd,
> Not for reflection of his face,
> But of his voice, the boy had mourn'd."

We do not find, it is true, in the works of Lawes,
the lofty conceptions of Purcell, nor those " tender
strokes of art " by which that unrivalled musician
reached the inmost recesses of the soul. But
Lawes was gifted with imagination, taste, and
feeling; and deserves a much higher place among
English composers than that which Burney and
other critics have thought proper to assign him.

Of Lawes' personal history not much is known.
He was admitted a gentleman of the Chapel Royal
in 1625 ; and afterwards was appointed one of the

public and private musicians of Charles I., with whom he was in great favour. Besides *Comus*, his principal dramatic production, he composed the music to several of the masques performed at court. On the fall of the monarchy, and the consequent abolition of the king's musical establishments, Lawes was deprived of his situations, and supported himself by teaching ladies to sing; and his subsistence derived from this source was probably scanty enough. In those days the fine arts were not, as now, supported by the patronage of the public. Wealth was little diffused, and taste and refinement still less. During the tranquil part of the reign of Charles I., it would appear that musicians must have subsisted chiefly by means of the royal household and chapel establishments, the munificence of the sovereign, and the patronage and employment of the great. There was no occupation for musicians in the families of the middle classes; nor were there concerts, or any public amusement, except the theatres, which employed but few hands, and those of an inferior order, the musical drama not yet having been introduced into public theatres. When the monarchy was overthrown, the abolition of every musical establishment, the prohibition of every entertainment of which music formed a part, and the prevalence of those opinions which discourage the use of music, even as a private amusement, must have reduced Lawes and his tuneful brethren to depend on the very limited patronage which the higher classes were still enabled to afford them. Lawes, accordingly, in the preface to the first book of his *Ayres*, published in 1653, says, " Now we live in so sullen an age, that our profession itself hath lost its encouragement."

In 1655, Lawes published his second book, and, in 1658, his third book of *Ayres and Dialogues*. There are some passages in his prefaces to these collections, which show, that the complaints made by English musicians, of the preference given to foreign music, merely because it is foreign, are of long standing. " Wise men have observed," he says, in the preface to his first book, " our generation so giddy, that whatsoever is native (be it ever so excellent) must lose its taste, because themselves have lost theirs. For my part, I profess (and such as know me can bear me witness) I desire to render every man his due, whether strangers or natives. I acknowledge the Italians the greatest masters of music, but yet not all. And (without depressing the honour of other countries) I may say our own nation hath had, and yet hath, as able musicians as any in Europe; and many now living (whose names I forbear) are excellent both for the voice and instruments. I never loved to set or sing words I do not understand. But this present generation is so sated with what is native, that nothing takes their care but what is sung in a language which (commonly) they understand as little as they do the music. And to make them a little sensible of the ridiculous humour, I took a table or index of old Italian songs (for one, two, and three voices), and this index (which read together made a strange medley of nonsense) I set to a varied air and gave out that it came from Italy, whereby it hath passed for a rare Italian song."—This ingenious hoax on his contemporaries is inserted as the last song in the book.—In the preface to the second book, he says, "There are knowing persons, who have been long bred in those worthily admired parts of Europe, who ascribe more to us than we to ourselves ; and able musicians returning from travel do wonder to see us so thirsty after foreigners. For they can tell us (if we knew it not) that music is the same in England as in Italy ; the concords and discords, the passions, spirits, majesty, and humours, are all the same they are in England ; their manner of composing is sufficiently known to us, their best compositions being brought over hither by those who are able enough to choose. But we must not here expect to find music at the highest, when all arts and sciences are at so low an ebb. As for myself, although I have lost my fortunes with my master (of blessed memory) I am not so low to bow for a subsistence to the follies of this age, and to humour such as will seem to understand our art better than we that have spent our lives in it."

At the Restoration Lawes recovered his place in the Chapel Royal, and composed the Coronation Anthem for Charles II. He died in 1662, and was buried in Westminster Abbey.

CHAPTER V.

THE COMMONWEALTH — SIR WILLIAM DAVENANT'S ENTERTAIN-
MENTS—HIS MUSICAL PIECES—FIRST FEMALE PERFORMANCES
—THEATRE ESTABLISHED AFTER THE RESTORATION—MATTHEW
LOCK—PSYCHE—MACBETH—DUCHESS OF MAZARIN.

IN the year 1647 rigorous ordinances were issued
by the parliament against stage-plays, and all
entertainments consisting of music and dancing,
by which not only the actors in such entertainments, but all such as should be present at them,
were subjected to severe punishment by fine and
imprisonment. There was thus a complete cessa-
tion of dramatic performances for about ten years.

In 1656, Sir William Davenant obtained permission to open a kind of theatre at Rutland-house,
in Charter-house-square, for the exhibition of what
he called " an Entertainment in Declamation and
Music, after the manner of the ancients." Anthony
Wood, imagining that this permission was to perform Italian operas, says : " Though Oliver Cromwell had now prohibited all other theatrical representations, he allowed of this, because, being in an
unknown language, it could not corrupt the morals
of the people." Sir William Davenant's *Entertainment* was wholly in the English language, nor was

it an opera, though he calls it so. It was merely
an imaginary dialogue or disputation between Dio-
genes, the Cynic philosopher, and Aristophanes,
the poet; the one attacking and the other defend-
ing dramatic representations. The author seems
to have intended it as the means of overcoming the
existing prejudices against dramatic representations, and of predisposing the public to receive
favourably a series of exhibitions of this kind,
which he had it in contemplation to give; and it
appears to have answered his purpose, for it was
immediately followed by a succession of dramatic
performances, which Davenant continued till his
death.

Davenant's " Entertainment after the manner of
the Ancients," was immediately succeeded by *The
Siege of Rhodes*, which was performed at Rutland
House, in 1656. Pope says, that "this was the
first opera sung in England;" and Langbaine, in
his *Account of the English Dramatic Poets*, says
that *The Siege of Rhodes*, and some other plays of
Sir William Davenant, in the times of the civil
wars, were acted *in stilo recitativo*. Burney disputes this; " I can find no proof," he says, " that
it was sung in recitative, either in the dedication
to Lord Clarendon, in the folio edition of 1673, or
the body of the drama." But we find conclusive
evidence on this point. Cibber says, that " Sir
W. Davenant opened a theatre in Lincoln's Inn
Fields, in 1662, where he produced *The Siege of
Rhodes*, with unprecedented splendour." A second

part was then added to it, which we find in Davenant's works. Evelyn, in his *Diary*, says, "1662, Jan. 9. I saw acted ' the Second Part of the Siege of Rhodes.' " " In this," he continues, "acted the fair and famous comedian, called Roxelana, from the part she performed; and I think it was the last, she being taken to be the Earl of Oxford's *Misse* (as at this time they began to call lewd women).* *It was in recitative musiq.*"

Davenant's next piece was *The Cruelty of the Spaniards in Peru*, which was produced in 1658. The scenes and decorations of this drama, (according to Downes, in his *Roscius Anglicanus*) were the first that were introduced on a public stage in England. Evelyn thus speaks of this piece: "5 May, 1659. I went to visit my brother in London, and next day to see a new *Opera after the Italian way, in recitative musiq, and sceanes*, much inferior to the Italian composure and magnificence: but it was prodigious, that, in a time of such publique consternation, such a vanity should be kept up or permitted. I being engaged with company, could not decently resist the going to see

---

* This actress was Mrs. Davenport. Lord Oxford, not having succeeded in his attempts to seduce her, had recourse to the stratagem of a sham marriage, by a pretended clergyman. When she discovered this infamous deception, she threw herself at the king's feet, to demand justice. Charles was not the sovereign from whom justice was to be obtained in a case like this ; but Lord Oxford allowed her an annuity of 300*l.*

it, though my heart smote me for it." The consternation here alluded to, was occasioned by the
recent death of Cromwell. We learn something
of the taste of that age, in regard to *spectacle*, from
a scene in this piece, which is thus described in
the stage directions: "A doleful pavin (a slow and
grave piece of music, so called from its resembling
the motion of the peacock), is played to prepare
the change of the scene, which represents a dark
prison at a great distance; and further to the view,
are discerned racks and other engines of torture,
with which the Spaniards are tormenting the
natives and English mariners, who may be supposed to be lately landed there to discover the
coast. Two Spaniards are likewise discovered
sitting in their cloaks, and appearing more solemn
in ruffs, with rapiers and daggers by their sides;
the one turning a spit, while the other is basting
an Indian prince, who is roasted at an artificial
fire."

The testimony of Evelyn, who, as we have
already seen, was acquainted with the state of the
opera in Italy, is decisive of the fact that these
dramas of Davenant's were operas after the Italian
way, and in recitative, however inferior they may
have been to the Italian operas which he had seen,
in respect to the composition of the music, and the
magnificence of the representation. It is evident,
too, that Davenant understood what were the peculiar features of the musical drama. In his piece,
called *The Playhouse to Let*, a musician, who

presents himself as a tenant for the playhouse, being asked what use he intended to make of it, answers, "I would have introduced heroic story in *stilo recitativo :*" and, upon being desired to explain himself further, he says, " Recitative musick is not composed of matter so familiar as may serve for every low occasion of discourse. In tragedy, the language of the stage is raised above the common dialect, our passions rising with the height of verse ; and vocal musick adds new wings to all the flights of poetry." No musical critic of our own day could more justly express the character and office of recitative.

Davenant's pieces, though they contributed greatly to the progress of the musical drama in England, have little poetical merit. Of their music there seem to be no remains. It was in these pieces that female performers first appeared on the stage. It has been said that there were no actresses on the English stage before the Restoration; and that the celebrated Mrs. Betterton was the first. It is true that the first formal licence for their appearance was contained in the patent granted to Sir William Davenant, immediately after the Restoration : but it appears to have been previously tolerated, for a Mrs. Coleman represented *Ianthe*, in the first part of *The Siege of Rhodes*, in 1656.

After the Restoration, two theatres were established in London by royal licence; the one was the *King's* theatre, in Drury-lane, and the other the

Duke's (which was Davenant's theatre), in Lincoln's-inn-fields. Cibber says, that, in the contest between the two companies for public favour, that of the King had the advantage; and that, therefore, " Sir William Davenant, master of the Duke's company, to make head against their success, was forced to add spectacle and music to action, and to introduce a new species of plays, since called dramatic operas, of which kind were *The Tempest*, *Psyche*, *Circe*, and others, all set off with the most expensive decorations of scenes and habits, with the best voices and dancers." This, however, is incorrect; for none of the above plays were performed under the management of Sir William Davenant, or even in his lifetime. Sir William died in 1668. *The Tempest*, made into an opera by Shadwell, and set to music by Matthew Lock, was first performed in 1673. In the same year appeared the opera of *Psyche*, also written by Shadwell and set to music by Lock and Battista Draghi; in 1674, *Macbeth* was brought out, as altered by Davenant; and in 1676 was produced the opera of *Circe*, written by Dr. Charles Davenant, Sir William's son, with music by John Banister. These pieces were got up at an enormous expense, in music, dancing, machinery, scenes, and decorations, in order to rival the performances of the French stage; and some of the most eminent Parisian dancers were brought over to perform in them. But at length, in 1682 (according to Cibber) the Duke's company not being able to support itself separately, united with the King's, and both were incorporated under the title of the King's Company of Comedians.

After the Restoration, the theatres, which in the time of James I. were no less than seventeen in number, were reduced to the two which have been mentioned. But their diminution in number was compensated by their increased magnitude and splendour. The old playhouses were either a large room in some noted tavern, or a slight building in a garden or open space behind it. The pit was unfloored; and the spectators either stood, or were badly accommodated with benches. There were hardly any attempts at scenery or decorations; and the music consisted of a few violins, hautboys, and flutes, on which vulgar tunes were played in unison, and in a wretched manner. But the two houses erected after the Restoration were truly and emphatically styled theatres, as being constructed so as to accommodate a large public assembly, adorned with painting and sculpture, provided with a proper stage, and with scenes and machinery, to gratify the eye and produce theatrical illusion. A regular band of musicians was placed in the orchestra, who, between the acts, performed pieces of music composed for that purpose, and called act-tunes; and also accompanied the vocal music sung on the stage, and played the music of the dances. Music thus became attached to the theatres, which, from this time, became the principal nurseries of musicians, both composers and performers. The most favourite music was that which was heard in the dramatic pieces of the day ; and to sing and play the songs, dances, and act-tunes of the theatres became a general amusement in fashionable society.

MATTHEW LOCK, the composer of *Psyche* and *Macbeth*, was born at Exeter, and brought up as a chorister in the cathedral of that city. We have no particulars of his life earlier than the year 1657, when he published a work called " a small consort of three parts, for viols or violins." He was employed to compose the music for the public entry of Charles II. at the Restoration, and was soon afterwards appointed composer in ordinary to the king. Some of his compositions appear in the second part of Playford's constitution of Hilton's collection, entitled *Catch that Catch can ;* and, among others, his three-part glee, " Ne'er trouble thyself about times or their turning," a simple and pleasing production. In the latter part of his life he became a Roman Catholic, and was appointed organist to Queen Catherine of Portugal, the consort of Charles II., who was permitted the exercise of her religion, and had a chapel with a regular establishment. Lock died in 1687.

The music of the opera of *Psyche* was printed in 1675, under the following title : " The English Opera, or the vocal music in *Psyche*, with the instrumental therein intermixed. To which is adjoined, the instrumental music in the *Tempest*. By Matthew Lock, composer in ordinary to his majesty, and organist to the queen." Prefixed to

it there is a preface of some length, written in a
rough and vigorous style, and strongly characteristic
of the irascible disposition which Lock is said to
have possessed. In this opera, Lock adopted the
method, which has been generally adhered to in
later times, of having the chief part of the dialogue
delivered in ordinary speech, intermixing it with
songs and choruses. In the songs for single voices,
the melody is a sort of compound of recitative and
air, with frequent changes of measure, in the style
of Lulli, which was fashionable at the court of
Charles II., and which Lock probably found it
necessary to imitate. We find in them many traits
of genius. There is one scene, in particular, " a
rocky desart full of dreadful caves and cliffs," in
which "two despairing men and two despairing
women enter," and sing the torments of unhappy
love: where there are bold and striking musical
phrases, expressing passion in a manner worthy of
Purcell. The choruses are generally superior to
the songs. They are more free and rhythmical in
movement, and contain a great deal of good, solid,
and pure harmony. One of them, a chorus of
devils and furies, at the beginning of the fifth act,
in six real parts (two trebles, counter tenor, tenor,
and two basses) is admirable. These choruses, in
short, appear to us to have much more merit than
has been generally ascribed to them, and to be by
no means unworthy (as they have been said to be),
of the author of the music in *Macbeth*.

The music composed by Lock for this tragedy,

which appeared only a year after *The Tempest* and *Psyche*, is of such transcendent excellence, that its beauties have suffered no decay at the distance of more than a century and a half, and it promises to partake of the immortality of the great work with which it is associated. Its superiority to Lock's previous works, and the circumstance of its not having been published with his name in his own time, have given rise to doubts of his claim to its authorship; but we cannot discover any good foundation for them. Lock is named as the composer of this music by contemporaries, and particularly by Downes, the author of the *Roscius Anglicanus*, who, from his own personal knowledge, gives a minute account of the proceedings of the Duke's theatre during the period in question.

The music in *Macbeth* is a pure emanation of genius. The author seems to have been inspired by his subject, and to have been freed, by the force of his imagination, from the trammels of imitation, and adherence to the style of his day. In the music of every period there is always a body of conventional forms and phrases which become, as it were, the common property of contemporary composers ; and from the use of which, the period to which a composition belongs may in general be pretty accurately assigned. In the music of Macbeth there is little of this. The melody, unlike that of the time, is flowing, and highly rhythmical, while it is full of energy and expression. The harmony is rich and grateful, free from elaborate intricacy or petty details, and thrown into masses of astonishing breadth and grandeur. The sort of recitative, or rather *aria parlante* of the opening dialogue, " Speak, sister, speak ;" is different from anything we have met with, either in ancient or modern music; and yet it is so simple and natural that one can hardly imagine the words uttered in any other accents. What genius there is in the chorus, "We should rejoice !" There is a character of demoniacal joy about it that would be absolutely appalling, if such pains were not taken, in our theatres, to mar the effect of this fine music, by the preposterous absurdity of the spectacle.* There are passages, too, of great elegance and beauty ; but the music is always characteristic. The air, for instance, " Let 's have a dance upon the heath," is exquisitely graceful; and yet there is a touch in it of gloomy melancholy, in perfect keeping with the unearthly scene. The music in Macbeth, in short, was not only a stupendous effort of genius, considering the state of music in England when it was written, but is, to this day, one of the noblest and most beautiful works that ever has been produced by an English musician.

* This abuse was reformed at Covent Garden, under the management of Mr. Macready.

CHAPTER VI.

DRYDEN—"THE STATE OF INNOCENCE—ALBION AND ALBA-
NIUS — PURCELL — DIDO AND ÆNEAS — PURCELL'S INSTRU-
MENTAL MUSIC—THE TEMPEST.

ABOUT this time Dryden turned his attention to
the musical drama. In 1678 he published his
play, called *The State of Innocence, and Fall of
Man*, which he formally denominated an opera.
This, however, is an improper designation; for the
piece contains no lyrical poetry, the music employed in it being entirely instrumental. It was
never performed, nor can we suppose that it was
ever intended for actual representation. Such
scenes as the following could not be exhibited on
the stage.

"Scene I. represents a chaos, or a confused
mass of matter; the stage is almost wholly dark:
a symphony of warlike music is heard for some
time; then from the heavens (which are opened)
fall the rebellious angels, wheeling in air, and
seeming transfixed with thunderbolts. The bottom
of the stage, being opened, receives the angels,
who fall out of sight. Tunes of victory are played
and an hymn sung; angels discovered above,
brandishing their swords; the music ceasing, and
the heavens being closed, the scene shifts, and on

a sudden represents hell; part of the scene is a
lake of brimstone, or rolling fire; the earth of a
burnt colour; the fallen angels appear on the lake,
lying prostrate : a tune of horror and lamentation
is heard." Lucifer, raising himself on the burning lake, begins the piece by exclaiming,—

> " Is this the seat our conqueror has given ?
> And this the climate we must change for heaven ? "

Other devils rise in succession; and an infernal
council is held, like that in the opening of the
Paradise Lost.

Adam and Eve are afterwards introduced, " as
just created." The manners and conversation of
the primeval pair, as represented by Dryden,
exhibit marks of the false and corrupted taste of
the age. There is a want of the purity and simplicity in the sentiments and images, which are so
beautifully preserved by Milton; and Eve especially, at the very outset, evinces no inconsiderable share of vanity, coquetry, and love of rule,
from which the " general mother" of the fair sex
must surely have been wholly free in the " state
of innocence." She enters, wondering at herself—

> " Like myself I see nothing : from each tree
> The feather'd kind peep down to look on me ;
> And beasts, with up-cast eyes, forsake their shade,
> And gaze, as if I were to be obey'd.
> Sure I am something which they wish to be,
> And cannot ; I myself am proud of me."

How quick-sighted to the general admiration she
excites; and what *naïveté* in " *I myself am proud*

of me! " In the same spirit is her apprehension that, when she grants her lover's suit, she will lose her much-loved sovereignty; and her fears of his *infidelity* have almost the effect of burlesque.

It is difficult to imagine what could have induced Dryden to think of this production. In his preface he gives some reasons for " publishing an opera which was never acted." Many incorrect copies, he says, had got abroad, full of errors and absurdities, so that he was obliged to publish, in self-defence. He confesses his obligations to Milton, and acknowledges the inferiority of his " mean production" to the sublime work of that poet. Knowing, perhaps, that Milton had taken the idea of the *Paradise Lost* from an Italian mystery, and that he had intended at first to give his poem a dramatic form, Dryden may have thought of accomplishing the design which Milton had abandoned. It is said by Aubrey, that Dryden made a personal application to Milton for permission to make the attempt; and that the old poet answered with indifference, " Aye, you may *tag* my verses if you will."*

* The Italian Mystery which suggested to Milton the subject of the Paradise Lost, is the *Adamo* of Adreini, in which the sacred subject, as usual with those productions, is unintentionally burlesqued. The drama opens with a grand chorus of angels, who sing thus :—

" Let the rainbow be the fiddle-stick of the fiddle of heaven,
Let the spheres be the strings, and the stars the musical notes ;
Let the new-born breezes make the pauses and sharps,
And let Time be careful to beat the measure."

Dryden's first opera, that was actually represented, was *Albion and Albanius*, which was performed at the Duke's Theatre, in 1685. This
piece was nearly finished in the lifetime of Charles
II., though not performed till after his death. It
had a political object, to favour the interest of the
court; and was an allegorical representation of the
restoration of the Stuart family to the throne, and
the king's recent victory over his Whig opponents.
It contains the leading incidents in the life of
Charles II.; the Restoration, and return of the
king and the Duke of York, under the names of
Albion and Albanius; and the popish plot, hatched
by a council of fiends, who send Democracy and
Zeal, with Dr. Titus Oates in their train, to propa-
gate it on earth. The return of the Duke of York
and his beautiful princess, and the rejoicings in
heaven and earth on the King's attaining complete power, were the intended termination of
the drama: but, in consequence of the death of
Charles, the conclusion was changed to the apo-
theosis of Albion, and the succession of Albanius
to the uncontrolled dominion over a willing people.

It may easily be imagined that a piece of this
political character, produced at a time when the
nation was almost ripe for the revolution which
took place within three years afterwards, could not
be very congenial to the public feeling. It was
brought upon the stage with great splendour, but
was coldly received. Its death-blow was the news
of Monmouth's invasion, which reached London on

Saturday the 13th of June, 1685, during its performance for the sixth time: the audience broke up in confusion, and it was never repeated.

This piece, notwithstanding its unhappy subject, is full of Dryden's characteristic vigour of thought and expression; and the lyrical poetry, in particular, is beautifully sweet and flowing.

When Dryden wrote this opera, the *Gallomania* raged at the English court; and Dryden, as the poet of the court, doubtless found it convenient to flatter the fashionable taste, of which the king himself was the principal votary. That Dryden was desirous to court the favour of Charles, by yielding to his French prepossessions, is evident from his employing Grabut, a Frenchman, to compose the music of *Albion and Albanius*, though he could not have been ignorant of the infinitely superior merit of his countryman Purcell, whose transcendent genius had already broke out in all its splendour. This Grabut was an obscure musician, whose name is not to be found in the French annals of the art. He appears to have come to England with Cambert, a musician of some eminence, who, about the year 1672, was made master of the king's band. Grabut composed the music to a translation of Cambert's French opera of *Ariadne*; or, more probably, only adapted Cambert's original music to the English words. This piece, which was performed with little success, in 1674, seems to have been the only work of Grabut's prior to *Albion and Albanius*: but he was in favour at court, and was consequently employed by Dryden.

The poet, however, appears to have thought that this step required some justification. In the preface he informs the public, that the opera had been rehearsed several times in presence of the king, "who had publicly declared, more than once, that the compositions and choruses were more just, and more beautiful, than any he had heard in England." Dryden then praises Grabut very warmly; and adds;—"This I say, not to flatter him, but to do him right: because, among some English musicians, and their scholars, who are sure to judge after them, the imputation of being a Frenchman is enough to make a party who maliciously endeavour to decry him. But the knowledge of Latin and Italian poets, both which he possesses, besides his skill in music, and his being acquainted with all the performances of the French operas, adding to these the good sense to which he is born, have raised him to a degree above any man who shall pretend to be his rival on our stage. When any of our countrymen excel him, I shall be glad, for the sake of Old England, to be shown my error: in the meantime, let virtue be commended, though in the person of a stranger." This passage gave great and general dissatisfaction. The original offence of giving the preference to an obscure and worthless musician was aggravated by the injurious and disparaging manner in which, to exalt his character, the English musicians,

including the already illustrious Purcell, were
treated. The consequence was, that Dryden was
exposed, not only to serious attacks, but to squibs
and lampoons of the most severe and poignant
description.

The following is the conclusion of the scene in
which the Popish Plot is hatched by a pandemonian
council of fiends and infernal deities. The description of the notorious Dr. Titus Oates could hardly
be paralleled in strength of invective. When
Zelota is about to be dismissed on her errand, to
stir up evil against the king, she says :—

> " You've all forgot
>   To forge a plot
> In seeming care of Albion's life ;
>   Inspire the crowd
>   With clamours loud,
> To involve his brother and his wife.

Alecto. Take, of a thousand souls at thy command,
   The basest, blackest of the Stygian band,
   One that will swear to all they can invent,
   So thoroughly damn'd that he ne'er can repent :
   One, often sent to earth
   And still at every birth
   He took a deeper stain :
   One, that in Adam's time was Cain ;
   One, that was burnt in Sodom's flame,
   For crimes even here too black to name :
   One, who through every flame of ill has run :
   One, who in Naboth's days was Belial's son :
   One, who has gain'd a body fit for sin :
   Where all his crimes
   Of former times
   Lie crowded in a skin.

Pluto.   Take him,
            Make him
            What you please ;
            For he can be
            A rogue with ease,
            One for mighty mischief born ;
            He can swear and be forsworn.

Pluto and Alecto.   Take him, make him, what you please,
                      For he can be a rogue with ease.*

  Pluto.   Let us laugh, let us laugh, let us laugh at our woes,
             The wretch that is damned hath nothing to lose.
                      Ye Furies, advance
                      With the ghosts in a dance :
             'Tis a jubilee when the world is in trouble ;
                      When the people rebel
                      We frolic in hell ;
             But when the king falls, the pleasure is double.

[*A single entry of a devil, followed by an entry of twelve devils.*]

Chorus.   Let us laugh, let us laugh, let us laugh, at our woes,
            The wretch that is damned hath nothing to lose."

In the preface to *Albion and Albanius,* Dryden
says that this opera " was only intended as a
prologue to a play of the nature of *The Tempest;*
which is a tragedy mixed with opera, or a drama
written in blank verse, adorned with scenes,
machines, songs, and dances ; so that the fable of

* Oates was alive at this time, and lived many years afterwards. He shook off, in some degree, the load of infamy which
had overwhelmed him ; regained some footing in society ; and
was rewarded for his virtues, by King William, with a pension
of 400*l.* a year !

it is all spoken and acted by the best of the comedians; the other part of the entertainment to be performed by the same singers and dancers who are introduced in the present opera." The only piece at all answering this description, subsequently produced by him, was *King Arthur*, which seems, therefore, to have been the tragedy here alluded to, though it did not make its appearance till the year 1691, six years afterwards.

During this interval, Dryden seems to have not only acquired a proper sense of the merits of Purcell, but to have entered into friendly intercourse with him. Before taking a review of their joint labours, it may be proper to give a slight sketch of the previous career of this illustrious musician.

Henry Purcell was born in the year 1658. His father, Henry Purcell, was a musician, and one of the gentlemen of the Chapel Royal at the restoration of Charles II. Some of his compositions, which are still extant, indicate a respectable degree of talent and knowledge of his art. He died in 1664, when his son was only six years old. It is not ascertained from whom young Purcell received his first instructions in music; but it was most probably from Captain Cook, who was then master of the children of the Chapel Royal. He afterwards received lessons from Dr. Blow; a circumstance in the life of that eminent musician which was considered of so much importance, that, in the inscription on his tomb, it is mentioned that he was "Master to the famous Mr. Henry Purcell."

His genius showed itself at a very early age. While he was yet a singing boy in the king's chapel, he composed several anthems, which are sung to this day. This is, perhaps, one of the most remarkable instances of precocity that has been recorded; for the anthem, demanding a knowledge of the laws of counterpoint which, in general, can be obtained only by long and severe study, seems to be in an especial manner beyond the reach of a juvenile composer. To have produced, therefore, pieces of this kind, which, for nearly two centuries, have kept their place among the standard works of our ecclesiastical musicians, indicated an inborn creative power, which, unless to a kindred spirit, is wholly inconceivable.

At the age of eighteen, Purcell received the honourable appointment of organist of Westminster Abbey; and in his twenty-fourth year he was chosen to be one of the three organists of the Chapel Royal. By this time he had composed many of those anthems which are considered as being among the noblest specimens of our cathedral music. Notwithstanding, however, his ecclesiastical situations and employments, he very early turned his attention to dramatic music, which seems to have been especially congenial to his inclination as well as his genius. Tom Brown, in his letters from the Dead to the Living, notices this bent of Purcell's mind. In a letter from Dr.

Blow to Purcell, he makes the writer say, that persons of their profession are equally attracted by the church and the playhouse, so that they are, like Mahomet's coffin, suspended between heaven and earth.*

His first essay in theatrical music was made when he was nineteen. Josiah Priest, a celebrated teacher of dancing, who had long been the composer of the court-ballets, and had consequently acquired a taste for the stage, wished to get up a private dramatic performance by his pupils. He accordingly got Tate to write a little opera, called *Dido and Æneas*, and prevailed on Purcell to compose the music for it. The piece was represented by some of the young ladies who attended Priest's school, before a select audience of their relatives and friends, with great applause. The music, in particular, was found to be beautiful; and, as it is extant, we are enabled to know that this opinion of it was perfectly just.

Dido and Æneas is a wonderful work, considering the youth of the composer. As a whole, it is deficient in the finish and mellowness which characterise the productions of his riper years. But, from beginning to end, it sparkles with genius, and contains beauties which even he himself has not surpassed. He was happy in his subject, which was treated by Mr. Tate with good dramatic effect. The piece opens with the arrival of

* This joke, by the way, is an anachronism; for Blow survived Purcell.

Æneas at Carthage, and ends with the death of Dido, after her desertion by her faithless lover. Dido's recitative, in which, after she has been listening to Æneas's story, she expresses her admiration of her guest, affords instances of that false expression, produced by seizing upon particular words, which is so common among composers, but is rarely to be found in Purcell's later works. Dido says,

> " Whence could so much virtue spring ?
> What storms, what battles, did he sing !
> Anchises' valour, mix'd with Venus' charms ;
> How soft in peace, and yet how fierce in arms ! "

One unmingled sentiment of pleasure and admiration pervades this passage: yet, when Dido comes to the word "soft" she falls upon it by a chromatic semitone, and repeats it twice with a languishing *appoggiatura;* and in an instant afterwards breaks out into a boisterous roulade upon the word " fierce." The word " storms," too, gives occasion for a little musical mimicry. Another fault of a similar kind occurs in the scene where Dido and Æneas are overtaken by the storm. Dido exclaims,

> " The skies are clouded ; hark how thunder
> Rends the mountain rocks asunder ! "

According to the approved principles of musical painting, the war of the elements should have been depicted by the tumultuous sounds of the orchestra, the voice using the simple accents of exclamation.

But, instead of this, Dido sets about mimicking
the thunder, by rolling out that word in a long,
rattling roulade. These things should be marked,
in the works of the greatest masters, as beacons to
be avoided; as students are fully as apt to copy
the faults as the beauties of their models.

The fault in the first passage above quoted is
redeemed by the true and beautiful expression
given to the phrase immediately following, where
Dido says, " But, ah ! I fear I pity him too much ! "
and by the lovely chorus,

> " Fear no danger to ensue,
> The hero loves as well as you ; "

sung, to re-assure her, by Anna and her other
attendants. Its graceful tranquillity is perfectly
delicious. The chorus " To the hills and the vales,
to the rocks and the mountains," is " redolent of
spring," and full of the most delightful freshness.
But, to our feeling, the flow of the melody is
checked, and its beauty impaired, by a single
crude note—the B *flat* suddenly introduced (the
key being G major) at the words " cool shady foun-
tains;" an unnecessary and unsuccessful attempt
at musical expression where it is not wanted.

The introduction of a malignant sorceress, by
whose machinations Æneas is made to abandon his
mistress, gives occasion for a great deal of admirable music. The invocation by the sorceress, and
the choral responses and wild laughter of the infernal spirits, are striking and unearthly, and would

have as powerful an effect as anything in the *Frei-schutz*. The little duet in this scene, between two of the witches, "But ere we this perform," in free canon, is remarkable for its ingenuity of contrivance, and easy flow of melody : and the full chorus which follows, and concludes the scene, has the broad simplicity of Matthew Lock.

The second act is full of beauties. In the scene in which the lovers and their attendants, while hunting, are overtaken by the storm, the chorus " Haste, haste, to the town," by the intricate movement of the parts, paints the confusion and agitation of the party. A chorus of Æneas's sailors, preparing to weigh anchor, is of a bold and somewhat comic character. We are again introduced to the infernal conclave, whose chorus of demoniacal exultation at Dido's approaching fate, is one of the most powerful of Purcell's compositions. The impassioned dialogue between the lovers, as they are about to part, is a beautiful specimen of true English recitative, in which the accents and inflexions of the language are made subservient to the purposes of musical expression. The last words of the queen are formed into a little air, "When I am laid in earth," which sounds like the dying murmurs of a broken heart. The melody is constructed on a ground bass ; a form of composition now obsolete, as imposing needless restrictions on the musician. Yet sometimes, as in the present instance, it is a source of beauty. The recurrence, over and over again, of the same few melancholy notes in the bass, strikes sadly on the ear, and deepens the expression of the song. The piece concludes with a soft mournful chorus.

This beautiful opera, which was produced in 1677, immediately attracted the attention of the managers of the theatres, and led to Purcell's being engaged in writing for the stage.

The musical drama not having yet a separate existence, it was still customary to introduce music into both tragedy and comedy. Most of the plays of that time had overtures and pieces to be performed between the acts, composed expressly for them; and incidental songs, not sung by the personages of the drama, but by singers introduced, as it were, for their entertainment. From this time, these overtures, act-tunes, and songs, were frequently composed by Purcell. In this manner, he embellished, as it may be called, the play of *Abelazor*, which appeared in 1677; *Timon of Athens* (altered from Shakspeare by Shadwell), in 1678; Lee's *Theodosius, or the force of Love*, in 1680; and other pieces which shall be afterwards mentioned.

A collection of these instrumental pieces was published, in 1697, after Purcell's death, by his widow, under the title of "A Collection of Ayres, composed for the Theatre, and on other occasions, by the late Mr. Henry Purcell." They are in four parts, for two violins, tenor and bass; and are so pleasing, that they were used in the theatres till the middle of the last century, when the progress of orchestral music necessarily caused them to be laid aside.

In 1683, he published twelve sonatas for two violins and a bass, with a preface containing the following interesting passage, in which he admits his obligations to the Italian composers. " The author has faithfully endeavoured a just imitation of the most famed Italian masters, principally to bring the seriousness and gravity of that sort of music into vogue and reputation among our countrymen, whose humour it is time now should begin to loathe the levity and balladry of our neighbours. The attempt he confesses to be bold and daring; there being pens and artists of more eminent abilities, much better qualified for the employment than his or himself, which he well hopes these his weak endeavours will in due time provoke and inflame to a more accurate under-taking. He is not ashamed to own his unskil-fulness in the Italian language, but that is the unhappiness of his education, which cannot justly be counted his fault; however, he thinks he may warrantably affirm, that he is not mistaken in the power of the Italian notes, or elegancy of their compositions." This work was so well re-ceived, that he soon afterwards published another set, containing ten sonatas, one of which, from its peculiar excellence, acquired the name of the *Golden Sonata*.

These sonatas, or trios, evidently belong to the

same school as those of Corelli. The trios of the great Italian composer were published in the same year, and could not have served as a model to Purcell, who, in acknowledging his obligation to "the most famed Italian masters" in this species of composition, must have alluded to Torelli and Bassani, the latter of whom was Corelli's master. Purcell's sonatas, in some respects, are even superior to those of the great Italian composer ;—for they contain movements which, in depth of learning and ingenuity of harmonical combination, without the least appearance of labour or restraint, surpass anything to be found in the works of Corelli : but Corelli had the advantage of being a great violinist, while Purcell, who was not only no performer himself, but probably had never heard a great performer, had no means, except the perusal of Italian scores, of forming an idea of the genius and powers of the instrument. This disadvantage prevented Purcell from striking out new and effective violin passages, and produced mechanical awkwardness which a master of the instrument would have avoided : but it did not disable him from exhibiting taste and fancy ; and every admirer of the works of Corelli will take pleasure in these sonatas of Purcell.

Dryden, who had done Purcell injustice, afterwards became his warm friend and one of his greatest admirers. After the death of Charles II. the poet must have found himself freed from the trammels imposed on him by the vitiated taste of

that monarch and his court, and a personal intercourse between Dryden and Purcell arose from the
circumstance of Purcell's having been the musical
instructor of Lady Elizabeth Howard, the poet's
wife. When the play of *The Tempest* was revived
in 1690, Purcell was employed to compose new
music for it.

The Tempest had been altered from Shakspeare
by Davenant and Dryden, and represented at
Davenant's theatre in 1667. In the preface, which
is written by Dryden, he says, " Sir William Davenant did me the honour to join me with him in the
alteration of this play ;" but what share Dryden had
in the alterations does not appear. They appear
to have been chiefly made by Davenant, though
they bear many marks of Dryden's hand. The
play, as thus altered, was published in the year
1670.

Shakspeare's play underwent these alterations
for the purpose, chiefly, of affording room for scenic
decoration and music. But this might have been
done without the interpolation of so much inferior
matter, and the introduction of those characters
which destroy the majestic simplicity of the original
design. The idea of contrasting Shakspeare's original character of a woman who has never seen a
man, with a man who has never seen a woman, is
puerile in itself, and, in its execution, wanting in
refinement and purity. That which, in Miranda,
is charming innocence and simplicity, becomes
unmanly silliness in the counterpart; and the cha-

racter of Dorinda, the sister given to Miranda, is not only unnecessary, but indelicate. The play, thus metamorphosed, cannot be read (for it is now never represented) without disgust; and it is surprising that Dryden (who, in the prologue to this very piece, has paid so noble a tribute to the genius of Shakspeare) could have lent his sanction to such an act of sacrilege.

When the music came to be composed by Purcell, several additions were made to the lyrical portion, which are not in the edition of the play published in 1670 ; and in other parts, the words are considerably altered.

The music of *The Tempest* consists almost entirely of the songs and choruses of the aërial inhabitants of Prospero's enchanted island, described by the poet as being

> "——— full of noises,
> Sounds and sweet airs, that give delight and hurt not."

The strange and wild character of these unearthly strains is beautifully supported, and the listener partakes of the feeling of the bewildered Ferdinand, when, amazed at the invisible chorus which reminds him of his drowned father, he exclaims,—

> " This is no mortal business, nor no sound
> That the earth owes !"

The scene of the spirits deputed to bewilder the conspirators contains the song, " Arise, ye subterranean winds"—a powerful composition, in which rolling divisions, finely adapted to a bass voice, are used with happy imitative effect. In this song, however, Purcell has fallen into the very common error of giving to particular words an expression at variance with the general tone of the poetry. The spirit is commanding the winds to

> " Drive these wretches to that part o' the isle,
> Where nature never yet did smile ;
> Cause fogs and damps, whirlwinds and earthquakes there ;
> There let them howl, and languish in despair."

On the word " howl," the singer howls on one note for two bars. This is a piece of musical mimicry inconsistent with the gravity of the style ; but it is not so bad as the next passage, in which, on the word " languish," the singer languishes, for three bars, through a drawling descent of semi-tones. Though the spirit desires that the wretches whom he is commissioned to punish may languish in despair, there is no reason that he should assume a languishing air in saying so. Nothing can be more exquisite than the fairy lightness of Ariel's little song, " Come unto these yellow sands," with its wild and simple burden. The masque, or pageant, presented by Prospero's spirits at the end of the play, is made a vehicle for some charming music. The recitative and air, for a bass (or rather baritone) voice in the character of Neptune, " Æolus, you must appear," is in a grand and dignified style. In the following air, " Come down, my blusterers," Æolus blusters through many long divisions ; but the passage,

"To your prisons below,
Down you must go,"

is remarkable for the very impressive utterance given to these words. The soprano air, "Halcyon days," sung by Amphitrite, is perfectly delicious. In this air it is impossible to overlook the beauty of the accompaniments. The charming passages given to the oboes, and the graceful motion of all the instrumental parts, show how much Purcell was in advance of his age, in this as well as other branches of his art. The chorus, "The Nereids and Tritons shall sing and shall play," is beautiful; and the famous duet and chorus, "No stars again shall hurt you," a piece of rich and resonant harmony, forms a brilliant conclusion to the whole. There is a song for Caliban, "The owl is abroad, the bat and the toad," which one might suppose Weber to have imagined.

Some parts of this music may still occasionally be heard at concerts; but it is long since the piece to which it belongs has been performed. We can hardly, however, imagine a more delightful theatrical entertainment than Shakspeare's beautiful play, unpolluted by Davenant's trash, and embellished by the music of Purcell.

CHAPTER VII.

KING ARTHUR—THE INDIAN QUEEN—TYRANNIC LOVE.

THE revival of *The Tempest*, with Purcell's music in 1690, was followed by the appearance of *King Arthur* in 1691. This piece was written by Dryden, and the music in it composed by Purcell. It was brought out in a splendid manner, and had great success.

King Arthur is a tale of love, war, and enchantment; its incidents are fantastic, but ingenious and entertaining. The story consists of the love of Arthur, the ancient British king, for Emmeline, the daughter of a tributary prince; her abduction by his rival Oswald, a heathen king of Kent; her recovery from his hands, and union with her lover. The evil designs of Oswald are favoured by Osmond, a Saxon magician, and his subservient evil spirits; while they are thwarted by Merlin, the famous enchanter, and the beneficent spirits under his command. The spirits are taken from the Rosicrucian philosophy; Grimbald, the malignant fiend, being a gnome, or spirit of earth, while his adversary, Philidel, is a sylph, or spirit of air. This machinery is well managed. There is a wild grandeur in the evil nature of Grimbald; and the character of Philidel, — an angel, who, though fallen, is not lost, but feels repentance and hopes for pardon,—is original and beautiful. The blindness of Emmeline adds interest to her innocent simplicity, and gives rise to many pretty and fanciful passages.

In the first scene, Arthur and Conon, Emmeline's father, are engaged in discourse. She enters.

" *Em.* O father, father, I am sure you're here,
Because I see your voice.
    Arth. No ; thou mistak'st thy hearing for thy sight :
He's gone, my Emmeline ;
And I but stay to gaze on those fair eyes,
Which cannot view the conquests they have made.
Oh starlike night, dark only to thyself,
But full of glory, as those lamps of heaven,
That see not, when they shine !
    Em. What is this heaven, and stars, and night, and day,
To which you thus compare my eyes and me ?
I understand you when you say you love ;
For, when my father clasps my hand in his,
That 's cold, and I can feel it hard and wrinkled ;
But when you grasp it, then I sigh and pant,
And something smarts and tickles at my heart.
    Arth. Oh artless love, where the soul moves the tongue,
And only nature speaks what nature thinks !
Had she but eyes !
    Em. Just now you said I had :
I see them : I have two.
    Arth. But neither see.
    Em. I 'm sure they hear you, then :
What can your eyes do more ?
    Arth. They see your beauties.

Em. Do not I see ?   You have a face like mine—
Two hands, and two round, pretty, rising breasts,
That heave like mine.

    Arth. But you describe a woman :
Nor is it sight, but touching with your hands.

    Em. Then 'tis my hand that sees, and that's all one,—
For is not seeing, touching with your eyes ?

    Arth. No ; for I see at distance, when I touch not.

    Em. If you can see so far, and yet not touch,
I fear you see my naked legs and feet
Quite through my clothes.   Pray do not see so well.

    Arth. Fear not, sweet innocence ;
I view the lovely features of your face,
Your lips' carnation, your dark-shaded eye-brows,
Black eyes and snow-white forehead ; all the colours
That make your beauty, and produce my love.

    Em. Nay, then, you do not love on equal terms ;—
I love you dearly without all these helps ;
I cannot see your lips' carnation,
Your shaded eyebrows, nor your milk-white eyes.

    Arth. You still mistake.

    Em. Indeed I thought you had a nose and eyes,
And such a face as mine : have not men faces ?

    Arth. Oh, none like yours, so excellently fair.

    Em. Then would I had no face, for I would be
Just such a one as you.

    Arth. Alas ! 'tis vain to instruct your innocence ;
You have no notion of light or colours.

                    [*Trumpet sounds within.*

    Em. Why, is not that a trumpet ?

    Arth. Yes.

    Em. I knew it,
And I can tell you how the sound on't looks ;
It looks as if it had an angry fighting face.

    Arth. 'Tis now indeed a sharp unpleasant sound,
Because it calls me hence from her I love,
To meet ten thousand foes.

Em. How do so many men e'er come to meet ?
This devil trumpet vexes them, and then
They feel about for one another's faces ;
And so they meet and kill.
    Arth. I 'll tell you all when we have gain'd the field.
One kiss of your fair hand the pledge of conquest,
And so a short farewell.   [*Exit.*
    Em. My heart and vows go with him to the fight.
May every foe be that which they call blind,
And none of all their swords have eyes to find him !
But lead me nearer to the trumpet's face ;
For that brave sound upholds my fainting heart ;
And, while I hear, methinks I fight my part."

The scene in which Emmeline recovers her sight
by means of Philidel, is calculated to produce a
charming effect on the stage; but we must turn to
the musical parts of the drama.

The scene in the first act, of the great sacrifice
offered by the Saxons before their battle with the
Britons, is full of barbarous grandeur. It opens
with the songs of the priests, accompanying the
sacrifice of three milk-white steeds to Woden,
Thor, and Freya. The choral shout, " We have
sacrificed ! " at the end of each recitation by a
single voice, is magnificent. The men who have
devoted themselves as voluntary victims, are addressed by the priests,—

     " Brave souls, to be renown'd in story ;
        Honour prizing, death despising,
         Fame acquiring by expiring,—
       Die, and reap the fruit of glory ! "

This chorus opens with a short but energetic

fugato, and passes into a dark and gloomy strain.
After a pause, a single voice sings, to a bold and
lively air—

> " I call you all
>   To Woden's hall,
>   Your temples round
>   With ivy bound,
>   In goblets crown'd
> And plenteous bowls of burnish'd gold.
>   Where ye shall laugh,
>   And dance, and quaff
> The juice that makes the Britons bold."

And the victims respond, in joyous chorus,

> " To Woden's hall,
>   All, all, all, all ;
> Where in plenteous bowls of burnish'd gold
>   We shall laugh,
>   And dance, and quaff
> The juice that makes the Britons bold."

The battle-song of the Britons, " Come if you
dare," is a noble burst of martial ardour, to which
the musician has given full expression. The choral
part written in plain counterpoint, may be conceived to be a whole army's shouts of defiance and
of victory.

Arthur being left alone in pursuit of the flying
foe, Grimbald, the malignant spirit, accosts him in
disguise, and attempts to lead him astray, while
Philidel, interposing, warns him of the deceit.
Philidel's song, with the chorus of her attendant
spirits,—" Hither, hither, this way bend," is exquisitely light and delicate.   Grimbald's air, " Let

not a moon-born elf mislead ye," has the plain simplicity of his assumed character, and is at the same
time smooth and beautiful. The dramatic effect
of this scene is admirable.

The celebrated frost-scene, so well-known to the
admirers of Purcell, is a sort of masque, exhibited
by the magician Osmond to Emmeline, after she
has recovered her sight, for the purpose of in-
ducing her to listen to his addresses. The poetry
and music are equally beautiful.

" *Emmeline.* I freeze, as if his impious art had fixed
My feet to earth.
    Osmond. But love shall thaw ye.
I 'll show his force in countries cak'd with ice,
Where the pale pole-star in the north of heaven
Sits high, and on the frosty winter broods,—
Yet there love reigns : For proof, this magic wand
Shall change the mildness of sweet Britain's clime
To Iceland, and the farthest Thule's frost,
Where the proud god, disdaining winter's bounds,
O'erleaps the fences of eternal snow,
And with his warmth supplies the distant sun.

> [*Osmond strikes the ground with his wand ; the scene
> changes to a prospect of winter in frozen countries.*

Cupid descends.

Cupid sings. What ho, thou genius of the clime, what ho !
    Ly'st thou asleep beneath those hills of snow ?
    Stretch out thy lazy limbs ; awake, awake,
    And winter from thy furry mantle shake.

Genius arises.

Genius. What power art thou, who from below
    Hast made me rise unwillingly and slow,
    From beds of everlasting snow ?

See'st thou how stiff and wondrous old,
Far unfit to bear the bitter cold ?
I can scarcely move, or draw my breath ;
Let me, let me freeze again to death.

Cupid. Thou doting fool, forbear, forbear !
What, dost thou dream of freezing here ?
At Love's appearing, all the sky clearing,
    The stormy winds their fury spare :
Winter subduing, and spring renewing,
    My beams create a more glorious year.
Thou doting fool, forbear, forbear !
What, dost thou dream of freezing here ?

Genius. Great Love, I know thee now ;
Eldest of the gods art thou :
Heaven and earth by thee were made ;
        Human nature
        Is thy creature,
Every where thou art obey'd.

Cupid. No part of my dominion shall be waste :
        To spread my sway, and sing my praise,
        Even here I will a people raise,
Of kind embracing lovers, and embrac'd.

[*Cupid waves his wand, upon which the scene opens, aud dis-*
    covers a prospect of ice and snow to the end of the stage.
    Singers and dancers, men and women, appear.

Man. See, see, we assemble,
        Thy revels to hold ;
        Though quivering with cold,
        We chatter and tremble.

Cupid. 'Tis I, 'tis I, 'tis I, that have warm'd ye ;
        In spite of cold weather,
        I 've brought you together ;
        'Tis I, 'tis I, 'tis I, that have warm'd ye.

Chorus. 'Tis Love, 'tis Love, 'tis Love, that has warm'd us;
        In spite of cold weather
        He brought us together :
        'Tis Love, 'tis Love, 'tis Love that has warm'd us.

Cupid. Sound a parley, ye fair, and surrender!
　　Set yourselves and your lovers at ease ;
　　　　He 's a grateful offender
　　　　Who pleasure dare seize ;
　　　　But the whining pretender
　　　　Is sure to displease.

　　Since the fruit of desire is possessing,
　　　　'Tis unmanly to sigh and complain ;
　　When we kneel for redressing
　　　　We move your disdain :
　　Love was made for a blessing,
　　　　And not for a pain.

　A dance ; after which the singers and dancers depart.

　Emmeline. I could be pleased with any one but thee,
Who entertain'd my sight with such gay shows,
As men and women moving here and there,
That, coursing one another in their steps,
Have made their feet a tune."

Cupid's invocation. " What, ho ! thou genius of
this isle," is called a recitative, though it is more
properly an *aria parlante.* The boundaries between recitative and air were not exactly defined
in Purcell's time. His recitatives often have the
protracted tones, the rhythmical movement, the
divisions, embellishments, and regular closes, which
are now considered as belonging entirely to the *air.*
A few bars of symphony form a picturesque introduction to the appearance of the genius ; there is
something freezing in the sounds he utters, as, with
a low and trembling voice, he rises, " unwillingly
and slow," through an octave of semitones; and

equally expressive is the descending octave with
which he murmurs, "Let me freeze again to
death," as if unable longer to suffer the pain of
utterance.   The influence of love, in gradually
warming his breast, is finely expressed; and the
chorus of the inhabitants of the regions of frost,
"'Tis love that has warmed us," is full of life and
spirit.   The construction of this effective chorus is
simple in the extreme; but it is that simplicity of
which the highest genius only is capable.

We now come to the romantic scene of Arthur's
temptations and dangers in the enchanted grove.
It is borrowed from the *Jerusalem Delivered* — the
same source from which Wieland derived the
similar scene in *Oberon*, which has been introduced in the opera composed by Weber.   Arthur,
before entering the scene of his trials, has been
warned that he has many perils to encounter; but
those he meets with are not such as he has prepared himself for.

"*Arthur (walking)*. No danger yet : I see no walls of fire,
No city of the fiends, with forms obscene,
To grin from far on flaming battlements.
This is indeed the grove I should destroy ;
But where 's the horror ? sure the prophet err'd.—
Hark ! music, and the warbling notes of birds !
                                        [*Soft music.*
Hell entertains me like some welcome guest.
More wonders yet ! yet all delightful too :
A silver current to forbid my passage,
And yet, to invite me, stands a golden bridge :
Perhaps a trap for my unwary feet,
To sink and whelm me underneath the waves,

With fire or water let him wage his war,
Or all the elements at once, I'll on.

> [*As he is going to the bridge, two Syrens arise from the*
> *water. They show themselves to the waist and sing.*

1st Syren. O pass not on, but stay,
       And waste the joyous day
         With us in gentle play;
      Unbend to love, unbend thee:
        O lay thy sword aside,
         And other arms provide;
      For other wars attend thee,
        And sweeter to be tried.
Chorus.   For other wars, &c.

Both sing. Two daughters of this aged stream are we;
      And both our sea-green locks have comb'd for thee:
      Come bathe with us an hour or two,
      Come naked in, for we are so;
      What danger from a naked foe?
      Come bathe with us, come bathe, and share
      What pleasures in the floods appear.
      We'll beat the waters till they bound,
      And circle round, around, around,
        And circle round, around.

Arthur. A lazy pleasure trickles through my veins!
Here could I stay, and well be cozen'd here.
But honour calls;—is honour in such haste?
Can it not bait at such a pleasing inn?
No, for the more I look, the more I long.
Farewell, ye fair illusions! I must leave ye,
While I have power to say that I must leave ye.
Farewell! with half my soul I stagger off.
How dear this flying victory has cost,
When, if I stay to struggle, I am lost!

> [*As he is going forward, Nymphs and Sylvans come*
> *out from behind the trees. A bass and two trebles*
> *sing the following song to a minuet.*

Dance with a song, all with branches in their hands.

Song. How happy the lover,
How easy his chain,
How pleasing his pain,
How sweet to discover
He sighs not in vain.
For love every creature
Is form'd by his nature ;
No joys are above
The pleasures of love.

The dance continues, with the same measure played alone.

In vain are our graces,
In vain are your eyes,
If love you despise ;
When age furrows faces
'Tis time to be wise.
Then use the short blessing,
That flies in possessing :
No joys are above
The pleasures of love.

Arthur. And what are the fantastic fairy joys
To love like mine ? false joys, false welcomes all.
Begone, ye sylvan trippers of the green ;
Fly after night, and overtake the moon.

[*The dancers, singers, and Syrens vanish.*''

The duet in this scene, " Two daughters of an aged stream are we," is one of the very happiest efforts of Purcell's genius.   In imagining it, he at once leaped over the space of a century and a half, and anticipated all the grace, refinement, and expression, which a long line of his successors, down to the present day, have been able to bestow

upon melody. This song of the Syrens is indeed
enchanting; and realises any idea that can be
formed of such bewitching accents as might shake
the constancy of a hero. Not only, too, is it fasci-
nating to every one who is capable of being moved
by sweet sounds, but it is full of exquisite beauties
as a work of art. How admirably chosen are the
gliding intervals in which the invitation, "Come,
come," is breathed out, and reiterated so gently!
and how persuasive the diminished fifth with
which the highest voice urges the remonstrance,
" *What danger* from a naked foe!" If we look to
the combination of the two parts, we find ingenious
contrivances, which, though charming to the ear,
give no idea whatever of art or labour. The passage, "We'll beat the waters till they bound,"
appears to the listener highly descriptive; but it
is, moreover, a canon in the unison very curiously
interwoven, till it breaks into a free imitation
between the parts, and the fine undulating strain
which continues to the end. This charming duet
wants nothing but the rich orchestral colouring
of Mozart; which Purcell would assuredly have
given to it, had he possessed the means which the
progress of instrumental music placed in the hands
of the modern composer.

The drama concludes with a masque, or pageant,
represented by Pan, Nereids, Venus, Æolus, and
other mythological personages, and consisting of
songs and dances, for the purpose of exhibiting to
King Arthur the future prosperity and greatness

of his country.   The following song, sung by
Venus, is a good specimen of Dryden's smooth
lyrical measures.   It is united to one of Purcell's
sweetest melodies.

> " Fairest isle, all isles excelling,
>   Seat of pleasures and of loves ;
> Venus here will choose her dwelling,
>   And forsake her Cyprian groves.
>
> Cupid, from his favourite nation,
>   Care and envy will remove ;
> Jealousy, that poisons passion,
>   And despair, that dies for love.
>
> Gentle murmurs, sweet complaining,
>   Sighs, that blow the fire of love ;
> Soft repulses, kind disdaining,
>   Shall be all the pains you prove ;
>
> Every swain shall pay his duty,
>   Grateful every nymph shall prove ;
> And as these excel in beauty,
>   Those shall be renown'd for love."

King Arthur has been adapted to the modern
stage, under the title of *Arthur and Emmeline*.   In this shape it has frequently been performed at different times; and the increasing taste
for Purcell's music will probably bring about the
permanent revival of this elegant and pleasing
drama.

The Indian Queen was written partly by Sir
Robert Howard, Dryden's brother-in-law, and
partly by Dryden himself.   It is in rhyme, according to the fashion of the day ; and the versification,
as well as the characters, bear evident marks of

Dryden's hand. The plot is extravagant enough; arising not only out of a war between Mexico and Peru, for which history affords no warrant, but a contest between the lawful sovereign of Mexico and an usurper. Montezuma, the Peruvian general, who, after having nearly completed the conquest of Mexico, demands, as a reward, the hand of the Inca's daughter, and, because he is refused, transfers his own prowess, and, consequently, victory, to the Mexican side, has a resemblance to the more celebrated and strongly-drawn Almanzor; and Zempoalla, the usurping Mexican queen, has a great deal of the indomitable pride which Dryden often makes an attribute of his female characters.

This play was acted in 1664, and received with great applause. In its original form there is very little music; and we are not informed by whom it was composed. There is an instrumental symphony, introducing the prologue; a song or chorus, sung by aërial spirits, in the incantation scene in the third act; and a short song, or chorus, in the scene of the sacrifice which opens the fifth act. The passages in the incantation scene, which are set to music by Purcell, seem to have been at first merely spoken; and the additional lyrical poetry was probably introduced for the purpose of being set by Purcell after Dryden became aware of his unrivalled genius.

In the scene of the Mexican sacrifice, the chorus of priests is a grand composition. The movement in F minor, "All dismal sounds thus on these offerings wait," is a most masterly piece of counter-point, equally remarkable for the simplicity of its effect, and the deep gloom of its expression. In the incantation scene, where the magician Ismeron invokes the infernal powers to reveal to Zempoalla her future destiny, Ismeron's recitative and air, "Ye twice ten hundred deities," is a striking in-stance of the power of musical sounds to illustrate poetical conceptions. After the dismal objects by which the God of Dreams is conjured to arise from his sleeping mansion, and open his unwilling eyes, how exquisitely smooth and tranquil is the strain that follows;—

> "While bubbling springs their music keep,
> That use to lull thee in thy sleep."

The appearance of the God of Dreams is heralded by a sweet symphony for oboes; and the air which he sings has a free and flowing oboe accompani-ment. Indeed the whole instrumental parts in the music of this play show an astonishing command of the limited resources which the composer had at his disposal, and enable us to imagine the uses he would have made of a complete and various or-chestra. This play, too, contains the ballad, "I attempt from Love's sickness to fly in vain," one of the most beautiful pieces of tender and expressive melody that ever flowed from the mind of a musi-cian. Of this song, Dr. Burney says, that "though it has been many years dead, it would soon be recalled into existence and fashion by the voice of some favourite singer, who should think it worth animation." This has been done in our day, by Mr. Hobbs, who has made the song his own by his exquisite manner of singing it.

Dryden's *Tyrannic Love* was first acted in 1668, and printed in 1670. We are not informed who was the author of the music originally performed: but other music was afterwards composed by Purcell.

This play is in many respects very characteristic of its author. It contains a great deal of tumid language and exaggerated sentiment, mixed with much grandeur and elevation of thought. The character of St. Catherine is too perfect, and too much raised above humanity, to excite interest. We cannot feel emotions of terror or pity, from anything that can happen to a person who knows that she is under the immediate protection of heaven, is in communication with beings of a higher world, and is indifferent about everything that can befall her in this.

The introduction of magic, and of the astral spirits, who have little to do with the story of the piece, was probably contrived for the sake of music and scenery. Dryden, in his preface, thus justifies his use of this machinery. "As for what I have said of astral or aërial spirits, it is no invention of mine, but taken from those who have written on that subject. Whether there are such beings or not, it concerns not me. It is sufficient for my purpose that many have believed the affirmative;

and that these heroic representations, which are of the same nature with the epic, are not limited, but with the extremest bounds of what is credible."

The duet "Hark, my Damilcar," * which has been rendered famous by Purcell's music, is sung by two spirits, Nakar and Damilcar, who have been evoked by the magician Nigrinus, to aid the designs of the emperor against the honour of the Christian saint. Of these spirits the enchanter gives the following imaginative description.

> " An earthly fiend by compact me obeys ;
> But him to light intents I must not raise.
> Some astral forms I must invoke by prayer,
> Framed all of purest atoms of the air ;
> Not in their natures simply good or ill,
> But most subservient to bad spirits' will.
> Nakar of these does lead the mighty band,
> For eighty legions move at his command ;
> Gentle to all, but far, above the rest,
> Mild Nakar loves his soft Damilcar best.
> In airy chariots they together ride,
> And sip the dew as through the clouds they glide :
> These are the spirits which in love have power."

Nigrinus uses incantations, which are pretty closely imitated from *Macbeth*. Nakar and Damilcar descend in clouds, and sing.

> " *Nakar*. Hark, my Damilcar, we are called below !
> *Damilcar*. Let us go, let us go !
> Go to relieve the care
> Of longing lovers in despair !

---

* In the copies of the music, this name is always turned into Daridcar.

Nakar. Merry, merry, merry, we sail from the east,
  Half tippled at a rainbow feast.

 Dam. In the bright moonshine while winds whistle loud,
  Tivy, tivy, tivy, we mount and we fly,
  All rocking along in a downy white cloud :
  And lest our leap from the sky should prove too far,
  We slide on the back of a new-falling star.

Nakar. And drop from above
  In a jelly of love !

 Dam. But now the sun 's down, and the elements red,
  The spirits of fire against us make head !

Nakar. They muster, they muster, like gnats in the air ;
  Alas ! I must leave thee, my fair ;
  And to my light horsemen repair.

 Dam. O stay, for you need not to fear them to-night :
  The wind is for us, and blows full in their sight :
  And o'er the wide ocean we fight !
  Like leaves in the autumn our foes will fall down,
  And hiss in the water,

 Both. And hiss in the water, and drown !

 Dam. Now mortals that spy
  How we tilt in the sky,
  With wonder will gaze,
  And fear such events as will ne'er come to pass.

Nakar. Stay you to perform what the men will have done.

 Dam. Then call me again when the battle is won.

 Both. So ready and quick is a spirit of air
  To pity the lover, and succour the fair,
  That, silent and swift, the little soft god
  Is here with a wish, and is gone with a nod.
   [*The clouds part ; Nakar flies up, and Damilcar
    down.*"

This extravagant rhapsody is abundantly open
to ridicule, and did not escape the lash of Buck-
ingham, who has given the following whimsical
parody of it in the *Rehearsal.*

" The two right Kings of Brentford descend in the clouds, sing-
  ing, in white garments; and three fiddlers sitting before
  them, in green.

Bayes. Now, because the two right kings descend from
above, I make 'em sing to the tune and style of our modern
spirits.

1st King. Haste, brother king, we are sent from above.

2nd King. Let us move, let us move;
        Move to remove the fate
        Of Brentford's long united state.

1st King. Tarra, tan tara, full east and by south.

2nd King. We sail with thunder in our mouth,
        In scorching noon-day, whilst the traveller stays,
          Busy, busy, busy, we bustle along
        Mounted upon warm Phœbus his rays,
          Through the heavenly throng
          Hasting to those
          Who feed us at night with a pig's petty-toes.

1st King. And we'll fall with our pate
        In an *olio* of hate.

2nd King. But now supper's done, the servitors try,
        Like soldiers, to storm a whole half-moon pie.

1st King. They gather, they gather hot custard in spoons,
        But, alas, I must leave these half-moons,
        And repair to my trusty dragoons.

2nd King. O stay, for you need not as yet go astray;
        The tide, like a friend, has brought ships in our way,
        And on their high ropes we will play:
      Like maggots in filberts, we'll snug in our shell,
          We'll frisk in our shell,
          We'll firk in our shell,
          And farewell.

1st King. But the ladies have all inclination to dance,
        And the green frogs croak out a coranto of France.

Bayes. Is not that pretty, now? The fiddlers are all in
green.

Smith. Ay, but they play no coranto.

Johnson. No, but they play a tune that's a great deal better.

Bayes. No coranto, quotha! That's a good one, with all my heart. Come, sing on.

2nd King. Now mortals that hear
How we tilt and career,
With wonder will fear
The event of such things as shall never appear.

1st King. Stay you to fulfil what the gods have decreed.

2nd King. Then call me to help you, if there shall be need.

1st King. So firmly resolv'd is a true Brentford king
To save the distressed, and help to 'em bring,
That ere a full pot of good ale you can swallow,
He's here with a whoop, and gone with a hollow.

[*Bayes fillips his finger, and sings after them.*

Bayes. He's here with a whoop, and gone with a hollow. This, sir, you must know, I thought once to have brought in with a conjuror.

Johnson. Ay, that would have been better.

Bayes. No, faith, not when you consider it : for thus 'tis more compendious, and does the thing every whit as well.

Smith. Thing! what thing?

Bayes. Why, bring them down again into the throne, sir ; what would you have?

Smith. Well, but methinks the sense of this song is not very plain.

Bayes. Plain? why, did you ever hear any people in clouds speak plain? They must be all for flight of fancy, at its full range, without the least check or control upon it. When once you tie up spirits and people in clouds to speak plain, you spoil all.

Smith. (*aside.*) Bless me, what a monster's this !

[*The two kings light out of the clouds and step into the throne.*

1st King. Come, now to serious counsel we'll advance.

2nd King. I do agree, but first let's have a dance."

Purcell, however, in the above duet, has redeemed the absurdity of Dryden's verses by the beauty of his own music. It is airy, animated, and tender; and has so much meaning in itself, that the listener forgets that the words are mere nonsense.

There is another pretty song in this piece. St. Catherine is discovered asleep on a couch, while images of love and pleasure are exhibited to her, in a dream, by the enchanter's spirits. The song is, " Ah, how sweet it is to love!" sung by Damilcar. Its expression is soft and voluptuous; though it is injured by an unmeaning reiteration of the word "all" half a dozen times, and a stiff division at the close.

It was for this play Dryden wrote the epilogue so celebrated for its whimsical beginning. It was spoken by Nell Gwynn, who, being left as dead on the stage, and about to be carried off, started up, exclaiming,

" Hold, are you mad? you damn'd confounded dog!
I am to rise and speak the epilogue."

CHAPTER VIII.

THE PROPHETESS—BONDUCA—DON QUIXOTE—PURCELL'S SONGS
IN VARIOUS PLAYS—HIS DEATH AND CHARACTER—PRINCIPAL
DRAMATIC SINGERS IN HIS TIME—DRYDEN'S SECULAR MASQUE
—ECCLES—JEREMY COLLIER'S ATTACK ON THE STAGE.

THE *Prophetess, or the History of Dioclesian*, by
Beaumont and Fletcher, was revived, with alterations and additions, " after the manner of an
opera," by Betterton, and performed in 1690, with
music by Purcell. The music was published by
Purcell in 1691, with a dedication to the Duke of
Somerset, in which he says, " Music is yet but in
its nonage, a forward child, which gives hope of
what it may be hereafter in England, when the
masters of it shall find more encouragement. 'Tis
now learning Italian, which is its best master, and
studying a little of the French air, to give it somewhat more of gaiety and fashion."

Dioclesian, as a drama, does not hold a high
place among the works of its authors; and Betterton's additions, " after the manner of an opera,"
are little better than doggrel. The music, though
it has many and great beauties, seems more unequal than that of any of Purcell's dramatic pieces
which have been already mentioned. The air of

the ballad, " What shall I do to show how much I love her ?" is charming, and well known from its union with the song, " Virgins are like the fair flower," in the *Beggar's Opera.* The duet, " Tell me why, my charming fair," contains many fine and characteristic ideas; but it is diffuse, and rambles through too many keys, and the melody is deformed by stiff and antiquated graces. The same observations are applicable to the duet, " Oh the sweet delights of love," and the air " When first I saw the bright Aurelia's eyes." The song, " Since the toils and hazards of war's at an end" (such is the poet's grammar), is embellished with a showy accompaniment for two flutes, and would be excellent, but for the long formal divisions through which a single syllable is frequently dragged for several bars together. In truth (and it is a rare thing in Purcell's music) the air and words are not at all suited to each other even in their general expression; the words being meant to be joyous, while the melody, let it be sung ever so briskly, is essentially sad. " Make room for the great god of wine," is a bacchanalian glee, which has served as a model for many such compositions in later times. " Sound, Fame, thy brazen trumpet," is a spirited trumpet-song; but its style has become antiquated. " Let the soldiers rejoice," is an animated and martial song and chorus.

Dioclesian was again revived at Covent Garden about the middle of the last century, but does not seem to have been performed since that time; and it is not probable that it will be again brought on the stage.

Among the last of Purcell's works was the music in *Bonduca*, another tragedy of Beaumont and Fletcher's, made into an opera by Betterton, in the same manner as *Dioclesian*. Neither the one nor the other of these pieces seems particularly calculated for being turned into a musical drama; and, in the one as well as the other, the music is introduced merely as belonging to shows or pageants, without being at all interwoven with the texture of the piece. *Bonduca* has some powerful and pathetic scenes, but not much general merit; and it is quite unfit for the modern stage. The subject, however, seems to have roused Purcell's patriotic feelings; for none of his compositions breathe a nobler or loftier spirit.

The chorus, " Hear us, great Rugwith, hear our prayers," sung by the British priests before the battle with the Romans, is a supplication full of the most sublime pathos. What grandeur there is in the few notes sung by a single voice—and

> " Descend in chariots of ethereal flame,
> And touch the altars you defend ! "

and how earnest and imploring the accents in which the whole choir join in the prayer,

> " O save us !
> O save our nation and our name ! "

The instrumental symphony which introduces this

chorus is a fine piece of solemn harmony, the effect of which could derive no addition from any modern improvements.

The solo for a bass voice, " Hear, ye gods of Britain ! " which is called an air, is a mixture of recitative and *aria parlante* or declamatory air. It is a model of the perfect adaptation of sound to sense. The notes not only aid the clear elocution of the words, but heighten their emphasis and expression. The accompaniments for the stringed instruments are beautifully wrought, and contain some harmony which in Purcell's time must have been quite new, and is still singularly bold and powerful.

The air for a treble voice, " O lead me to some peaceful gloom," has all the freedom and grace of the finest modern melody, and is beautifully in accordance with the sentiment of the words. In one place, however, the author has been led astray by a word which has ofted proved an *ignis fatuus* to composers. In the passage,

" Where the shrill trumpets never sound,
  But one eternal hush goes round,"

the singer breaks out into a loud and dashing passage, in imitation of the sound of a trumpet ; although the whole song is an aspiration after peace, repose, and silence. Even where the trumpet is introduced, it is *negatively*,* in expressing a

* A whimsical proof of the prevalence of this error was given in the setting of Sir Walter Scott's famous song of

wish for some peaceful gloom, where its sound may never be heard. The " eternal hush," in the succeeding line, is exquisitely expressed.

The chorus; " To arms, to arms ! your ensigns straight display," is one of the most inspiring martial strains that ever was heard. The concluding duet and chorus, " Britons, strike home," has long taken its place among the warlike national songs of England.

The music in *Bonduca* was composed in 1695, the last year of Purcell's life ; and the piece was brought out in the following year after his death.

Durfey's three parts of *Don Quixote*, which are three consecutive plays, were brought out, the first in 1694, and the last in 1696.* For these plays

---

" County Guy." Many composers essayed it ; and most of them, when they came to the words,

" The lark, his lay that trill'd all day,
Sits hush'd, his partner by,"

set about imitating the trill of a lark, either by the voice or the accompaniment ; forgetting that the lay of the lark (like the trumpet in Purcell's song) is mentioned *negatively,* and for the purpose of intimating that it is *hushed.*

* Thomas (familiarly called Tom) D'Urfey was a native of Devonshire, and bred to the profession of the law, which a love of idleness and pleasure led him to abandon. He took to writing for the stage, and produced a considerable number of plays and operas, several of which were very popular. He produced also a great many songs, and other fugitive pieces, which are contained in the well-known collection published by him in the year 1719, under the title of *Wit* and *Mirth, or Pills to Purge Melancholy.*

D'Urfey was a man of gay and convivial, if not dissolute

Purcell produced the finest of all his dramatic compositions, the two songs, "Let the dreadful engines," and "From rosy bowers."

"Let the dreadful engines," is a soliloquy of Cardenio, while he is wandering among the wilds of the Sierra Morena. It is a wonderful picture of every variety of human passion — love, hatred, tender melancholy, fury, and despair—raging with unrestrained violence, as in rapid succession they chase each other through the mind of a maniac. Except some other works of Purcell himself, there is nothing in music like it, or comparable to it. In

habits. He was very popular among the licentious London society of Charles the Second's time, and a great favourite of that monarch himself. That his character, however, was not depraved, appears from the great kindness with which he is mentioned by some of the most respectable writers of his time, especially Addison, who gives a very pleasing description of him in the sixty-seventh number of the *Guardian*. Addison there tells his female readers that his old friend and contemporary had often made their grandmothers merry, and that his sonnets had perhaps lulled asleep many a toast among the ladies then living, when she lay in her cradle. The paper, which was written for the purpose of recommending a play to be performed for D'Urfey's benefit, concludes with this character of him :—

"As my friend, after the manner of the old Lyrics, accompanies his works with his own voice, he has been the delight of the most polite companies and conversations from the beginning of King Charles the Second's reign to the present time. Many an honest gentleman has got a reputation in his country by pretending to have been in company with Tom D'Urfey.

"I might here mention several other merits in my friend, as

the play it forms an entire scene. Cardenio rushes
distractedly upon the stage, and, after giving vent
in this monologue to his frenzy, disappears among
the rocks and thickets of his haunt. Delivered by
a performer (if there was any such) capable of
conceiving and expressing it, this scene must have
been appalling, heart-rending, overpowering to a
degree beyond anything which our experience of
dramatic music has led us even to imagine. It is
to be lamented that this astonishing composition
can never again be heard in this manner, as the
play for which it was written has long disappeared

his enriching our language with a multitude of rhymes, and
bringing words together that, without his good offices, would
never have been acquainted with one another so long as it had
been a tongue. But I must not omit that my old friend angles
for a trout the best of any man in England. May-flies come
in late this season, or I myself should before now have had a
trout of his hooking.

"After what I have said, and much more that I might say
on this subject, I question not but the world will think that my
old friend ought not to pass the remainder of his life in a cage
like a singing-bird, but enjoy all that Pandarick liberty which
is suitable to a man of his genius. He has made the world
merry, and I hope they will make him easy so long as he stays
among us. This I will take upon me to say, they cannot do a
kindness to a more diverting companion, or a more cheerful,
honest, and good-natured man."

From this and other passages it appears that D'Urfey, as is
generally the case with persons of his disposition and habits,
was in necessitous circumstances in his old age. He died ten
years afterwards, in 1723. There is a great deal of wit and
humour in his plays and poems; but his writings are polluted
by grossness and indecency.

for ever from the stage: and every one has felt
how much the music of the theatre is chilled and
enfeebled by being transferred to the concert-room.
But it is there that we must now be content to
hear it, and many other of Purcell's dramatic
compositions: and, even under this disadvantage,
they are calculated to afford more delight than
any other music of which the English school can
boast.

"From rosy bowers" was the song of the swan.
"It was," says the *Orpheus Britannicus*, "the last
song the author set, being in his sickness." It is
the passionate raving of a girl crazed with love,
and thus forms the counterpart to the song of Cardenio. It wants the fierce and terrible features
of that song, but is equally fantastical, and has
a charming feminine air throughout, even in its
wildest flights and most violent bursts of passion.
This song, unlike that of Cardenio, is not injured
by its separation from the play for which it was
composed. It belongs to the character of Altisidora, and is sung by that witty damsel while she is
persecuting the Knight of the Rueful Countenance
with her pretended passion: but it is by far too
beautiful and too pathetic for such a purpose. It
is evident that Purcell was quite in earnest in composing it; so should the performer be in singing it,
and the auditor in listening to it. It would be
quite shocking to hear this exquisite effusion of
feeling given as a joke, like the crying song in
Love in a Village, with which Rosetta mystifies her

gouty lover, Justice Woodcock, whimpering to him,
but all the while laughing behind her fan. It was
a favourite song of several great English vocalists
of past times, and will unquestionably be so again,
though none of our present singers seem to have
sufficient strength or courage to attempt it.

Purcell also composed vocal pieces for *The
Fairy Queen*, a play altered from *The Midsummer
Night's Dream*, and performed in 1692; *Timon
of Athens*, altered from Shakspeare by Shadwell;
The Libertine and *Epsom Wells*, by that dramatist;
Dryden's *Aurungzebe;* and a mask in the tragedy
of *Œdipus*. The well-known mad song, " I'll sail
upon the dog-star," was sung in a play called *The
Fool's Preferment*. Many of these, as well as his
occasional or miscellaneous songs, duets, &c., are
contained in the *Orpheus Britannicus*.

This illustrious musician died on the 21st of
November, 1695, in the thirty-seventh year of his
age. It is said that his death was caused by a
cold, occasioned by his having been kept standing
one night at his own door for a considerable time,
in consequence of his wife's irritation at his having
stayed too late at a convivial party. This story has
been told and repeated again and again, accompanied with many harsh comments on the character
and conduct of Mrs. Purcell. It has been told,
however, without evidence, and in the face of circumstances which render it incredible. Though
he possessed many good and amiable qualities,
Purcell's domestic character cannot be rated high.

He was too much addicted to the society of mean
and dissolute companions; and the irregularity of
his habits must, to his wife, have been a source of
grief, anxiety, and well-grounded displeasure. That
she was destitute of affection for him, however,
and treated him with such harshness as to cause
his death in the manner that has been mentioned,
is entirely inconsistent with the language of grief
and tenderness which she made use of in her dedication of the posthumous collection of his works;
expressions which, if hypocritical, she durst hardly
have ventured to use at a time when her habits
of life with her husband must have been so well
known to many. Purcell's death, moreover, appears to have been the consequence of illness of
some duration. One of his finest songs was composed "during his sickness;" and in his will,
dated three weeks before his death, he describes
himself as " of sound mind, though *very ill in constitution ;* " a phrase which induces the belief that
he died of a gradual decay. By this will, too, he
leaves all his effects to his loving wife Frances,
and appoints her his sole executrix. Would he
have bestowed this mark of love and confidence on
a woman whose unkind usage had brought him to
the brink of the grave? It is time, therefore, that
there should be an end to these idle and un-
warrantable attacks on the memory of poor Mrs.
Purcell.

Though, unhappily, fond of society unworthy of
his character and genius, he was not exclusively

given to such society. He enjoyed the esteem and friendship of many persons distinguished both by rank and talents. Pepys, in his Diary, speaks of meeting him in the fashionable circles of the day. The Lord Keeper North, an eminent patron of literature and the arts, was among his friends; and Dryden appears to have regarded him with warm affection.

Purcell left several children, one of whom, Edward, became an organist of small reputation, and died in 1751; of the others there is no account. Daniel Purcell, his brother, was a musician of respectable abilities. He composed many songs for the dramatic pieces of the day; all of which, however, are now forgotten.

Purcell was buried in Westminster Abbey. His monument was erected by Lady Elizabeth Howard, Dryden's wife; and the epitaph inscribed on it was written by the poet himself.

" Here lies
HENRY PURCELL, ESQUIRE ;
Who left this life
And is gone to that blessed place
Where only his own harmony can be exceeded.
Obiit 21mo die Novembris,
Anno ætatis suæ 37mo,
Annoque Domini 1695."

Though Purcell's genius ranged through every walk of his art, yet its bent was towards the music of the theatre; and he has left behind him a large body of dramatic compositions, which to this hour remain unrivalled among the works of the English school. In variety of character, beauty of melody, truth and force of expression, and nice adaptation to the genius of the English language, they are to this hour unparalleled. Their imperfections must be ascribed to the state of music, as a practical art, in his day; and when this is considered, it is wonderful that these imperfections are so small and so few. In regard to composition, it must be remembered that English secular melody was almost created by Purcell; the greatness of his predecessors having been derived, with slight exceptions, from their achievements in vocal harmony. It was not then in England as it was in Italy, where the melody of the stage had been polished by a succession of distinguished masters. It was still worse in regard to performance: for, though Purcell could, and did, obtain ideas of the Italian melody by reading the scores of the Italian composers, yet he could obtain no conception of the delicacies and graces of Italian singing. His principal vocalists, probably, had as fine voices, and as much native feeling, as any of their successors: but the powers of the voice were not then developed by cultivation; nor was expression heightened and varied by the thousand refinements of modern execution. Of all the qualities of an artist, the taste is that which is most slowly matured; and it is to immaturity of taste, therefore, that Purcell's defects are to be wholly ascribed. Still, we repeat, it is wonderful to observe how free his works are from defects even of taste. His innate sense of the beautiful gave rise to conceptions, which, to himself, were never realised. What would have been his feelings, had he heard " Bess of Bedlam," " From rosy bowers," or, " Let the dreadful engines," sung by Madame Mara, Mrs. Sheridan, Bartleman, or Braham !

But the highest quality of Purcell's music is its genuine English character. In this respect it remains wholly unrivalled. Purcell was fully aware of the great principle, that the vocal music of every country must be founded upon the peculiar accent, or modulation, of its spoken language. Addison (who, though not a musician, was well acquainted with those fundamental laws of taste and criticism which are applicable to all the fine arts), has so clearly explained this principle, and so elegantly and happily illustrated it, that his remarks deserve the attention of every musical artist. Their value has suffered no abatement by the lapse of a century.*

" The only fault," says Addison, " I can find in our present practice, is the making use of the Italian *recitativo* with English words.

" To go to the bottom of this matter, I must observe, that the tone, or (as the French call it) the accent of every nation in their ordinary speech, is altogether different from that of every other people ; as we may see even in the Welsh and Scotch who border so near upon us. By the tone

* Spectator, No. 29. April 3, 1711.

or accent, I do not mean the pronunciation of each particular word, but the sound of the whole sentence. Thus it is very common for an English gentleman, when he hears a French tragedy, to complain that the actors all of them speak in a tone; and therefore he very wisely prefers his own countrymen, not considering that a foreigner complains of the same tone in an English actor.

" For this reason, the recitative music, in every language, should be as different as the tone or accent of each language; for otherwise, what may properly express a passion in one language will not do it in another. Every one who has been long in Italy knows very well, that the cadences in the recitative bear a remote affinity to the tone of their voices in ordinary conversation; or, to speak more properly, are only the accents of their language made more musical and tuneful. Thus the notes of interrogation, or admiration, in the Italian music (if one may so call them) which resemble their accents in discourse on such occasions, are not unlike the ordinary tones of an English voice when we are angry: insomuch, that I have often seen our audiences extremely mistaken as to what has been doing upon the stage, and expecting to see the hero knock down a messenger when he has been asking him a question; or fancying that he quarrels with his friend when he only bids him good-morrow.

" For this reason, the Italian artists cannot agree with our English musicians, in admiring Purcell's compositions, and thinking his tunes so wonderfully adapted to his words; because both nations do not always express the same passions by the same sounds.

" I am, therefore, humbly of opinion, that an English composer should not follow the Italian recitative too servilely, but make use of many gentle deviations from it, in compliance with his own native language. He may copy out of it all the lulling softness and *dying* falls (as Shakspeare calls them), but should still remember that he ought to accommodate himself to an English audience; and, by humouring the tone of our voices in ordinary conversation, have the same regard to the accent of his own language as those persons had to theirs whom he professes to imitate. It is observed that several of the singing-birds of our own country learn to sweeten their voices and mellow the harshness of their natural notes, by practising under those that come from warmer climates. In the same manner I would allow the Italian opera to lend our English music as much as may grace and soften it, but never entirely to annihilate and destroy it. Let the infusion be as strong as you please, but still let the subject-matter of it be English.*

" A composer should fit his music to the genius of the people, and consider that the delicacy of hearing, and taste of harmony, have been formed

* Addison's musical language is not technically accurate, but this does not affect his principles.

upon those sounds which every country abounds
with: in short, that music is of a relative nature,
and what is harmony to one ear may be dissonance
to another.

"The same observations which I have made
upon the recitative part of music, may be applied
to all our songs and airs in general."

These important considerations are, in a great
measure, disregarded by English composers. English recitative, instead of being founded on what
may be 'called the natural melody of English
speech, is generally made up of a tissue of musical
phrases borrowed from the Italian composers; so
that an English singer, delivering a piece of recitative in his own language, has the appearance of
a foreigner declaiming in broken English. The
same thing, though in a lesser degree, is perceptible in our English airs; which, being made up of
passages originally suggested by the modulations
of Italian speech, are destructive of the emphasis
and accent of the words to which they are united
by the English composer. Similar effects are produced by the present imitation of the German
music. Our composers act precisely as a painter
would do, who, in painting an English landscape,
instead of looking upon the scenery around him,
should compose his picture by copying his rocks
from Salvata Rosa, his blue distances from Poussin,
his sunshine from Claud, his trees from Ruysdael,
and his cattle from Cuyp. The evil has been
aggravated of late years by the practice of adapting

Italian, German, and French operas to the English
stage; a practice which has almost put an end to
the existence of English melody. Even when
setting an English ballad, our composers show that
their heads are full of Rossini, Spohr, Weber, or
Auber. Compare their exotic productions with
the genuine English strains of Purcell, Arne,
Linley, Arnold, Dibdin, and Shield; and the difference is at once perceived between copying from
art and copying from nature. But let us not be
misunderstood. A knowledge of art, and a study
of its most exquisite productions, are necessary to
enable the artist to bestow grace and refinement on
his copies from nature. Purcell, the most natural
and the most truly English of all our composers,
sought for models among the French and Italian
masters of his time. He himself has said, that
" he has faithfully endeavoured a just imitation of
the most far-famed Italian masters : but this imitation (as the present writer has elsewhere observed)
did not consist in stringing together fragments of
Italian melody, and trying to force these into an
union with English words. He studied the genius
of the Italian music ; observed that its excellencies
consisted in its smoothness and expression, and in
the exquisite adaptation of the melody to what
may be called the accent and modulation of the
Italian language ; and he endeavoured to give to
his own music corresponding qualities. It thus
arises, that Purcell's music, while it does possess
the excellencies of the Italian music which he

studied, is perfectly original, and much more truly
and essentially English than that of any composer
who has appeared before or since."*—" Though
Purcell's dramatic style and recitative," says Burney, "were formed, in a great measure, on French
models, there is a latent power and force in his expression of English words, whatever be the subject,
that will make an unprejudiced native of this island
feel, more than all the elegance, grace, and refinement of modern music, less happily applied, can
do : and this pleasure is communicated to us, not
by the symmetry or rhythm of modern melody, but
by his having tuned to the true accents of our
mother-tongue, those notes of passion which an
inhabitant of this island would breathe in such
situations as the words describe.   And these indi-
genous expressions of passion Purcell had the
power to enforce by the energy of modulation,
which, on some occasions, was bold, affecting, and
sublime." — " Handel," adds the same writer,
" who flourished in a less barbarous age for his art,
has been acknowledged Purcell's superior in many
particulars; but in none more than the art and
grandeur of his choruses, the harmony and texture
of his organ fugues, as well as his great style of
playing that instrument : the majesty of his grand
concertos ; the ingenuity of his accompaniments to
his songs and choruses; and even in the general
melody of the airs themselves : yet, in the accent,
passion, and expression *of English words*, the vocal

* Musical History, Biography, and Criticism.

music of Purcell is, sometimes, to my feelings, as superior to Handel's as an original poem to a translation."

Every English student of composition ought to "give his days and nights" to the music of Purcell: not for the purpose of learning to copy him, but of learning, from him, to copy nature.

The principal dramatic singers in Purcell's time were Mr. James Bowen, Mr. Harris, Mr. Freeman, Mr. Pate, and Mr. Mountfort, performers at the theatres; Mr. Damascene, Mr. Woodson, Mr. Turner, and Mr. Bouchier, gentlemen of the Chapel Royal; Mrs. Mary Davis, Miss Shore (afterwards Mrs. Cibber), Mrs. Cross, Miss Campion, Mrs. Butler, and Mrs. Bracegirdle.

None of the above male theatrical performers are much spoken of as singers, though they are described as excellent actors. The gentlemen of the Chapel Royal, about this time, occasionally assisted in musical performances on the stage ; but this practice was afterwards prohibited by Queen Anne.

Mrs. Davis was one of the actresses belonging to Sir William Davenant's company, who boarded in his house. Downes says that she played the part of Celania in a play called *The Rivals ;* and in this part, which was that of a shepherdess mad for love, sang the well known ballad, " My lodging is on the cold ground," so beautifully, that she captivated King Charles II., who took her off the stage, and had a daughter by her, who was named

Mary Tudor, and was married to Francis Lord Ratcliffe, afterwards Earl of Derwentwater. Mrs. Davis was also admired as a dancer.

Miss Shore was daughter of Matthias Shore, serjeant-trumpeter in the King's household. She was a beautiful and amiable young woman, and at an early age showed great musical talents, and became a favourite pupil of Purcell. Colley Cibber, having accidentally heard her perform on the harpsichord, fell in love with her, and married her, when he himself was only two-and-twenty, and she still younger. At that time, as Cibber tells us, he had no other income than twenty pounds a year allowed him by his father, and twenty shillings a week from the theatre. The marriage having taken place without the consent of the lady's father, he refused to do anything for them ; upon this Mrs. Cibber betook herself to the stage ; and, after having distinguished herself as a singer, became an actress of the highest celebrity.

Miss Cross was an eminent actress, especially in musical parts. She performed the character of Altisidora in the third part of *Don Quixote*, in which she sang the song, " From rosy bowers."

Miss Campion was a young woman of low birth, but, unhappily for herself, possessed a beautiful person and a fine voice. William, the first Duke of Devonshire, then an old man, took her off the stage, and made her his mistress. She died in 1706, in her nineteenth year, and the Duke buried

her in the church of Latimers, in Buckingham-
shire, the burial-place of his family. In the chancel
of that church he erected a monument for her, on
which there is a Latin inscription, importing that
she was wise beyond her years, and bountiful to
the poor even beyond her abilities; and at the
theatre, where she had sometime acted, modest and
untainted; that being seized with a hectic fever,
she had submitted to her fate with a firm confidence and christian piety; and that, William, Duke
of Devonshire, had, upon her beloved remains,
erected that tomb as sacred to her memory. This
ostentatious proof of attachment to an object of
illicit love was properly looked upon as an insult
to religion and good manners, and very generally
censured.

Mrs. Butler is described by Cibber as an excellent actress and singer. In speaking, she had a
sweet-toned voice, which, with her genteel air and
sensible pronunciation, rendered her very interesting in many serious parts, though she excelled
also in characters of humour. She gave great
attraction, both by her acting and singing, to
the part of Philidel, the good spirit, in *King
Arthur*.

Mrs. Bracegirdle was the most favourite performer of her time. Cibber gives a captivating
description of her, as she was in the year 1690.
She was then, he says, just blooming to her maturity, her reputation as an actress gradually rising
with the beauty of her person. There never was

any woman in such general favour with the public ; a favour which, to the very end of her theatrical life, she preserved by maintaining strict propriety of conduct. She was a brunette, with so lively an aspect, and such a glow of health and cheerfulness in her countenance, that she was surrounded by lovers and admirers.

Among these was a Captain Hill, a man of a profligate and brutal character, who had long persecuted her with addresses which she rejected with merited contempt. Hill ascribed this rejection, not to his own unworthiness, but to the lady's preference of some other person; and as Mountfort the actor was a handsome man, frequently performed with her, and was on terms of friendly intercourse with her, Hill fixed on him, though a married man, as the object of his suspicion. Having obtained the assistance of Lord Mohun, a noted *roué* of that day, and hired some soldiers, he attempted to force Mrs. Bracegirdle into a coach, as she came out of a house where she had supped. But her mother and the gentleman of the house, having resisted and called for help, she was rescued and safely guarded home. Hill and Lord Mohun, thus disappointed of their prey, vowed vengeance, with dreadful imprecations, against Mountfort. Mrs. Bracegirdle's friends, hearing these threats, immediately sent to Mrs. Mountfort, advising her to warn her husband not to come home that night; but, unfortunately, Mrs. Mountfort's messengers were unable to find him. In the meantime Lord

Mohun and Captain Hill paraded the street with their swords drawn till about midnight, when they met Mountfort on his return home. Lord Mohun saluted him in a friendly manner, and while they were in conversation, Hill, coming behind Mountfort, gave him a violent blow on the head with his left hand, and before Mountfort had time to draw and stand on his defence, ran him through the body with his sword. This last circumstance Mountfort declared, as a dying man, to the surgeon who attended him. He died on the following day. Hill immediately made his escape; but Lord Mohun was seized. He was brought to trial on the 31st January, 1693, when he was acquitted, strangely enough, on the ground that he had not directly assisted Hill in the murder; fourteen peers voting that he was guilty, and sixteen not guilty. Mountfort, who was in his thirty-third year, was, says Cibber, generally lamented by his friends and all lovers of the theatre.

Mrs. Bracegirdle's name appears as a principal performer in many of the comedies that were performed about the end of the seventeenth and the earlier part of the eighteenth century. She appears to have made an extraordinary impression by her manner of singing an impassioned song, composed by Eccles, in the character of Marcella, in the second part of *Don Quixote*. In the *Orpheus Britannicus* there is a song, " Whilst I with grief on you did look," addressed to her in compliment to that performance.

" Mrs. Bracegirdle," says Aston, a contemporary writer, " that Diana of the stage, had many assailants on her virtue, as Lord Lovelace and Mr. Congreve, the last of which had her company most. But she ever resisted his vicious attacks, and yet was always uneasy at his leaving her. She was very shy of Lord Lovelace's company, as being an engaging man who dressed well; and as every day his servant came to her to ask her how she did, she always returned her answer in the most obeisant words and behaviour, that she was indifferent well, she humbly thanked his lordship. She was of a lovely height, with dark brown hair and eyebrows, black sparkling eyes, and a fresh blushy complexion; and, whenever she exerted herself, had an involuntary flushing in her breast, neck, and face, having continually a cheerful aspect, and a fine set of even white teeth; never making an exit but that she left the audience in an imitation of her pleasant countenance. Her virtue had its reward both in applause and specie; for it happened, that as the Dukes of Dorset and Devonshire, Lord Halifax, and other nobles, over a bottle, were extolling Mrs. Bracegirdle's virtuous behaviour; ' Come,' says Lord Halifax, ' you all commend her virtue, but why do we not present this incomparable woman with something worthy her acceptance?' His lordship deposited two hundred guineas, which the rest made up eight hundred, and sent to her, with encomiums on her virtue. She was, when on the stage, diurnally charitable, going often into Clare-market and giving money to the poor unemployed basket-women, insomuch that she could not pass that neighbourhood without the thankful acclamations of people of all degrees; so that if any person had affronted her, they would have been in danger of being killed directly; and yet this good woman was an actress."

The character of this remarkable woman did not escape obloquy. She was grossly attacked by the notorious Tom Brown; and Gildon (in his *Comparison between the two Stages*, 1702) says, " her virtue is all a juggle, 'tis legerdemain; the best on't is, she falls into good hands, and the secrecy of the intrigue secures her; but as to her inno-cence, I believe no more on't than I believe of John Mandeville." The circumstances of her life, how-ever, in so far as they are known, do not give countenance to these accusations, which are pro-bably calumnies resulting from personal enmity. Gildon also says, that, after the appearance of Jeremy Collier's book, she, along with one or two other performers, were fined for uttering profane or indecent expressions on the stage. Whatever grounds there may have been, however, for charg-ing Mrs. Bracegirdle with secret irregularities, it is certain that she conducted herself with decency and prudence, passed through life with credit, supported the respectability of her profession, and never, by her own example, gave countenance or encouragement to the impropriety of others.

Mrs. Bracegirdle continued to perform till the year 1707, when she left the stage. In the latter part of her life she resided in the family of Francis Chute, Esq., one of the king's counsel, at his house in Norfolk-street in the Strand, where she died, in 1748, in the eighty-fifth year of her age.

Dryden, who had furnished Purcell with subjects worthy of his genius, did not long survive him. The poet's last production was *The Secular Masque*, which was written about the end of the year 1699, and, from its title, seems to have been intended to celebrate the conclusion of the century; Dryden having erroneously supposed that the century terminated with the year 1699. It is a mythological satire on the reigns of the Stuarts, the predecessors of King William. By the introduction of the deities of the chase, of war, and of love, as governing the various changes of the seventeenth century, Dryden alludes to the sylvan sports of James I., the bloody wars of his son, and the licentious gallantry which prevailed in the court of Charles II., and of James, his successor. It was performed in 1700, but it does not seem certain whether or not the poet was then alive. It was favourably received; and the music, which is said to have been composed by Daniel Purcell, was much approved. Though this piece is a mere trifle, it was revived with success at Drury Lane, in 1749, with new music, by Dr. Boyce.

John Eccles holds a high rank among the mu-

sicians of this period, and many of his compositions
are still well known to the lovers of the old English music. He was much employed in writing for
the stage. He composed the music in a tragedy,
by Dennis, called *Rinaldo and Armida*, which was
performed in 1690; and in which the song, "The
jolly breeze," was long popular. He composed
the music to Congreve's Masque, *The Judgment of
Paris*, which was published entire. A collection
of his theatrical compositions, consisting of act-
tunes, dances, and incidental songs, in a number
of dramatic pieces, was published by him with a
dedication to Queen Anne. It contains many
admirable songs, which are indeed inferior only
to those of Purcell. The mad song, "I burn, my
brain consumes to ashes," sung by Mrs. Bracegirdle, in the character of Marcella, in *Don Quixote*, was one of the masterpieces of that favourite
actress. In the *Orpheus Britannicus* there is a
song by Purcell, in compliment to Mrs. Bracegirdle's performance of Eccles's song. In the
latter part of his life, Eccles was master of the
queen's band, and was known to the musical world
only by the odes on her majesty's birth-day, the
new year, &c., which he composed in the course of
his duty.

Eccles had two brothers, Henry and Thomas,
both musicians. Henry was an eminent violinist,
in the service of the French court, and the author
of a set of excellent violin solos, published at Paris
in 1720. Thomas is remarkable as having been

perhaps the last of those itinerant musicians who used to frequent taverns, and play for the entertainment of the guests. He was a man of talent in his profession, but reduced by dissolute habits to this degrading exercise of it. The following account of him and his performance was given to Sir John Hawkins, by a good judge of music who heard him play. "It was about the month of November, in the year 1735, that I, with some friends, were met to spend the evening at a tavern in the city, when this man, in a mean but decent garb, was introduced to us by the waiter. Immediately on opening the door, I heard the twang of one of his strings from under his coat, which was accompanied by the question, 'Gentlemen, will you please to hear any music?' Our curiosity and the modesty of the man's deportment inclined us to say yes; and music he gave us, such as I had never heard before, nor shall again, under the same circumstances. With as fine and delicate a hand as I ever heard, he played the whole fifth and ninth solos of Corelli, two songs of Mr. Handel, 'Del minacciar' in *Otho*, and 'Spero si, mio caro bene,' in *Admetus:* in short, his performance was such as would command the attention of the nicest ear, and left us, his auditors, much at a loss to guess what it was that constrained him to seek his living in a way so disreputable. He made no secret of his name; he said he was the youngest of three brothers, and that Henry, the middle one, had been his master, and was then in the service of the King of France. We were very little disposed to credit the account he gave us of his brother's situation in France; but the collection of solos, above mentioned to have been published by him at Paris, put it out of question." Upon inquiry some time afterwards, it appeared that he was idle and given to drinking. He was well known to the musicians of the time, who thought themselves disgraced by this practice of his, which was called going a-busking.*

In 1698, Jeremy Collier published his celebrated "View of the Immorality and Profaneness of the English Stage;" a book in which he assailed most of the living writers, from Dryden to Durfey.

* There are many allusions, in old English writers, to the practice of entertaining the guests at inns and taverns with music. Fynes Moryson, in his *Itinerary*, giving an account of the manner in which it was customary to receive and treat a traveller at an English inn, says, " Then the host and hostesse visits him, and if he will eate with the host, or at a common table with others, his meale will cost him sixpence, or in some places but fourpence (yet this course is less honourable, and not used by gentlemen): but if he will eate in his chamber, he commands what meate he will, according to his appetite, and as much as he thinks fit for him and his companie ; yea, the kitchen is open to him to command the meat to be dressed as he best likes ; and when he sits at table, the host or hostesse will accompany him, or, if they have many guests, will at least visit him, taking it for curtesie to be bid sit down. While he eates, if he have company especially, he shall be offered musicke, which he may freely take or refuse ; and if he be solitary, the musicians will give him the good day with musicke in the morning."

This book made a great impression on the public, who were confounded when they contemplated the mass of profanity, immorality, and indecency, which was thus concentrated and brought all at once before their eyes. "The wise and the pious," says Dr. Johnson, "caught the alarm; and the nation wondered why it had so long suffered irreligion and licentiousness to be openly taught at the public charge." Dryden, to his honour, admitted the justice of the accusation against himself. "I shall say the less of Mr. Collier," said the veteran poet, in the preface to his *Fables*, "because in many things he has taxed me justly; and I have pleaded guilty to all thoughts and expressions of mine, which can be truly argued of obscenity, profaneness, or immorality, and retract them. If he be my enemy, let him triumph; if he be my friend, as I have given him no personal occasion to be otherwise, he will be glad of my repentance. It becomes me not to draw my pen in the defence of a bad cause, when I have so often drawn it for a good one." It does not appear that such an *amende honorable* as this was made by any other of the dramatic writers whom Mr. Collier had chastised; but his book contributed to the reformation of a great evil. " Collier's attack on the stage," says Sir Walter Scott, " was attended with good consequences, which that active disputant lived to witness. Indecencies were no longer either fashionable or tolerated; and by degrees the ladies began to fill the boxes at a new play, without either the necessity of wearing masks, or the risk of incurring censure. Later times have carried this laudable restraint still farther; till at last, if we have lost almost all the wit of our predecessors, we at least have retained none of their licentiousness."

CHAPTER IX.

DEGENERACY OF THE ITALIAN OPERA AT THE COMMENCEMENT OF THE LAST CENTURY — MARCELLO'S SATIRE, IL TEATRO ALLA MODA—PRINCIPAL COMPOSERS OF THAT PERIOD—SCARLATTI—CALDARA — LOTTI — VIVALDI — IMPROVEMENTS EFFECTED BY THEM — DRAMATIC POETS — APOSTOLO ZENO—METASTASIO—HIS APPEARANCE AN ERA IN THE ITALIAN OPERA.

ABOUT the end of the seventeenth and beginning of the eighteenth century, the Italian musical drama appears, for a time, to have degenerated, and to have become liable to many abuses. As public theatres multiplied in the different towns, and each department of the drama became a profession giving employment to numbers of people in the capacities of dramatists, composers, actors, and singers, these occupations came to be exercised by ignorant and worthless pretenders: so that, notwithstanding the genius of a few eminent individuals, the general standard of excellence, in every branch of the art, was much lowered. The Italian musical dramas of that period were full of the most ridiculous absurdities. Regularity of construction, consistency of character, and poetical beauty, were disregarded, provided the eye and ear were gratified with splendid sights and feats of vocal execution. In one of these pieces, which represented the siege of Persepolis, a mine exploded and blew up a part of the city. In another, Alcibiades, the Athenian general, came on the stage in a fashionable carriage, preceded by couriers and outriders, according to the mode of the day. In an opera called *Dido*, written by Businelli, a Venetian poet, the first act comprehended the burning of Troy; the second, the arrival of Æneas after seven years' wandering on the shores of Carthage; the third, the flight of Æneas, and suicide of the deserted queen. These dramas, too, contained a mixture of tragedy and comedy which had neither the grandeur of the one, nor the vivacity of the other. Gods and heroes were mixed with buffoons, tragical incidents with farcical jokes, and lofty or impassioned declamation with doggrel or ribaldry. In *Giasone*, an opera by Giacinto Andrea Cicognini, of Florence, an eminent poet of that day, there is the following dialogue between King Egeus and Demos, a stuttering servant. The situation is sufficiently serious, the aged king inquiring anxiously about the departure of his son.

" *Egeo.* E verso dove andranno ?
  Demo. (*Balbutante*) S'imbarcano per co, co, co, per co, co, co.
  Egeo. Per Coimbra ?
  Demo. Per co, co, co.
  Egeo. Per Coralto ?
  Demo. Oibò ! per co, co, co.
  Egeo. Per Cosandro ?
  Demo. Nemmeno ; per co, co, co.

> *Egeo.* Per Corinto.
> *Demo.* Ah ! ah ! bene
> Mi cavasti di pene."

In these dramas, love was always introduced as the principal topic; and it was often treated in a childish as well as indecent manner. In one of them there is a duet between two lovers, the subject of which is their alternately asking, refusing, and giving each other kisses; the performers, while singing it, "suiting the action to the word."

One of the musical beauties of that time was the mimicry of various sounds by means of instruments. In an *Opera buffa*, called *Il podestà di Coloniola*, the following verses were sung, while the composer, in his accompaniments, imitated the sounds of the animals described by the singer;

> " Talor la granocchiella nel pantano
> Per allegrezza canta qua quarà ;
> Tribbia il grillo tre, tre, tre ;
> L'agnellino bè, bè, bè ;
> L'assinuolo whu, whu, whu,
> Ed il gal cucchericù ;
> Ogni bestia sta gaia, io sempre carico
> Di guidaleschi a ogni otta mi rammarico."

And in a piece called *L'Amore in Cucina*, performed at Bologna, the composer imitated with the orchestra the crowing of the cock and the sound of cannon; solely because some mention was made of the bird, and because one of the characters said,

> " Io del canone al suon
> Solo risponderò bun-ban-bun-bon."

Imitations of the cries of animals, or other natural sounds, by means of instruments, when discreetly used, may really be a musical beauty. But the excess to which they were carried by the composers of those days was most ridiculous.

Although Cicognini was one of the chief corruptors of the Italian musical drama, by introducing into it these follies and absurdities, yet, in his own time, he was looked upon as a restorer of the drama. His pieces were many times reprinted; and the Italian critics held him up as a model for imitation.

In the year 1720, there appeared a satirical work of Benedetto Marcello, the celebrated author of the *Psalms*, which gives a lively picture of the musical drama at that period. Marcello was a Venetian nobleman, still more distinguished by his genius and various accomplishments than by his rank. Besides his great sacred work, which has rendered his name illustrious, he wrote the poetry and music of several operas, besides sonnets and other lyrical pieces. His book, which we have just mentioned, is called *Il Teatro alla moda*, and is a curious satire on the manners as well as the music of the time. It is described in the title-page as being " an easy and sure method of composing and performing Italian operas in the modern fashion ; " and professes to give useful and necessary advice to poets, composers, singers, managers, orchestra-players, machinists, scene-painters, prompters, copyists, the actresses' mothers and

protectors, and other persons belonging to the
theatre. A few of these ironical counsels will
give an idea of the whole.

The author begins by telling the poet, that there
is no occasion for his reading, or having read, the
old Greek and Latin authors: for this good reason,
that the ancients never read any of the works of
the moderns. He will not ask any questions about
the ability of the performers, but will rather inquire
whether the theatre is provided with a good bear,
a good lion, a good nightingale, good thunder,
lightning, and earthquakes. He will introduce a
magnificent show in his last scene, and conclude
with the usual chorus in honour of the sun, the
moon, or the manager. In dedicating his *libretto*
to some great personage, he will select him for his
riches rather than his learning, and will give a
share of the gratuity to his patron's cook, or *maître
d'hôtel*, from whom he will obtain all his titles,
that he may blazon them on his title pages, with
an &c. &c. He will exalt the great man's family
and ancestors; make an abundant use of such
phrases as liberality, and generosity of soul; and
if he cannot find any subject of eulogy (as is often
the case), he will say, that he is silent through
fear of hurting his patron's modesty, but that
Fame, with her hundred brazen trumpets, will
spread his immortal name from pole to pole. He
will do well to protest to the reader that his opera
was composed in his youth, and may add that it
was written in a few days: by this he will show

that he is a true *modern*, and has a proper contempt for the antiquated precept, *nonumque pre-*
matur in annum. He may add, too, that he became
a poet solely for his amusement, and to divert his
mind from graver occupations: but that he had
published his work by the advice of his friends and
the command of his patron, and by no means from
any love of praise or desire of profit. He will take
care not to neglect the usual explanation of the
three great points of every drama, the place, time,
and action; the place signifying in such-and-
such a theatre; the time, from eight to twelve
o'clock at night; the action, the ruin of the manager. The incidents of the piece should consist
of dungeons, daggers, poison, boar-hunts, earthquakes, sacrifices, madness, and so forth; because
the people are always greatly moved by such unexpected things. A good *modern* poet ought to know
nothing about music, because the ancients, according to Strabo, Pliny, &c., thought this knowledge
necessary. At the rehearsals he should never tell
his meaning to any of the performers, wisely re-
flecting that they always want to do everything in
their own way. If a husband and wife are discovered in prison, and one of them is led away to
die, it is indispensable that the other remain to
sing an air, which should be to lively words, to
relieve the feelings of the audience, and make
them understand that the whole affair is a joke.
If two of the characters make love, or plot a conspiracy, it should always be in the presence of

servants and attendants. The part of a father, or
a tyrant, when it is the principal character, should
always be given to a soprano; reserving the tenors
and basses for captains of the guard, confidants,
shepherds, messengers, and so forth.

The modern composer is told that there is no
occasion for his being master of the principles of
composition; a little practice being all that is
necessary. He need not know anything of poetry,
or give himself any trouble about the meaning of
the words, or even the quantities of the syllables.
Neither is it necessary that he should study the
properties of the stringed or wind instruments; if
he can play on the harpsichord, it will do very well.
It will, however, be not amiss for him to have been
for some years a violin-player, or music-copier for
some celebrated composer, whose original scenes
he may treasure up, and thus supply himself with
subjects for his airs, recitatives, or choruses. He
will by no means think of reading the opera
through, but will compose it line by line; using
for the airs, *motivi* which he has lying by him:
and if the words do not go well below the notes,
he will torment the poet till they are altered to his
mind. When the singer comes to a cadence, the
composer will make all the instruments stop,
leaving it to the singer to do whatever he pleases.
He will serve the manager on very low terms, considering the thousands of crowns that the singers
cost him :—he will therefore content himself with
an inferior salary to the lowest of these, provided

that he is not wronged by the bear, the attendants, or the scene-shifters, being put above him. When he is walking with the singers, he will always give them the wall, keep his hat in his hand, and remain a step in the rear ; considering that the lowest of them, on the stage, is at least a general, a captain of the guards, or some such personage. All the airs should be formed of the same materials—long divisions, holding notes, and repetitions of insignificant words, as *amore amore, impero impero, Europa Europa, furori furori, orgoglio orgoglio,* &c. and therefore the composer should have before him a memorandum of the things necessary for the termination of every air. This will enable him to eschew variety, which is no longer in use. After ending a recitative in a flat key, he will suddenly begin an air in three or four sharps ; and this by way of novelty. If the modern composer wishes to write in four parts, two of them must proceed in unison or octave, only taking care that there shall be a diversity of movement : so that if the one part proceeds by minims or crotchets, the other will be in quavers or semiquavers. He will charm the audience with airs accompanied by the instruments *pizzicati* or *con sordini,* trumpets, and other *effective* contrivances. He will not compose airs with a simple bass accompaniment, because this is no longer the custom ; and, besides, he would take as much time to compose one of these as a dozen with the orchestra. The modern composer will oblige the manager to furnish him with a large orchestra of violins, oboes, horns, &c., saving him rather the expense of double basses, of which there is no occasion to make any use, except in tuning at the outset. The overture will be a movement in the French style, or a *prestissimo* in semiquavers in a major key, to which will succeed a *piano* in the minor; concluding with a minuet, gavot, or jig, again in the major key. In this manner the composer will avoid all fugues, syncopations, and treatment of subjects, as being antiquated contrivances, quite banished from modern music. The modern composer will be most attentive to all the ladies of the theatre, supplying them with plenty of old songs transposed to suit their voices, and telling each of them that the opera is supported by her talent alone. He will bring every night some of his friends, and seat them in the orchestra; giving the double bass or violoncello (as being the most useless instruments) leave of absence to make room for them.

The singer is informed that there is no occasion for having practised the *solfeggio*; because he would thus be in danger of acquiring a firm voice, just intonation, and the power of singing in tune; things wholly useless in modern music. Nor is it very necessary that he should be able to read or write, know how to pronounce the words or understand their meaning, provided he can run divisions, make shakes, cadences, &c. He will always complain of his part, saying that it is not in his way, that the airs are not in his style, and so on: and

he will sing an air by some other composer, pro-
testing that at such a court, or in the presence of
such a great personage, that air carried away all
the applause, and he was obliged to repeat it a
dozen times in an evening. At the rehearsals he
will merely hum his airs, and will insist on having
the time in his own way. He will stand with one
hand in his waistcoat and the other in his breeches'
pocket, and take care not to allow a syllable to be
heard. He will always keep his hat on his head,
though a person of quality should speak to him, in
order to avoid catching cold : and he will not bow
his head to anybody, remembering the kings,
princes, and emperors whom he is in the habit of
personating. On the stage he will sing with shut
teeth, doing all he can to prevent a word he says
from being understood, and, in the recitatives,
paying no respect either to commas or periods.
While another performer is reciting a soliloquy, or
singing an air, he will be saluting the company in
the boxes, or tittering with musicians in the orchestra, or the attendants ; because the audience
knows very well that he is Signor So-and-so, the
musico, and not prince Zoroastro, whom he is representing. A modern virtuoso will be hard to
prevail on to sing at a private party. When he
arrives, he will walk up to the mirror, settle his
wig, draw down his ruffles, and pull up his cravat
to show his diamond brooch. He will then touch
the harpsichord very carelessly, and begin his air
three or four times, as if he could not recollect it.

Having granted this great favour, he will begin talking (by way of gathering applause) with some lady, telling her stories about his travels, correspondence, and professional intrigues; all the while ogling his companion with passionate glances, and throwing back the curls of his peruke, sometimes on one shoulder, sometimes on the other. He will every minute offer the lady snuff in a different box, in one of which he will point out his own portrait; and will show her some magnificent diamond, the gift of a distinguished patron, saying that he would offer it for her acceptance were it not for delicacy. Thus he will perhaps make an impression on her heart, and, at all events, make a great figure in the eyes of the company. In the society of literary men, however eminent, he will always take precedence, because, with most people, the singer has the credit of being an artist, while the literary man has no consideration at all. He will even advise them to embrace his profession, as the singer has plenty of money as well as fame, while the man of letters is very apt to die of hunger. If the singer is a bass, he should constantly sing tenor passages as high as he can. If a tenor, he ought to go as low as he can in the scale of the bass, or get up, with a falsetto voice, into the regions of the contralto, without minding whether he sings through his nose or his throat. He will pay his court to all the principal *cantatrices* and their protectors; and need not despair, by means of his talent and exemplary modesty, to acquire the title of a count, marquis, or chevalier.

The *prima donna* receives ample instructions in her duties both on and off the stage. She is taught how to make engagements, and to screw the manager up to exorbitant terms; how to obtain the " protection " of rash amateurs, who are to attend her at all times, pay her expenses, make her presents, and submit to her caprices. She is taught to be careless at rehearsals, to be insolent to the other performers, and to perform all manner of musical absurdities on the stage. She must have a music-master to teach her variations, passages, and embellishments to her airs; and some familiar friend, an advocate or a doctor, to teach her how to move her arms, turn her head, and use her handkerchief, without telling her why, for that would only confuse her head. She is to endeavour to vary her airs every night; and though the variations may be at cross purposes with the bass, or the violin part, or the harmony of the accompaniments, that matters little, as a modern conductor is deaf and dumb. In her airs and recitatives, in action she will take care every night to use the same motions of her hand, her head, her fan, and her handkerchief. If she orders a character to be put in chains, and addresses him in an air of rage or disdain, during the symphony she should talk and laugh with him, point out to him people in the boxes, and show how very little she is in earnest. She will get hold of a new passage in rapid triplets, and introduce it in all her airs, quick, slow, lively, or sad; and the higher she can rise in the scale, the surer she will be of having all the principal parts allotted to her.

A modern manager, says our author, ought to have no knowledge of music, acting, poetry, painting, or anything belonging to a theatre. He will engage his composers, and others, at the suggestion of his friends, taking care to be as narrow as possible in his terms, except with the singers, particularly the ladies, who must be well paid. He will put an opera into the hands of the composer on the fourth of the month, telling him that it must positively be brought out on the twelfth, and that therefore he need not be very nice about the correctness of his score. The greater part of his company should consist of women; and if two ladies dispute about having the first part, he will get two parts composed, precisely equal in airs, recitatives, and everything else; taking care even that the names of the characters shall contain the same number of letters. He will engage singers of small reputation, having a view rather to their looks than to their talent; for, if pretty, they will find plenty of "protectors," which will be of advantage to his theatre. In playing his violoncello and double bass, he will abate all the second parts of the airs which they have not played; desiring, for that purpose, his composer to write these second parts without putting a note of bass to them. If the house is thin, he will allow the performers to leave out their

recitatives and sing half their songs, and make game
with each other on the stage. On such nights he
will not insist on the orchestra rosining their bows,
nor make any objection to the attendants smoking
behind the scenes.

In the directions to the orchestra, "the oboes,
flutes, trumpets, bassoons, &c.," are advised to be
always out of tune. From this it would appear
that wind-instruments were in common use in the
Italian opera at an earlier period than is generally
supposed. The author goes on to instruct the
machinists, scene-painters, attendants, dressmakers,
dancers, prompters: the amateur patrons of the
theatre and protectors of the *cantatrices*, with their
mothers (a set of persons on whom he bestows very
particular attention) in the same sarcastic vein.
The grave irony and quaint style of the book are
very amusing; and the author makes his theatrical
ladies talk a *patois* so rude as to be almost unintelligible—an indication of their want of education and breeding, and the low position which
they then held in the scale of society.

In a sketch professedly satirical, some allowance
must be made for exaggeration and caricature: but
it bears every mark of having been drawn from the
life; and its general truth is confirmed by the number of particulars in which it resembles the musical
stage, even after the lapse of a century. In the
days of Marcello, as in our own, there were distinguished dramatic poets, composers, and singers;
but the bulk of them were in many respects such

as he describes, and are so to this hour. The Italian playwright, called, *par excellence*, "poeta," is still generally an ignorant, despised creature, the *serf* of some particular theatre, and cringingly obsequious to the popular composer and fashionable singers, who requite his humility by making him the butt of their ridicule.* In the sarcastic advices which Marcello gives to this class of persons, as well as to the composers and performers, we recognise many approved practices of the present day. One difference there is; the present Italian stage, among its poets and composers, can boast of no such names as adorned it in the time of Marcello.

The greatest of the Italian composers for the theatre, who flourished at the beginning of the last century, was the celebrated ALESSANDRO SCARLATTI. This great musician was born at Naples in 1650, and spent the greater part of his life in his native city, where he died in 1728. He was a voluminous writer for the church and the chamber, as well as the theatre. He is said to have composed above a hundred operas, which are now forgotten; but his numerous cantatas are still the admiration of musicians. ANTONIO CALDARA was also a great dramatic composer, though it is only by his works for the church that he is now known. He produced his first opera at Venice in 1697, and his last (Metastasio's *Achille in Sciro*) at Vienna

* See the anecdote of Rossini and Tottola, the "poeta" of the theatre of San-Carlo, in Stendhal's *Vie de Rossini*.

in 1736. He was during the greatest part of his life in the imperial service, and died at Vienna in 1763, at the age of ninety. ANTONIO LOTTI, whose fine compositions for the church are still extant, composed a number of operas for the Venetian theatre between 1698 and 1717. ANTONIO VIVALDI was a great violinist as well as a dramatic composer. He was for some time *maestro di capella* to the landgrave of Hesse Darmstadt, but afterwards became director of the conservatory of *La Pietà* at Venice, where he resided from the year 1713 till his death. He was an ecclesiastic; and it is related of him, that one day, while he was saying mass, a theme for a fugue having suddenly struck him, he quitted the altar to the surprise of the congregation, hastened into the sacristy to write it down, and, having done so, returned to finish his office. For this misdemeanour he was brought before the inquisition; but the fault having been considered as an aberration of genius, he received no further punishment than a prohibition from saying mass for the future.

These were the principal composers of the beginning of the last century who had produced operas before the date of Marcello's satire, and who contributed to those improvements in dramatic music which were carried further by Leo, Vinci, and others who came after them.

Similar improvements gradually took place in the dramatic composition of Italian operas. They became more regular and rational in their structure and incidents. It was no longer necessary that their subjects should be drawn from the classic mythology, or the marvels and enchantments of the middle ages. " Gods and devils," says Arteaga, " were banished from the stage, as soon as poets discovered the art of making men speak with dignity." It was found better that the feelings should be roused by an interesting story, and the heart touched by noble or pathetic sentiments, than that the eye should be dazzled by glittering shows, or the fancy amused, at the expense of reason and common sense, by absurd adventures and incredible prodigies. The opera, too, received dignity and congruity by being cleared of the low buffoonery which it had been usual to introduce into the most lofty and serious scenes.

Many poets, whose names are now forgotten, even in Italy, had the merit of contributing to this reformation of the musical drama. Of some of the poets of this period we shall have occasion to speak, in tracing the introduction of the Italian opera into England. The first musical dramatist of lasting celebrity was APOSTOLO ZENO, who, for a time, was the idol of his countrymen, till he was thrown into the shade by the far greater splendour of his successor Metastasio.

Apostolo Zeno was not only an eminent poet, but a learned critic and antiquary. He was born in the year 1669, and descended from a noble Venetian family. At an early age he applied himself to literature and the study of the history and antiquities of his country. In 1696 he instituted at Venice a distinguished literary society, called the Academy *Degli Animosi*, and was the editor of the *Giornale de' Letterati d'Italia*, which he carried on from 1710 till 1719. His first musical drama, *L' Inganni felici*, was performed at Venice in 1695. In 1718 he entered into the service of the emperor Charles VI., in the capacity of imperial poet-laureate; in which situation he resided at Vienna till 1731, when he returned to Venice, his native city, where he died in 1750, at the age of eighty-one. Previous to the time of his quitting Vienna, Zeno had produced forty-six operas and seventeen oratorios, besides a number of other dramatic pieces. After his return to Venice, he employed his latter days in the composition of several learned and valuable works on subjects of history, anti-quities, and criticism. His dramatic works were published at Venice in 1744, in ten volumes, by Count Gozzi; and in 1752 his letters were pub-lished in three volumes by Forcellini. His com-mentary on the *Bibl. dell' Eloquenza Italiana*, one of the best of his critical works, was published in 1753, with a preface dictated by himself imme-diately before his death. He was a man of great modesty, and, as appears from passages in his let-ters, thought diffidently of his own talents. Being conscious of the decay of his poetical powers, he recommended, some years before he quitted Vienna, that Metastasio should be associated with him in the office of poet-laureate; and, after the arrival of his young colleague, seems to have attempted nothing but oratorios.

Apostolo Zeno was called the Corneille of the musical drama; and, in the bold and original genius which enabled him to leave his contemporaries so far behind him, he certainly resembled the father of French tragedy. But the quality of his works was much injured by the quickness with which he produced them. He took only eight days, as Maffei informs us, to write an opera; and this haste led him into innumerable negligences, both of construction and style. He was not sufficiently aware of the rapidity of action which the musical drama requires. Hence his scenes are often too long, and his plots so complex and crowded with incident, that one of his pieces might furnish materials for two or three. His language is rich in poetical beauties, and possesses great vigour and energy; but he has neither the delicacy of thought and feeling, nor the exquisite sweetness of versification, which so eminently distinguish the incomparable Metastasio.

The appearance of Metastasio may be considered as an era in the history of the Italian opera, not only in regard to its poetry, but its music. Though not an artist, he possessed the mind of a musician; and his judgment and taste had a powerful influence on the greatest dramatic composers of his time. Before entering upon this new era, we shall now notice the progress which, previous to its commencement, the Italian opera had made in other countries.

CHAPTER X.

THE EARLY MUSICAL DRAMA IN GERMANY—GERMAN OPERAS—
INTRODUCTION OF THE ITALIAN OPERA—GERMAN COMPOSERS
OF THE SEVENTEENTH CENTURY—MATTHESON—KEISER—
ARRIVAL OF METASTASIO.

DURING the seventeenth century the musical drama made little progress in Germany. The music of that country resembled its literature; it was learned and profound, with little imagination, elegance, or grace. There were many great organists and composers for the church; men deeply versed in the mysteries of counterpoint, with whom music was the art of constructing fugues and resolving harmonical puzzles, and by whom, consequently, simple and popular melody was looked upon as unworthy of notice.

We are told, indeed, that operas in the German language and by German composers, were performed at the courts of German sovereigns early in the seventeenth century. But they must have been very rude productions; as all traces of them, even the names of their authors, seem to be lost.

The first operas which have been commemorated as performed in Germany, were imported from Italy. About the year 1630, Martin Opitz, who has been called the father of the German drama, translated from the Italian the *Dafne* of Rinuccini; and the music having been adapted to the German words by a composer of the name of Schutz, the opera was performed at the court of Dresden, on the occasion of the marriage of the Landgrave of Hesse with the sister of the elector of Saxony. Soon afterwards, several other Italian operas were adapted to German words, and performed at Ratisbon, Munich, and other places.

Italian operas now began to be performed in their original language. About the middle of the seventeenth century, the imperial court, under the Emperor Leopold, was full of Italian ministers and nobles, and the emperor himself was fond of Italian music. Such, indeed, was this sovereign's love of the art, that it was exhibited as " his ruling passion, strong in death." It is related, that, when on his deathbed, and after he had performed his last devotions with his confessor, he ordered his band to be called in, and expired while listening to their music. Leopold retained in his service several Italian poets and composers, to furnish operas for the imperial court. Among these was Antonio Draghi, a composer of celebrity, who remained in the imperial service nearly forty years. Several dramas were written for the emperor's court by the Marchese Santinelli, an Italian nobleman.

Hitherto, musical dramas, as in other countries, had been performed only at the courts of princes ; but they now began to make their appearance in public theatres. The first opera, publicly exhibited on a German stage, was Thiele's *Adam and Eve*, which was performed in the German language, at Hamburg, in 1678. The second was *Orontes*, performed the same year. After this period many German operas were performed at Hamburg, the principal composers of which were Strunck,* Franck, Förtsch, Conradi, and Cousser; the last of whom afterwards came to England, where he obtained the place of master of the state band in Ireland. About the close of the century, the celebrated Keiser began to compose for the Hamburg theatre; and the operas of the Abate Steffani, which he had set to Italian words for the court of

* Strunck was violinist to the elector of Hanover, and was chiefly celebrated for his wonderful powers as a performer on that instrument. While travelling in Italy, he paid a visit to Corelli at Rome. Corelli, not knowing his person, but finding, from his conversation, that he was a musical performer, inquired what was his instrument. Strunck said that he played a little on the violin, and begged the favour that the great Italian master would let him hear his performance. Corelli readily complied, and exerted his abilities for the gratification of the unknown amateur. On laying down the violin, he requested Strunck to play something in his turn. Strunck began to play rather carelessly, but yet in such a style as to obtain a compliment on the freedom of his bow, and a remark that he promised, with practice, to become an excellent player. Strunck, with a quiet smile, put all the strings out of tune, and then began to play with amazing execution, correcting with his fingers the false tuning of the instrument ; till at last, Corelli, in utter amazement, exclaimed, " They call me *Arcangelo*; but, by heaven, Sir, you must be *Arcidiavolo!* "

Hanover, began to be performed at Hamburg in the German language, except the airs, which were usually sung in Italian. We shall afterwards see, that a similar medley of Italian and English was made use of when the Italian opera was first introduced into this country. This custom (absurd as it seems) prevailed in Germany so late as the year 1733, when Graun's opera of *Pharao*, a German version of the *Gianguir* of Apostolo Zeno, was performed at Brunswick;—the recitatives only being translated into German, while the airs were sung in the original Italian.

Mattheson, whose name will be immortalized as the youthful friend and rival of Handel, was a composer for the Hamburg stage. Mattheson was not only a composer, but an actor, singer, and instrumental performer. On the harpsichord he was considered equal, if not superior, to Handel. As a composer, he seems to have had little genius, and to have been given to pedantry and puerile conceits. His biographers tell us, that, towards the close of his life, he composed his own funeral anthem; and that, in setting the words, from the Revelations, "And there was a rainbow round about the throne," he contrived, in a very full score, to make every part form an arch by a gradual ascent and descent of the notes on the paper; conceiving, it would seem, that this appearance to the eyes of the performers would convey the idea of a rainbow to the ears of the hearers. One of Mattheson's operas caused a duel between the two young rivals, which nearly cost Handel his life. This was *Cleopatra*, in which the composer himself performed the part of Antony, while Handel, as conductor, sat at the harpsichord in the orchestra. On the death of Antony, which happened early in the piece, Mattheson divested himself of his royal trappings, and came into the orchestra to take his usual place at the harpsichord. Handel, however, would not give it up, and a violent quarrel ensued. As they were leaving the theatre, Mattheson gave Handel a slap in the face ; they drew their swords, and a desperate encounter ensued in the market-place, which was fortunately terminated by Mattheson's sword breaking against one of his adversary's buttons, or, as others say, against the score of Mattheson's opera, which Handel had buttoned under his coat.

The greatest German composer of this period was Keiser, whose once splendid reputation, contrasted with the oblivion into which he has now fallen, affords a striking instance of the instability of musical fame. Keiser was born in 1673, and died in 1739. He kept possession of the Hamburg stage for more than forty years, and composed above a hundred operas. " This master," says Burney, " was as sure of fancy and originality, whenever he put pen to paper, as Haydn is at present. In a manuscript collection of near seventy cantatas by the greatest composers of his time, both of Italy and Germany, in which there are twelve by Keiser, in opening the book by chance, in any part of it where his cantatas are inserted, it is instantly known to be his music at the first glance; so new are the passages, and so different the arrangement of the notes from that of his companions in the collection, amounting to near thirty of the first order. For grace and facility I do not recommend him; indeed they were little sought or known during his time; but for modulation, ingenuity, and new ideas, he had scarcely his equal." The famous Hasse said to Dr. Burney, that "Keiser was one of the greatest musicians the world had ever seen;" and yet, with all his greatness, he is now almost as completely forgotten as if he had never existed.

We are informed by Riccoboni, in his *General History of the Stage*, that, in the beginning of the last century, the performers in the German operas at Hamburg, were all tradesmen or handicrafts. "Your shoemaker," he says, "was often the first performer on the stage; and you might have bought fruit and sweetmeats of the same girl whom the night before you saw in the character of Armida or Semiramis." But this account must be taken with considerable qualification: for, as has been already mentioned, Mattheson was a performer on the Hamburg stage; and Hasse, before he went to Italy, was a tenor-singer on the same stage, in the operas of Keiser.

Such was the state of the musical drama in Germany till the period when it received a new impulse by the arrival of Metastasio, who spent almost his whole life at Vienna, in the service of the imperial court.

CHAPTER XI.

THE ITALIAN OPERA INTRODUCED INTO ENGLAND — BATTISTA DRAGHI — ARRIVAL OF ITALIAN SINGERS — MARGHERITA DE L'EPINE—MRS. TOFTS—MUSICAL FACTIONS—OPERA OF ARSINOE —CAMILLA—ROSAMOND—ADDISON AND CLAYTON—NICOLINI— PYRRHUS AND DEMETRIUS — THE TATLER — LEVERIDGE — ALMAHIDE—HYDASPES—THE SPECTATOR.

WE have already seen, that, during the time of Charles the Second, the English dramatic music was in the French style, and that it so continued till an English school was founded by the genius of Purcell. Before that time, however, Italian music had begun to be heard in England: and Purcell himself acknowledged the benefit he had derived from the study of the Italian masters. It had become fashionable for English gentlemen to visit Italy; and they returned with a taste for the music, painting, and poetry of that classic land. We have given, in a preceding chapter, Evelyn's account of the Italian opera at Venice: and the following passage in Pepys's *Diary* gives a curious view of the progress of Italian music, and the general state of the art, in this country.

" January 12th, 1667. With my Lord Brouncker to his house, there to hear some Italian musique,

and here we met Tom Killigrew, Sir Robert
Murray, and the Italian, Signor Baptista,* who
hath prepared a play in Italian for the opera, which
Sir T. Killigrew do intend to have up ; and here
he did sing one of the acts. He himself is the
poet as well as the musician, and did sing the
whole from the words without any musique prickt,
and played all along upon a harpsicon most admirably, and the composition most excellent. The
words I did not understand, and so knew not how
they were fitted, but believe very well, and all the
recitativo very fine. But I perceive there is a
proper accent in every country's discourse, and
that do reach in their setting of notes to words,
which, therefore cannot be natural to anybody else
but them ; so that I am not so much smitten with
it as if I were acquainted with their accent. But
the whole composition is certainly most excellent ;
and the poetry, Sir T. Killigrew and Sir R. Murray,
who understood the words, did say was most excellent. I confess I was most mightily pleased
with the musique." Pepys adds : " He (Sir T.
Killigrew) tells me that he hath gone several
times (eight or ten times he tells me) hence to
Rome, to hear good musique ; so much he loves it,
though he never did sing or play a note. That he
hath ever endeavoured, in the late king's time,
and in this, to introduce good musique ; but he
never could do it, there never having been any
musique there better than ballads and songs.

* Battista Draghi.

' Hermitt Poore,' and ' Chiny Chase ' [Chevy Chase] was all the musique we had; and yet no ordinary fiddlers get so much money as ours do here, which speaks our rudeness still." A sad account of the state of music at that time!

The Italian opera which Pepys speaks of does not seem ever to have been represented; and there is no account of the production of any Italian opera on our stage till many years afterwards. Italian music, as Burney observes, was long talked of and performed in England, before we heard of Italian singing. Even in the time of Queen Elizabeth, the works of the great Italian madrigalists were well known to our amateurs as well as composers: and Purcell, as we have seen, studied the Italian vocal music of his time. But we do not hear of the arrival of Italian singers till about the close of the seventeenth century. In 1692, an advertisement in the London Gazette announces that "the Italian lady, that is lately come over, that is so famous for singing," will sing at the concerts in York-buildings during the season. In April, 1693, Signor Tosi, the author of the celebrated treatise on singing, advertises a concert: and, from that time, the announcements of concerts by Italian performers became frequent.

The " Italian lady," announced in 1692 as being so famous for her singing, was FRANCESCA MARGHERITA DE L'EPINE, the first Italian singer of any note who appeared in England. She came to this country with a German musician, of the name of Greber; and hence we find her in some of the musical squibs of the day, called "Greber's Peg." She sang in Italian operas, and at concerts and other musical entertainments, till the year 1718; when she retired, and married the celebrated Dr. Pepusch. She was an excellent musician; being not only an accomplished singer, but an extraordinary performer on the harpsichord. She was so swarthy and ill-favoured that her husband used to call her Hecate, a name to which she answered with perfect good-humour; but her want of personal charms did not prevent her from enjoying the uninterrupted favour of the public. By her marriage with Dr. Pepusch she brought him a fortune of 10,000*l*.; a sum which, by relieving him from the daily cares and toils of his profession, enabled him to follow his favourite pursuit of learned researches into the history and antiquities of his art. She was a person of perfect respectability; but, nevertheless, was unceremoniously treated by some of the writers of the day, who had no love for foreign players and musicians. She had a sister, who came to England in 1703; and these ladies are thus mentioned by Swift in his Journal to Stella: "August 6, 1711. We have a music-meeting in our town (Windsor) to-night. I went to the rehearsal of it, and there was *Margarita*, and her sister, and another drab, and a parcel of fiddlers. I was weary, and would not go to the meeting, which I am sorry for, because I heard it was a great assembly." The dean frequently speaks of the music-meetings at Windsor in the course of this season; always with spleen and an affectation of contempt; saying, for example, "In half an hour I was tired of their *fine stuff*," and so on: merely showing how little even a great man can make himself by talking flippantly of what he does not understand.

In the year 1703, we first hear of the celebrated Mrs. TOFTS, who is mentioned in advertisements of the day, as singing English and Italian songs, at the theatre in Lincoln's-inn-fields. This lady became the rival of Margherita de l'Epine; and their competition gave rise to the first musical feud that we read of in England. The public was divided into an Italian and English party; the one composed of the partizans of Margherita, the other of the admirers of Mrs. Tofts. The spirit of faction appears to have run high among the amateurs, both high and low. When Margherita made her appearance at Drury-Lane, there was a disturbance in the theatre while she was singing, which was supposed to have been created by the emissaries of Mrs. Tofts; a supposition which derived some colour from the circumstance that her own female servant was a ringleader in the uproar. In her own vindication, however, Mrs. Tofts had the following paragraph inserted in the *Daily Courant* of February 8, 1704:—

"Ann Barwick having occasioned a disturbance at the theatre-royal Drury Lane, on Saturday night last, the 5th of February, and being thereupon taken into custody, Mrs. Tofts, in vindication of her innocency, sent a letter to Mr. Rich, master of the said theatre, which is as followeth: —'Sir, I was very much surprised when I was informed that Ann Barwick, who was lately my servant, had committed a rudeness last night at the playhouse, by throwing of oranges and hissing when Mrs. L'Epine, the Italian gentlewoman, sung. I hope no one will think that it was in the least with my privity, as I assure you it was not. I abhor such practices; and I hope you will cause her to be prosecuted, that she may be punished as she deserves. I am, Sir, your humble servant,

'KATHARINE TOFTS.'"

The musical feuds among the aristocracy, to which the rivalry of the British and foreign songstresses gave rise, are thus alluded to by Hughes, the author of the *Siege of Damascus:*

> " Music has learn'd the discords of the state,
> And concerts jar with Whig and Tory hate.
> Here Somerset and Devonshire attend
> The British Tofts, and every note commend ;
> To native merit just, and pleas'd to see
> We've Roman hearts, from Roman bondage free.
> There famed L'Epine does equal skill employ,
> While listening peers crowd to the ecstatic joy :
> Bedford to hear her song his dice forsakes ;
> And Nottingham is raptured when she shakes.
> Lull'd statesmen melt away their drowsy cares,
> Of England's safety, in Italian airs."

The actual introduction of the Italian opera into England was preceded by adaptations of Italian pieces to the English stage. The first of these was *Arsinoe, Queen of Cyprus*, a translation of an opera then popular in Italy, with music composed for the English words, by Thomas Clayton, a composer whose name has acquired an unmerited celebrity from his connexion with Addison. Clayton had been in Italy; and, though destitute of genius, laid claim to the character of a reformer of the English musical drama, and talked so big that he contrived to persuade the public of his capacity for the task. In the preface to the book of the words of this opera, he thus sets forth its pretensions. "The design of this entertainment being to introduce the Italian manner of singing to the English stage, which has not been before attempted, I was obliged to have an Italian opera translated; in which the words, however mean in several places, suited much better with that manner of music than others more poetical would do. The style of this music is to express the passions, which is the soul of music; and though the voices are not equal to the Italian, yet I have engaged the best that were to be found in England; and I have not been wanting, to the utmost of my diligence, in the instructing of them. The music, being recitative, may not at first meet with that general acceptation, as is to be hoped for, from the audience's being better acquainted with it; but if this attempt shall be a means of bringing this manner of music to be used in my native country, I shall think my study and pains very well employed."

This opera was first performed at Drury-lane, on the 16th of January, 1705. The singers were all English, consisting of Mrs. Tofts, Mrs. Cross, and Mrs. Lyndsay, with Messrs. Hughes, Leveridge, and Cook. At this time Signora de l'Epine sang Italian songs before or after the opera. The music, as well as the words, of this piece were utterly contemptible; yet such was the charm of novelty, and so effectually had Clayton persuaded the public that he was a great man, that this worthless production was performed twenty-four times the first season, and eleven times the second.*

The next opera after the Italian manner was *Camilla*, performed for the first time at Drury-lane,

* Though *Arsinoe* is utterly unworthy of criticism, yet there is something amusing in the folly of the composer. The very first song may be taken as a specimen. The words are :

> " Queen of Darkness, sable Night,
> Ease a wandering lover's pain ;
> Guide me, lead me,
> Where the Nymph whom I adore,
> Sleeping, dreaming,
> Thinks of love and me no more."

The first two lines are spoken in a meagre sort of recitative. Then there is a miserable air, the first part of which consists of the next two lines, and concludes with a perfect close. The second part of the air is on the last two lines; after which there is, as usual, a *da capo*, and the first part is repeated ; the song finishing in the middle of a sentence—

> " Guide me, lead me,
> Where the nymph whom I adore ! "

on the 30th of April, 1706. It was translated from
the Italian of Silvio Stampiglio, by Owen M'Swiney,
a person who was for some time manager of that
theatre, and the English words were adapted to the
original music of Marc Antonio Buononcini, the
brother of Giovanni Buononcini, the celebrated
rival of Handel. It was performed by the same
company as *Arsinoe*, and met with great success ;
having been frequently performed, alternately with
Arsinoe, and *Thomyris, Queen of Scythia*, another
opera of the same kind, till a change in the taste
of the town was effected by the arrival of the first
Italian dramatic singers.

These were Valentini Urbani, and a lady known
only by the name of the Baroness, a native of Germany, who had been educated in Italy, and had
acquired a considerable reputation on the Continent. Along with them, Signora de l'Epine was
engaged at Drury-lane ; and then the opera of
Camilla was performed half in English and half in
Italian ; the English singers, as formerly, making
use of the translation, while the Italians performed
their parts in the original language. The part of
Camilla, the heroine, continued to be performed by
Mrs. Tofts, in English, while Valentini enacted
Turnus in Italian. This absurdity was ridiculed
by the wits of the day, but passed current with the
public, who looked upon it as one of those conventional licences which must always, to a greater or
smaller extent, be tolerated in dramatic performances. It was an absurdity not peculiar to Eng-

land; for Riccoboni says, that, when Italian operas were first performed at Hamburg, the recitative was delivered in the German language, and the airs generally sung in Italian.

The music of *Camilla* has considerable merit. The airs are very short, consisting of two parts (the second of which is almost always in the relative minor key), and ending with a repetition of the first part. This form was adhered to, in defiance of sense and meaning, by every dramatic composer, for the best part of a century, till it was got rid of by Gluck and Piccini. The melodies exhibit invention and expression, and are accompanied by solid and ingenious basses. The song in the part of *Turnus*, "Frail are a lover's hopes," has many strokes of feeling, and would please the most modern ear. The air, "Fortune ever known to vary," sung by Mrs. Tofts, contains a number of passages in triplets, each triplet being sung to a syllable, exactly in the manner of Rossini. The air,—

> " I was born of a royal race,
> Yet must wander in disgrace,"

sung by Mrs. Tofts in the opening of the piece, consists of only *fourteen bars;* and yet there is so much meaning in these few notes, that it is easy to conceive the effect which Mrs. Tofts is said to have produced in singing them.

This lady acquired great celebrity by her performance of the character of *Camilla.* There is a pleasant allusion to it in the *Spectator*, in the form of a letter from the actor who personated the wild boar killed by the Amazonian heroine. " Mr. Spectator," says this correspondent, " your having been so humble as to take notice of the epistles of other animals, emboldens me, who am the wild boar that was killed by Mrs. Tofts, to represent to you, that I think I was hardly used in not having the part of the lion in *Hydaspes* given to me. It would have been but a natural step for me to have personated that noble creature, after having behaved myself to satisfaction in the part above mentioned ; but that of a lion is too great a character for one that never trode the stage before but upon two legs. As for the little resistance which I made, I hope it may be excused, when it is considered that the dart was thrown at me by so fair a hand. I must confess I had but just put on my brutality ; and *Camilla's* charms were such, that beholding her erect mien, hearing her charming voice, and astonished with her grateful motion, I could not keep up to my assumed fierceness, but died like a man."

Mrs. Tofts retired from the stage in 1709. Cibber, who speaks of her from his own knowledge, says, " Whatever defect the fashionably skilful might find in her manner, she had, in the general sense of her hearers, charms that few of the most learned singers ever arrive at." — "The beauty," he adds, " of her finely proportioned figure, and exquisitely sweet, silver tone of voice, with peculiar rapid swiftness of her throat, were perfections not

to be imitated by art or labour." It appears from
the music of the operas in which she performed,
that her voice was a *soprano* of moderate compass,
and that her passages of execution were by no
means either various or difficult.

Her retirement from the stage was caused by a
mental malady, under the influence of which she
imagined herself to be some one or other of the
characters she represented. This calamity is un-
feelingly alluded to by Steele, in the *Tatler*.*
After saying, that " the theatre is breaking," and
that " there is a great desolation among the gentlemen and ladies who were the ornaments of the
town and used to shine in plumes and diadems,
the heroes being most of them pressed and the
queens beating hemp," the writer adds, " The
great revolutions of this nature bring to my mind
the distresses of the unfortunate *Camilla*, who has
had the ill luck to break before her voice, and to
disappear at a time when her beauty was in the
height of its bloom. This lady entered so thoroughly into the great characters she acted, that
when she had finished her part she could not think
of retrenching her equipage, but would appear in
her own lodgings with the same magnificence as
she did upon the stage. This greatness of soul
has reduced that unhappy princess to a voluntary
retirement, where she now passes her time among
the woods and forests, thinking on the crowns and

* No. 20, May 26th, 1709.

sceptres she has lost, and often humming over in her solitude,

> ' I was born of royal race,
> Yet must wander in disgrace,' &c.

But for fear of being overheard, and her quality known, she usually sings it in Italian ;

> ' Nacqui al regno, nacqui al trono,
> E pur sono
> Sventurata pastorella.' "

Burney says, that it seems doubtful whether we are to take this account literally, and refers his readers to the *Tatler*, leaving the comments to their own ingenuity. But there is no doubt that Steele alluded to the state of insanity under which she then laboured, and into which, though she recovered from it for a time, she again fell in the latter period of her life. "In the meridian of her beauty," says Hawkins, "and possessed of a large sum of money which she had acquired by singing, Mrs. Tofts quitted the stage, and was married to Mr. Joseph Smith, a gentleman, who being appointed consul for the English nation at Venice, she went thither with him. Mr. Smith was a great collector of books and patron of the arts. He lived in great state and magnificence; but the disorder of his wife returning, she dwelt sequestered from the world in a remote part of the house, and had a large garden to range in, in which she would frequently walk, singing, and giving way to that innocent frenzy which had seized her in the early part of her life." In this unhappy state she continued many years, and died about 1760.*

The favour with which the public received these importations from the Italian stage, induced Addison to undertake an opera in the same style, but entirely of English workmanship. He accordingly wrote his celebrated *Rosamond:* but unfortunately partook so much of the general delusion as to commit the composition of the music to the worthless pretender Clayton. It was performed for the first time on the 4th of March, 1707. The part of *Queen Eleanor* was performed by Mrs. Tofts; *Rosamond,* by Signora Maria Gallia, a singer of whom we have not met with any account; the *King,* by Mr. Hughes; and the two comic characters, *Sir Trusty* and *Grideline,* by Mr. Leveridge and Mrs. Lyndsay. Notwithstanding the favourable prepossessions of the public, and the poetical merit of the piece, it was received with the utmost coldness, and struggled with difficulty through three representations. It was then laid aside, and never again performed

* In the French translation of the *Tatler,* there is the following note. "La célèbre Madame Tofts, après avoir brillé par la douceur et la beauté de sa voix, eut, je ne sais pas comment, la mortification de se voir negligée avant que d'avoir perdu les agrémens qui la rendaient si fameuse. De chagrin, elle prit la résolution d'aller à Rome, où l'on dit qu'elle se fit Papiste. Le Pape Clement XI., devant qui elle chanta, fut charmé de sa voix, et la chronique scandaleuse en publia même quelque chose de plus." No authority, however, is given for this piece of scandal.

in the life-time of the author; though it was revived thirty years afterwards, with new music by
Dr. Arne.

Rosamond is a very pleasing dramatic poem,
though it cannot be called a good opera. It is
better calculated for reading than for representation. Its versification is polished and elegant, containing many lively and graceful turns of expression, poetical thoughts, and touches of tenderness.
But it lacks dramatic action and movement; and
the interest of the story is made to terminate long
before the conclusion of the piece, the latter part
of which is spun out by forced and clumsy buffoonery, and by a tissue of fulsome compliments to
the Duke of Marlborough, which would not now
be tolerated, but were considered as matters of
course in an age when men of the highest literary
distinction were not ashamed to pay their court to
the great by the grossest adulation. *Rosamond*
owed its failure in a great measure to the worth-
lessness of Clayton's music, which the audience
were now able to compare with better things: but
the defects of the drama must also be taken into
account; for even when it was afterwards performed
with the pretty music of Arne, it was unable to
acquire a permanent hold of the public favour.
Addison's mortification at this ill success appears
to have been the cause of the constant hostility he
ever afterwards exhibited to the Italian opera.

The year 1708 was rendered memorable by the
arrival of the celebrated Cavaliere Nicolino Gri-

MALDI, generally known by the name of NICOLINI. This distinguished performer was a Neapolitan; and is classed by Quadrio among the great singers who began to appear between 1690 and 1700. He had acquired a high reputation at Venice, Milan, and other cities of Italy where the musical drama was established, when he was attracted to England (according to Cibber), by the report of our passion for foreign operas, without any particular invitation or engagement.

The first opera in which Nicolini appeared was *Pyrrhus and Demetrius*, a translation of the *Pirro e Demetrio* of Adriano Morselli, first performed at Naples, with the music of Alessandro Scarlatti, in 1694. The translation was executed by M'Swiney, the manager, and the music was arranged to the English words by Nicola Haym, a composer of some merit, then resident in London, who composed a new overture and several additional airs. It was performed, for the first time, on the 14th of December, 1708, and continued for a long time to draw crowded audiences. The performers were a mixture of Italians and English, who acted and sang in their respective languages: the Italians being Nicolini, Valentini, Margherita de l'Epine, and the Baroness; and the English, Mrs. Tofts, Mr. Cook, and Mr. Ramondon. The airs of this opera are in general excellent. Many of them are deformed, of course, by antiquated divisions; but others are in that pure and simple style which will always please; and it is only doing justice to Haym

to say that the airs added by him are not inferior
to those of the more celebrated author of the original music.

The successful representation of this opera produced the following remarks from Sir Richard
Steele, in the fourth number of the *Tatler*.—
" Letters from the Haymarket inform us that on
Saturday night last the opera of *Pyrrhus and
Demetrius* was performed with great applause.
This intelligence is not very acceptable to us friends
of the theatre; for the stage being an entertainment of the reason and all our faculties, this way of
being pleased with the suspense of them for three
hours together, and being given up to the shallow
satisfaction of the ears and eyes only, seems to arise
rather from the degeneracy of our understanding
than an improvement of our diversions.   That the
understanding has no part in the pleasure is evident from what these letters very positively assert ;
to wit, that a great part of the performance was
done in Italian: and a great critic fell into fits in
the gallery at seeing not only time and place, but
language and nations, confused in the most incor-
rigible manner.   His spleen is so extremely moved
on this occasion, that he is going to publish another
treatise against the introduction of operas, which,
he thinks, has already inclined us to thoughts of
peace, and, if tolerated, must infallibly dispirit us
from carrying on the war.   He has communicated
his scheme to the whole room, and declared in
what manner things of this kind were first intro-

duced. He has on this occasion considered the
nature of sounds in general, and made a very
elaborate digression upon the London cries, where-
in he has shown, from reason and philosophy, why
oysters are cried, card-matches sung, and turnips
and all other vegetables neither cried, sung, nor
said, but sold with an accent and tone neither
natural to man nor beast." Notwithstanding
Steele's propensity, however, to indulge his satirical
vein at the expense of the Italian opera, he afterwards admits *Pyrrhus and Demetrius* to be "a
noble entertainment," and pays a tribute to the
talents of Nicolini.* " For my own part," he
says, " I was fully satisfied with the sight of an
actor, who, by the grace and propriety of his action
and gesture, does honour to the human figure.
Every one will imagine I mean Signor Nicolini,
who sets off the character he bears in an opera by
his action, as much as he does the words of it by
his voice. Every limb and every finger contri-
butes to the part he acts, inasmuch that a deaf
man may go along with him in the sense of it.
There is scarce a beautiful posture in an old statue
which he does not plant himself in, as the different
circumstances of the story give occasion for it.
He performs the most ordinary action in a manner
suitable to the greatness of his character, and
shows the prince even in the giving of a letter, or
despatching of a messenger. Our best actors,"
he adds, " are somewhat at a loss to support them-

* Tatler, No. 113.

selves with proper gesture, as they move from any considerable distance to the front of the stage; but I have seen the person of whom I am now speaking enter alone at the remotest part of it, and advance from it with such greatness of air and mien as seemed to fill the stage, and, at the same time, commanded the attention of the audience with the majesty of his appearance." The two passages just quoted are very inconsistent with each other. That the understanding had no share in the pleasure derived from the Italian opera could not be said of an entertainment in which, by Steele's own account, so much intellectual gratification was produced by the noble performance of Nicolini. But Steele's fine taste and excellent sense were warped, on this subject, by his feelings of personal interest; for he was a patentee of an English theatre, and was suffering from the successful rivalry of the Italian opera.

Pyrrhus and Demetrius was the last opera which was performed partly in Italian and partly in English. From that time Italian operas, performed entirely in their original form, completely engrossed the musical stage. The English singers disappeard, and the English opera, for a time, was in abeyance. Mrs. Tofts, as has been already mentioned, retired in 1709; and Mr. Hughes, who had performed principal parts in the Anglo-Italian operas, is no more heard of after this period. Leveridge, who, from Purcell's time, had been an eminent dramatic singer, appears also, at this time, to have been deprived of his occupation. Leveridge had acquired some reputation as a composer as well as a singer. In 1699 he appeared at Drury Lane in an opera called the *Island Princess*, composed jointly by Daniel Purcell, Jeremiah Clarke, and himself. When operas in the Italian style were introduced, he had a part in all of them, as long as the English performers were allowed to sing in their own language. After this he sang in pantomimes, at the theatres in Lincoln's Inn Fields and Covent Garden, till after the middle of the last century, when he was more than eighty years old. "I remember," says Dr. Burney, "his singing 'Ghosts of every occupation,' and several of Purcell's bass songs, occasionally, in a style which forty years ago seemed antediluvian; but as he generally was the representative of Pluto, Neptune, or some ancient divinity, it corresponded perfectly with his figure and character. He was not only a celebrated singer of convivial songs, but the writer and composer of many that were in great favour with singers and hearers of a certain class, who more piously performed the rites of Comus and Bacchus than those of Minerva and Apollo. He quitted this sublunary world in 1758, at eighty-eight years of age."

The first opera performed entirely in Italian was *Almahide*, supposed to be the composition of Buononcini. It appeared in January 1710, and was received with favour. The singers were Valentini, Nicolini, Margherita de l'Epine, Cassani, and Isabella Girardeau, called Signora Isabella. The music is fuller of divisions and feats of execution, in the airs for the principal singers, than that of any of the previous operas; but it is not remarkable on any other account.

In the same year, *Hydaspes*, composed by Francesco Mancini, was brought on the stage by Nicolini, who performed the principal character. The other performers were the same as in *Almahide*, with the addition of Lawrence, a tenor singer of some ability, who had knowledge enough of Italian to perform an inferior part in it.

Hydaspes, as a drama, contains many puerilities, and possesses less musical merit than several operas which preceded it. Its success, however, was very great; and indeed, for a time, it was quite the rage in the fashionable world.

The combat between Hydaspes and the lion was a favourite subject for satire among the wits of the day. Hydaspes is the brother of Artaxerxes, king of Persia, and his rival in the love of the Princess Berenice. Falling into the tyrant's power, he is condemned to be devoured by a lion in the public amphitheatre, and in the presence of his mistress. The third act opens with a scene representing the amphitheatre, filled with a crowd of spectators. Hydaspes is brought in, guarded by soldiers; a tender dialogue between him and Berenice is broken off by the sound of a trumpet; the Princess resumes her seat among the royal spectators; a monstrous lion rushes into the arena, and, after a desperate combat, is slain by the hero amid the shouts and acclamations of the surrounding multitude.

This scene must have had a most whimsical effect on the stage. Hydaspes addresses the lion in a long bravura song, " Mostro crudel che fai?" full of divisions and flourishes; first calling on the "cruel monster," in a tone of defiance, to come on, and then telling him, with a sentimental air, and in a *largo* movement in the minor key, that he may tear his bosom, but shall not touch his heart, which he has kept faithful to his beloved.   The exhibition of Nicolini, alternately vapouring and gesticulating to a poor biped in a lion's skin, then breathing a love-tale in the pseudo-monster's ear, and at last fairly throttling him on the stage, must have been ludicrous in the extreme, and sufficient to throw ridicule on the Italian opera.

The thirteenth number of the *Spectator* is an admirable *jeu d'esprit* on the subject of Nicolini's combat with the lion, "which," says Addison, "has been very often exhibited to the general satisfaction of most of the nobility and gentry in the kingdom of Great Britain." After a playful imaginary description of the various representatives of the lion, the *Spectator* concludes in a more serious strain : " I would not be thought," he says, "in any part of this relation, to reflect upon Signor Nicolini, who in acting this part only complies with the wretched taste of his audience. He knows very well that the lion has many more admirers than himself; as they say of the famous equestrian statue on the Pont Neuf at Paris, that more people go to see the horse than the king who sits upon it. On the contrary, it gives me a just indignation to see a person whose action gives new dignity to kings, resolution to heroes, and softness to lovers, thus sinking from the greatness of his behaviour, and degraded into the character of *The London Prentice*. I have often wished that our tragedians would copy after this great master in action. Could they make the same use of their arms and legs, and inform their faces with as significant looks and passions, how glorious would an English tragedy appear with that action which is capable of giving a dignity to the forced thoughts, cold conceits, and unnatural expressions of an Italian opera: in the mean time I have related this combat of the lion, to show what are at present the reigning entertainments of the politer part of Great Britain. Audiences have often been reproached by writers for the coarseness of their taste ; but our present grievance does not seem to be the want of a good taste, but of common sense."

In another number* of the same journal, there are some keen strokes of satire in a letter from " Toby Rent-free."—" You are to know," says this correspondent, " that I am naturally brave, and love fighting as well as any man in England. This gallant temper of mine makes me extremely delighted with battles on the stage. I give you this

* No. 314.

trouble to complain to you, that Nicolini refused
to gratify me in that part of the opera for which I
have most taste. I observe it is become a custom, that whenever any gentlemen are particularly
pleased with a song, at their crying out *encore* or
altra volta, the performer is so obliging as to sing
it over again. I was at the opera the last time
Hydaspes was performed. At that part of it where
the hero engages with the lion, the graceful manner in which he put that terrible monster to death
gave me so great a pleasure, and at the same time
so just a sense of that gentleman's intrepidity and
conduct, that I could not forbear desiring a repetition of it, by crying out *altra volta*, in a very
audible voice; and my friends flatter me that I
pronounced those words with a tolerably good accent, considering that this was but the third opera
I had ever seen in my life. Yet, notwithstanding
all this, there was so little regard had to me, that
the lion was carried off and went to bed without
being killed any more that night. Now, Sir, pray
consider that I did not understand a word of what
Mr. Nicolini said to this cruel creature; besides, I
have no ear for music; so that during the long
dispute between them, the whole entertainment I
had was from my eyes. Why then have I not as
much right to have a graceful action repeated as
another has a pleasing sound, since he only hears
as I see, and we neither of us know that there is
any reasonable thing a doing? Pray, Sir, settle
the business of this claim in the audience, and let us

know when we may cry *altra volta, Anglicè, again, again*, for the future. I am an Englishman, and expect some reason or other to be given me, and perhaps an ordinary one may serve; but I expect an answer." In another paper a foolish projector is introduced, entertaining a coffee-house audience with a proposal for an opera of a new species, caricaturing, of course, all the absurdities laid to the charge of the fashionable amusement. The opera is to be entitled, *The Expedition of Alexander the Great;* and the projector gives a humorous account of the way in which he intends to dispose of all the remarkable shows about town among the scenes and decorations of the piece. "This project," continues the *Spectator*, "was received with very great applause by the whole table. Upon which the undertaker told us that he had not communicated to us above half his design; for that, Alexander being a Greek, it was his intention that the whole opera should be acted in that language, which was a tongue he was sure would wonderfully please the ladies, especially when it was a little raised and rounded by the Ionic dialect; and could not but be acceptable to the whole audience, *because there are fewer of them who understand Greek than Italian.* The only difficulty that remained was how to get performers, unless we could persuade some gentlemen of the universities to learn to sing, in order to qualify themselves for the stage; but this objection soon vanished, when the projector informed us that the Greeks were at present the only musicians in the Turkish empire, and that it would be very easy for our factory at Smyrna to furnish us every year with a colony of musicians by the opportunity of the Turkey fleet; besides, says he, if we want any single voice for any lower part in the opera, Lawrence can learn to speak Greek, *as well as he does Italian,* in a fortnight's time."

CHAPTER XII.

ARRIVAL OF HANDEL IN ENGLAND — RINALDO — ADDISON'S OPINIONS RESPECTING THE ITALIAN OPERA, AND OBSERVATIONS ON THEM.

SUCH was the state of the Italian opera when Handel arrived in England, towards the end of the year 1710. This illustrious musician was then in the twenty-seventh year of his age, and had already acquired a high reputation, both in Germany and Italy, as a dramatic composer. He came to England upon the invitation of several noblemen with whom he had become acquainted at the court of Hanover, where he then resided, and on a temporary leave of absence from the elector, afterwards George the First.

The theatre in the Haymarket was at this time under the management of Aaron Hill, who, hearing of the arrival of so great a musician, immediately applied to him to compose an opera. Handel having consented, Hill sketched out the plan of a drama, taking the subject from the famous episode of Rinaldo and Armida in Tasso's Jerusalem Delivered; and the piece was written by Rossi, a poet of considerable merit, who afterwards produced several other dramas for the opera stage. In an

advertisement prefixed to the *libretto*, the poet says
that the composer proceeded so rapidly as hardly
to allow him time to write; and that the music of
the opera was produced in a fortnight.

Rinaldo appeared for the first time on the 24th
of February, 1711. The romantic interest of the
subject, the charms of the music, and the splendour
of the spectacle, made it an object of general
attraction; and it was performed to crowded
audiences, without interruption, to the end of the
season. This extraordinary success appears to have
induced Addison to write down, if possible, the
Italian opera, on which, since the fate of his own
Rosamond, he looked with an evil eye. Accordingly the *Spectator*, then newly established, contains a series of attacks, in rapid succession, on
the Italian stage in general, and on the favourite
opera in particular, in which this delightful writer
employs alternately playful raillery, cutting sar-
casm, and grave remonstrance. Notwithstanding
the influence which the *Spectator* exercised over
the taste and manners of the age, its attacks on
the Italian opera seem to have had little effect in
turning the public from an entertainment which,
in spite of the absurdities (partly with justice) laid
to its charge, they found delightful. People
laughed with the *Spectator*, but still flocked to see
Rinaldo.

What Addison has said on this subject, however,
is worthy of attention, even at the distance of more
than a century. He wrote under the influence of

spleen and jealousy ; but the shafts of his wit are
frequently pointed by its justice; and he had too
much perspicacity of judgment to be entirely in
the wrong, even where he was, in some measure,
blinded by prejudice.

On the 6th of March, ten days after the first
performance of *Rinaldo*, the fifth number of the
Spectator contained an article on the opera. The
absurdities introduced into the *spectacle* are ridiculed in the first place. "An opera," says Addison,
" may be allowed to be extravagantly lavish in its
decorations, as its only design is to gratify the
senses, and keep up an indolent attention in the
audience. Common sense, however, requires that
there should be nothing in the scenes and machines
which may appear childish and absurd. How would
the wits of King Charles's time have laughed to
have seen Nicolini exposed to a tempest in robes
of ermine, and sailing in an open boat upon a sea
of pasteboard ! What a field of raillery would they
have been let into, had they been entertained with
painted dragons spitting wildfire, enchanted chariots
drawn by Flanders mares, and real cascades in
artificial landscapes ! A little skill in criticism
would inform us, that shadows and realities ought
not to be mixed together in the same piece ; and
that the scenes which are designed as the representations of nature should be filled with resem-
blances, and not with the things themselves. If
one would represent a wide champaign country
filled with herds and flocks, it would be ridiculous

to draw the country only upon the scenes, and to crowd several parts of the stage with sheep and oxen. This is joining together inconsistencies, and making the decoration partly real and partly imaginary. I would recommend what I have said here, to the directors as well as to the admirers of our modern opera." This passage might be recommended, too, to the directors of *our* modern opera; for it contains the true principle of stage-decoration, which is still too often lost sight of. The writer goes on to give an amusing instance of the absurdity he reprehends. " As I was walking in the streets about a fortnight ago, I saw an ordinary fellow carrying a cage full of little birds upon his shoulders; and as I was wondering with myself what use he would put them to, he was met very luckily by an acquaintance who had the same curiosity. Upon his asking him what he had upon his shoulders, he told him that he had been buying sparrows for the opera. 'Sparrows for the opera!' says his friend, licking his lips,—'what, are they to be roasted?' 'No, no,' says the other, 'they are to enter towards the end of the first act, and to fly about the stage.' This strange dialogue awakened my curiosity so far, that I immediately bought the opera, by which means I perceived that the sparrows were to act the part of singing birds in a delightful grove: though, upon a nearer inquiry, I found the sparrows put the same trick upon the audience that Sir Martin Mar-all practised upon his mistress: for, though they flew in sight, the music proceeded from a consort of flageolets and bird-calls, which were planted behind the scenes." This ridiculous way of imitating nature was actually attempted in *Rinaldo*, in the scene in which the heroine, Almirena, wandering amid the enchanted groves of Armida, calls upon the feathered song-sters, and the breezes which murmur around, to tell her of her absent lover—

> " Augelletti che cantate,
> Zeffiretti che spirate,
> Aure dolce intorno a me,
> Il mio ben dite dov' è."

This charming song is introduced, in the ori-ginal score, by a long symphony of twenty bars for octave flutes, in imitation of birds, which is not inserted in the printed music, but its place is merely indicated by a mark of twenty bars' rest. During the performance of this symphony, the sparrows were let loose, and flew about the stage — real birds among painted groves.

But Addison is not so just or so successful when he proceeds to attack the dramatist and the com-poser. "To give you a taste," he says, "of the poet after the conjuror, I shall give you a taste of the Italian from the first lines of his preface. *Eccoti, benigno lettore, un parto di poche sere; che se ben nato di notte, non è però aborto di tenebre, mà si farà conoscere figlio d'Apollo con qualche raggio di Parnasso.* Behold, gentle reader, the birth of a few evenings, which, though it be the offspring of the night, is not the abortion of darkness, but will make *itself known to be the son of Apollo, with a certain ray of Parnassus.* He afterwards proceeds to call Mynheer Handel the Orpheus of our age, and to acquaint us, in the same sublimity of style, that he composed this opera in a fortnight. Such are the wits to whose tastes we so ambitiously conform ourselves. The truth of it is, the finest writers among the modern Italians express themselves in such a florid form of words, and such tedious circumlocutions as are used by none but pedants in our own country; and at the same time fill their writings with such poor imaginations and conceits as our youths are ashamed of before they have been two years at the university. Some may be apt to think that it is the difference of genius which produces this difference in the works of the two nations: but to show there is nothing in this, if we look into the writings of the old Italians, such as Cicero and Virgil, we shall find that the English writers, in their way of thinking and expressing themselves, resemble those authors much more than the modern Italians pretend to do. And as for the poet himself, from whom the dreams of this opera are taken, I must entirely agree with Monsieur Boileau, that one verse of Virgil is worth all the *clinquant*, or tinsel, of Tasso."

Sheer ignorance dictated the above sneer against Handel, whose character, as a musician, Addison was wholly unable to appreciate. His remarks on the Italian writers betray an ignorance which is rather more surprising. The Italian prose, especially of the older writers, is more verbose and figurative than ours; and such passages as that ridiculed by Addison are to be found in their best authors. Though now considerably changed, it was then the national manner, and no more to be ridiculed, in any particular writer, than the peculiar genius and idiom of the language. It is a mere sophism to bring Cicero and Virgil into the argument in the character of *old* Italians, there being little or nothing in common between the ancient Romans and the modern Italians, besides the circumstance of the one occupying the same portion of the globe which the other occupied two thousand years before. When Addison talked of the writings of the Italians being filled with poor imaginations and conceits, he must have shut his eyes to the thousand forms of sublimity, beauty, grace, and elegance, presented by the host of Italian poets whose writings *ought*, at least, to have been well known to him. But what can we think of his character as a critic in Italian literature, when we find him taking his opinion of Tasso from the flippant antithesis of Boileau?

In a subsequent paper* Addison professes to deliver down to posterity a faithful account of the Italian opera, and of the gradual progress which it has made upon the English stage; " for there is no question (he says) but our great-grandchildren will be very curious to know the reason why their forefathers used to sit together like an audience of

* Spectator, No. 18.

foreigners in their own country, and to hear whole plays acted before them in a tongue which they did not understand." He proceeds thus to account for this singular phenomenon :

"*Arsinoe* was the first opera that gave us a taste of Italian music. The great success this opera met with produced some attempts of forming pieces upon Italian plans, which should give a more natural and reasonable entertainment than what can be met with in the elaborate trifles of that nation. This alarmed the poetasters and fiddlers of the town, who were used to deal in a more ordinary kind of ware ; and therefore laid down an established rule, which is received as such to this day, *That nothing is capable of being well set to music, that is not nonsense.*

"This maxim was no sooner received but we immediately fell to translating the Italian operas ; and as there was no great danger of hurting the sense of those extraordinary pieces, our authors would often make words of their own which were entirely foreign to the meaning of the passages they pretended to translate ; their chief care being to make the numbers of the English verse answer to those of the Italian, that both of them might go to the same tune. Thus the famous song in *Camilla*,

' Barbara, si, t'intendo,' &c.

"Barbarous woman, yes, I know your meaning,' which expresses the resentments of an angry lover, was translated into that English lamentation,

' Frail are a lover's hopes,' &c.

And it was pleasant enough to see the most refined persons of the British nation dying away and languishing to notes that were filled with a spirit of rage and indignation. It happened also very frequently, where the sense was rightly translated, the necessary transposition of words, which were drawn out of the phrase of one tongue into that of another, made the music appear very absurd in one tongue that was very natural in the other. I remember an Italian verse that ran thus, word for word,

'And turn'd my rage into pity,'

which the English for rhyme's sake translated.

'And into pity turn'd my rage.'

By this means the soft notes that were adapted to *pity* in the Italian, fell upon the word *rage* in the English; and the angry sounds that were turned to *rage* in the original were made to express *pity* in the translation. It oftentimes happened, likewise, that the finest notes in the air fell upon the most insignificant words in the sentence. I have known the word *And* pursued through the whole gamut, have been entertained with many a melodious *The*, and have heard the most beautiful graces, quavers, and divisions bestowed upon *Then, For,* and *From;* to the eternal honour of our English particles.

" The next step to our refinement was the introduction of Italian writers into our opera; who sung their parts in their own language, at the same time that our countrymen performed theirs in our native tongue. The king or hero of the play generally spoke in Italian, and his slaves answered him in English; the lover frequently made his court, and gained the heart of his princess, in a language which she did not understand. One would have thought it very difficult to have carried on dialogues after this manner without an interpreter between the persons that conversed together; but this was the state of the English stage for about three years.

"At length the audience got tired of understanding half the opera; and, therefore, to ease themselves entirely of the fatigue of thinking, have so ordered it at present, that the whole opera is performed in an unknown tongue. We no longer understand the language of our own stage; insomuch that I have often been afraid, when I have seen our Italian performers chattering in the vehemence of action, that they have been calling us names and abusing us among themselves: but I hope, since we do put such entire confidence in them, they will not talk against us before our faces, though they may do it with the same safety as if it were behind our backs. In the meantime I cannot forbear thinking how naturally an historian who writes two or three hundred years hence, and does not know the taste of his wise forefathers, will make the following reflection: *In the beginning of the eighteenth century the Italian tongue was so well understood in England, that operas were acted on the public stage in that language.*

" One scarce knows how to be serious in the confutation of an absurdity that shows itself at the first sight. It does not want any great measure of sense to see the ridicule of this monstrous practice; but what makes it the more astonishing, it is not the taste of the rabble, but of persons of the greatest politeness, which has established it.

" If the Italians have a genius for music above the English, the English have a genius for other performances of much higher nature, and capable of giving the mind a much nobler entertainment. Would one think it was possible (at a time when an author lived that was able to write the *Phedra and Hippolitus*) for a people to be so stupidly fond of the Italian opera as scarce to give a third day's hearing to that admirable tragedy? Music is certainly a very agreeable entertainment: but if it would take entire possession of our ears, if it would make us incapable of hearing sense, if it would exclude arts that have a much greater tendency to the refinement of human nature, I must confess I would allow it no better quarter than Plato has done, who banishes it out of his commonwealth.

" At present our notions of music are so very uncertain, that we do not know what it is we like; only, in general, we are transported with anything that is not English: so it be of foreign growth, let it be Italian, French, or High Dutch, it is the same thing. In short, our English music is quite rooted out, and nothing yet planted in its stead."

There is good sense and just criticism in all this,

though certainly mingled with error. Much allowance must be made for the state of things when Addison wrote. It was perfectly true that, at that time, " our English music was quite rooted out," and this truth could not be palatable to an Englishman. It was natural to feel some dislike for the music which had usurped the place of that of our own country. Purcell, though not twenty years dead, was as clean forgotten as if he had never been ; and the bright dawn of a national opera, by his untimely death, had fallen back to dark midnight. No English composer of the smallest genius had appeared ; and the growing love for the sweet strains of the south prevented the want of native talent from being felt. At that time Addison entertained the patriotic wish of creating an English opera; and he rightly judged that this object was to be accomplished by producing English pieces upon the model of the Italian stage. He accordingly wrote his *Rosamond.* Had Purcell yet lived, the fame of the fellow-labourer of Dryden would at once have pointed him out to Addison as his partner in the work; and Addison, in all probability, would have stood in our musical annals as the founder of the regular English opera. Addison, however, marred his own design by his choice of Clayton; an error for which he has undergone the indignant censure of almost every musical writer. But, after all, he was more unfortunate than blamable. In choosing Clayton, his fault was more venial than that of Dryden in choosing Grabut; for

Dryden chose a worthless Frenchman in preference to his gifted countrymen; while Addison chose the only Englishman who appears at that time to have had any pretensions to musical reputation. It is true that Clayton was a mere pretender, but he was a specious and plausible one, and his pretensions had passed current with the public. He had produced an opera which had been most favourably received; and it was not wonderful that Addison (who, like many other lyric poets, laid no claim to musical connoisseurship) should have fallen into the general error in estimating his character. It is hardly fair, therefore, to visit Addison with any severe blame for the failure of his praiseworthy, and (with this single exception) judicious and able endeavour to give a local habitation and a name to the English musical drama.

Many of Addison's censures, moreover, were perfectly just, and his sarcasms well founded. It has been shown in a previous chapter that the Italian stage was in a low state at the beginning of the eighteenth century: and the dramas which we then imported from Italy were, of course, in the prevailing fashion; made up of frivolous incidents, feeble poetry, and showy, but ridiculous scenic exhibitions. The reign of taste and reason, under Apostolo Zeno and Metastasio, had not yet begun.

But, on the other hand, his attacks were too sweeping and indiscriminate. He goes too far when he maintains that an opera in a language different from that of the country in which it is represented, is an absurdity. The best proof of the contrary is the unvarying delight which the Italian opera has given to the inhabitants of every country into which it has been introduced. An absurdity in manners, dress, or amusement, may be in vogue for a time, and may acquire a currency through the influence of fashion ; but whatever preserves its ascendancy from age to age, is sure to be founded on some permanent principle of taste or reason. The opera is of a twofold nature : it is a dramatic representation and a musical entertainment. The music is not merely the language in which the personages of the drama express their sentiments and feelings, but is calculated to produce a separate and very intense pleasure, that which is derived from "the concord of sweet sounds." A song may charm the ear, and even affect the heart, though we do not understand its words or know its subject. Music, in itself, is "most eloquent;" it speaks more powerfully than words. The delicious tones of Grisi might "lap us in Elysium;" her soft complaining accents might dissolve us in tenderness ; we might be roused and excited by the spirit-stirring energy of Pasta, were we ignorant of the very names of the characters represented by these accomplished performers. But, among the thousands who listen to them, is there a single individual who is so ignorant? Surely not. Did any one who witnessed Pasta's beautiful and terrible representation of Medea not know enough of the history of the enchantress—her base desertion and

terrible revenge—to enter deeply into the spirit of
the scene ? When, with desperate fondness, she
hung over her little children, exclaiming, in tones
of the bitterist anguish,

> " Miseri pargoletti,
> Ah, che innocenti siete ! "

did any of the audience, however ignorant of the
language, feel at a loss, from not understanding the
words, to know what was passing before them?

In listening to an air, very little attention is paid
to the words. Indeed, unless they are already
known, they can rarely be followed, even when in
the vernacular tongue. The protracted tones, the
embellishments, the repetitions, make it very frequently impossible for the most skilful singer to
make them intelligible. It is only in the case of
ballads, or narrative songs of many stanzas, that we
ever think of making an effort to follow the words.
But such songs do not occur in the Italian opera.
The words of an air are of small importance to the
comprehension of the business of the piece. They
merely express a sentiment, a reflection, a feeling :
it is quite enough if their general import is known;
and this may most frequently be gathered from the
situation, aided by the character and expression
of the music. " The German composers," says
Madame de Staël, " follow too closely the sense of
the words. This, it is true, is a great merit in the
opinion of those who love the words better than the
music; and, indeed, it cannot be denied, that a
disagreement between the sense of the one and the

expression of the other would be offensive: but the Italians, who are truly the musicians of nature, make the air and the words conform to each other only in a general way. As in popular ballads there is not much music, the little that there is may be subjected to the words; but in the great effects of melody we should endeavour to reach the soul by an immediate sensation." Such a *contresens* as that mentioned by Addison, where, in consequence of an inversion of the words in the translation of an Italian verse, "the soft notes that were adapted to *pity* in the Italian, fell upon the word *rage* in the English, and the angry sounds that were turned to *rage* in the original, were made to express *pity* in the translation," has often happened in the verbal method of musical composition ascribed by Madame de Staël to the Germans, but it could not arise in the music of a composer who, attending only to the general spirit of the words, would never dream of putting soft notes into one part of his air and angry sounds into another, because he found the word *pity* in the beginning of a sentence, and *rage* in the end of it.

It is not merely because the words of an Italian opera are foreign, but because they are *sung*, that we are obliged (at least till we become acquainted with the piece) to follow them by the help of a *libretto*. The Italians themselves use the *libretto* as well as we do.

If there is anything in the objection that the audience cannot follow the words of an opera, it is not confined to the Italian opera. Wherever words are sung, they must also be read, in the first instance at least; and this we every day find to be the case on the English as well as the Italian stage. To enjoy a really good opera, it must be heard over and over again; and those who do so soon understand its plot, incidents, situations, sentiments, and passions, whether it be English or Italian. Those who form the habitual audience of the Italian opera-house are as well acquainted with the favourite Italian pieces as the frequenters of the English theatres with the popular productions of our own stage.

Addison's complaint of the preference of foreign music, and the neglect of native talent, has continued to be made down to the present day, and repeated till it has become a sort of cant. It was greatly exaggerated by Addison; and where it existed, there was considerable reason for it. We encouraged foreign composers, because we had none of our own worthy of the name. The English composer, patronised by Addison, and on whose behalf he made this complaint, met with a reception infinitely beyond his deserts. We preferred the Italian singers, because we could not be deaf to their superiority: and yet (as has been seen in the preceding pages) our native singers of that day, when they deserved applause and encouragement, received it abundantly. Of the grounds of the complaint in later times we shall hereafter have occasion to speak.

Having traced the progress of the Italian opera, not only in its native country, but in France, Germany, and England, down to the era of the appearance of Metastasio, we shall take a review of the life and writings of that great poet, and then follow the further progress of the musical drama in Italy. No account of the Italian opera in other countries, at any period, can be made intelligible, unless its situation at its source is understood.

CHAPTER XIII.

LIFE OF METASTASIO.

METASTASIO was born at Rome, on the 6th of January, 1698. His real name was Pietro Trapasso. His father, Felice Trapasso, was of a respectable, decayed family of Assisi. Such was the poverty of its representative, that he was compelled, in his youth, to enlist as a soldier, and was in that situation when he married, and became the father of so illustrious a son. Having served the usual time, and by great economy saved a little money, he entered into business at Rome, as a dealer in oil, flour, pastry, and other culinary articles, the profits of which enabled him to place his son at a grammar school.

The young Pietro discovered his passion for poetry at a very early age, and exhibited a power of *improvising* on any given subject, before he was ten years old. He was in the custom of exercising this faculty, after school hours, in his father's shop: and crowds of persons used to assemble round the door to hear him sing his extempore verses. On one of these occasions, the celebrated civilian Gravina chanced to pass by.

Struck with the sweetness of the boy's voice, he stopped to listen, and soon discovered that the verses he was singing were his own. Surprised and delighted with the precocity of the little poet's genius, the lawyer entered into conversation with him, and was equally charmed with his modesty and intelligence. Gravina became warmly interested in his behalf; and immediately conceived the idea of adopting him as his son, in order that such talents might receive due cultivation. He made his proposal to the boy's parents; and so advantageous an offer was joyfully and thankfully accepted. Next morning Pietro was taken by his father and mother to Gravina's house, and received into his family.

Gravina was not only a profound and eminent lawyer, but a man of letters, and an enthusiastic votary of poetry and the arts. Being a great lover of Grecian literature, he took the somewhat affected step of translating the name of his *protégé* from Italian to Greek; calling him *Metastasio* instead of *Trapasso*. His object was to turn the young man's natural eloquence to the best account, by making him an orator instead of a poet; and, for this purpose, he determined that he should embrace the honourable and lucrative profession of the law. The young poet applied himself to the studies pointed out to him by his adopted father; but his ruling passion could not be restrained: and Gravina wisely resolved to allow him to read the best and most classical poetical authors. Into these congenial studies Metastasio entered with ardour; and, their first-fruits was a tragedy *(Giustino)* written at the age of fourteen. With his production, his maturer judgment, as might be expected, was far from being satisfied. In a letter to the Italian poet Calsabigi, he thus speaks of it: " I should have wished that none of my early productions, which savour so much of adolescence, had appeared in the Paris edition, particularly the tragedy of *Giustino*, written at fourteen years of age; when the authority of my illustrious master did not suffer me to move a step from the most devout imitation of the Greeks; and when my inexperience and want of discernment were unable to distinguish gold from lead, even in those mines themselves of which he then began to show me the treasures." There are many beauties, however, in this tragedy; and its story is affecting. Though Metastasio cannot be supposed to have read Shakspeare, there is a singular coincidence between one of the incidents and that in *Romeo and Juliet*, where Juliet revives after Romeo, supposing her dead, has swallowed poison. In this play, Sophia, supposing Giustino to have perished, poisons herself, and is then informed that he still lives. There are some pieces of lyric poetry at the end of each act. It does not appear whether it was ever performed. It is quite different from the opera of the same name performed in England, with Handel's music, in 1737.

From this time Gravina appears to have not only permitted, but encouraged, his pupil's poetical pursuits. When he was eighteen, Gravina took him to Naples, for the purpose of affording him an opportunity of exercising his talent for improvisation, along with some of the greatest masters of that truly Italian art. In one of his letters, speaking modestly of his youthful talent as an *improvisatore*, Metastasio says: " This phenomenon so dazzled my great master Gravina, that he was partial to it, and cherished me as a soil worthy of his cultivation. So late as the year 1716, he exhibited me to speak verses, God knows how, upon all kinds of subjects; at which time I had for competitors the illustrious Rolli, Vagnini, and the Cavaliere Perfetti; men who were then arrived at full maturity, and veterans in Pindaric battles." He excited universal admiration among the susceptible and enthusiastic Neapolitans. The method, clearness, and richness of classical allusion, with which he treated his subject, the beauty of his verses, the sweetness of his voice, and his graceful manner in reciting them, his handsome and expressive features, and the mingled dignity and modesty of his deportment, made him the idol of every one who heard and saw him.

He still continued to pursue the study of the law, and also entered into the church, and took the minor orders of priesthood. Hence he always received the title of the Abate Metastasio. This step he took in compliance with the advice of

Gravina, the law and the church being the most promising roads to preferment at Rome.

In 1718, Metastasio lost his kind friend and patron, who died at the age of fifty-four; Meta-stasio being then twenty. By a will made the previous year, Gravina, who was unmarried and childless, made his adopted son heir to his property, amounting to fifteen thousand crowns, or between 3000l. and 4000l. sterling. Metastasio deeply mourned the death of his benefactor, and paid a beautiful tribute to his memory in the elegy entitled *La Strada della Gloria*, read by him at an assembly of the members of the Arcadian Academy, a literary institution of which Gravina was the founder.

Metastasio thus became his own master, and the possessor of a considerable fortune, at too early an age to make a prudent use of his independence. His poetry found plenty of admirers, and his table was in no want of guests. He abandoned the dry study of the law, and, intoxicated by perpetual applause, thought of nothing but furnishing matter for it. Surrounded by flatterers and parasites, whom, in his youthful inexperience, he imagined to be his frinds, he thought not of the morrow, till he was rudely awakened from his dream of enjoyment by the discovery that Gravina's legacy was dissipated, and that his dear friends were falling from him.

Finding himself, in the space of two years, thus reduced to the verge of poverty, and having his eyes opened to the folly of the life he had been leading, Metastasio removed to Naples, with the view of resuming the study of the law. He placed himself under the guidance of an advocate named Pagliotti, one of the most eminent lawyers in Naples, and so rigidly devoted to his profession, that he disliked and despised every kind of ornamental literature. Poetry he held in especial abhorrence, as the most deadly sin of which a lawyer could be guilty. It required no small exertion of fortitude on the part of the youthful poet to place himself under the control of such a man, aware, as he was, of his rigid notions and austere disposition. Metastasio's poetical fame was very far from increasing the complacency or indulgence of the stern lawyer. But Metastasio submitted patiently to the severity of his discipline, and for some time applied himself so steadily to his tasks, that Pagliotti began to have hopes of making him a good lawyer, and treated him as kindly as the bitterness of his temper would allow.

But this did not last. Metastasio was a general favourite at Naples, and his society was sought by persons of eminence and distinction. In 1721, he was tempted to deviate from the strict line of duty he had laid down for himself, by the solicitations of the Countess Althan, who prevailed on him to write an epithalamium for the nuptials of a member of her family. This gave rise to *Endymion*, the first of his operas, which was afterwards published, with a dedication to this lady, dated 30th May.

The ice was now broken, and Metastasio was a poet for life. His backsliding, however, was for some time concealed from his legal Mentor. Having been requested, by no less a personage than the Viceroy of Naples, to write a musical drama, to be performed on the birthday of the Empress Elizabeth, the consort of the Emperor Charles VI., Metastasio complied, with much hesitation, and on condition that his delinquency should be kept a profound secret. In perpetual fear of the vigilant lawyer, he sacrificed his hours of sleep to what was to him a labour of love; and speedily produced *Gli Orti Esperidi,* one of the most beautiful of his early works. The viceroy, on receiving the manuscript, presented the poet with two hundred ducats. The music was composed by the celebrated Porpora; and so well was the secret kept, that the piece was performed without even the composer or the singers knowing who was the author. Its success, however, seems to have determined Metastasio to put an end to all further concealment of his poetical pursuits: for it was immediately published at Naples, and with a dedication to the Vice-Queen, dated 28th August, 1724, and subscribed with his name. In the following year he produced his *Angelica,* which was also set by Porpora, and first performed on the birthday of the Empress.

These dramas were received at Naples with unbounded delight and applause. The principal character in *Gli Orti Esperidi* was performed by Marianna Bulgarini (called La Romanina from her birthplace), the greatest singer and actress of her time. Inspired with admiration of the beauty of the piece, and gratitude for the distinguished reception it had procured for herself, she ardently desired to be acquainted with the author, and having found that one of her intimate friends knew him, she prevailed on him to try and bring the poet to her house. Metastasio resisted a temptation which, he felt, would draw him farther than ever from the study of the law; but he was at last persuaded by the importunities of his friend to pay her a visit. La Bulgarini was one of the most beautiful and highly gifted women of her time, possessing a strong and cultivated mind along with all the charms and accomplishments of her sex. A warm and intimate friendship sprang up between them, which endured for a long course of years, and was not broken but by the hand of death.

All these doings were any thing but pleasing to the old advocate. The young poet and he became every day more disagreeable to each other; and at last Metastasio determined to leave him, and abandon the study of a profession for which Nature never intended him. He was stimulated to devote himself to poetry, by the encouragement and counsels of his female friend, by whom and her husband he was pressingly invited to live with them; an invitation which, after much hesitation, he accepted.

His biographer, Saverio Mattei, relates an anecdote of his life at this period, which, while it shows the power of his extemporaneous poetry, gives a strange view of the state of jurisprudence in the kingdom of Naples. During his residence at Naples, after the death of Gravina, Metastasio was involved in a lawsuit for part of the possessions in that kingdom bequeathed him by the civilian. Having applied to the Princess Belmonte (who herself told the story to his biographer) for her interest with the judges, she told him that if he would first make her acquainted with the merits of the case, and convince her that justice was on his side, by pleading his cause in verse *all' improvista*, she would use her influence in his behalf. Accordingly he pleaded his cause in a song, in so pathetic a manner, that he drew tears from the princess. Next day she applied to the judges, to whom she stated the merits of the cause, expatiating at the same time on the wonderful talents of her client, and entreating them to listen to a pleading such as he had made to her. The judges accordingly assembled in the princess's palace, and Metastasio, without repeating a word of what he had sung before, defended his cause with such fire, elegance, and enthusiasm, that there was not a dry eye in the room. Soon afterwards the question was regularly decided in his favour; and his adversary lost his cause, not because he was in the wrong, but because he was not a poet and a musician, an eloquent declaimer, and a beautiful singer. All this is supremely ridiculous, and indeed much worse; but there seems to be no doubt of the truth of the story.

Metastasio's next opera, *La Didone Abbandonata*, was produced at Naples during the carnival of 1724. The part of Eneas was performed by the celebrated Nicolini, and Dido by Bulgarini; this subject having been chosen by the poet in order to afford her an opportunity of displaying all her powers. Mattei says that Bulgarini was a great actress, and that Metastasio himself was obliged to her for suggesting to him the finest situations in this opera; such as the fourteenth and fifteenth scenes of the second act, which were entirely of her invention. *Didone* was received with acclamations by the Neapolitans. Many editions of it were published, and it was soon performed in the other principal theatres of Italy. The original music was composed by Sarro; but it employed the talents of many of the greatest dramatic composers, almost down to the end of the last century.

Few particulars are preserved of the life of Signora Bulgarini. In 1709 she was at Venice, standing in the highest rank of her profession; and it does not appear that she ever sang on the stage after she quitted Venice in 1726. She could not, therefore, have been very young in 1722, when her intimacy with Metastasio began.

During the carnival of 1726, *Didone* was performed at Rome, with music by Leonardo Vinci. The impression it produced is thus described by the celebrated ex-jesuit Cordara, in his *éloge* on Metastasio. " Every scene produced incessant applause. But who can describe the rapture of the

audience, when the Queen of Carthage, rising dis-
dainfully from her throne, represses the insolent
pretensions of the King of Mauritania, with the
dignity of an independent princess, by the spirited
air, ' Son Regina?' The acclamations seemed to
shake the theatre to its foundation. I was not
there myself, as my habit did not allow me to be
present at such spectacles; but I almost heard the
sounds in my cell, so filled was all Rome with the
fame of this production."

In 1727, Metastasio, with Signora Bulgarini and
her husband, removed to Rome: he having stipulated that, in return for the hospitality he had
received under her roof at Naples, she and her
family should become his guests at Rome. A
house was provided sufficient for the accommoda-
tion of the two families, and they continued to
dwell under one roof till the poet's departure for
Germany.

The first drama produced by Metastasio for
the Roman theatre, was *Catone in Utica*, which was
performed in 1728, with the music of Vinci, and,
in the following year, at Venice, with the music of
Leonardo Leo. His next operas were *Ezio* and
Semiramide Riconosciuta, both composed by Porpora. Both these operas were most favourably
received; but hitherto his productions seem to
have gained him more applause than profit. His
necessities still compelled him to accept pecuniary
assistance from Signora Bulgarini. He was humbled
and mortified; and his circumstances so preyed

on his mind, that he fell into a state of deep despondency.

While in this situation he unexpectedly received a letter from Prince Pio of Savoy, written from Vienna, and containing, in consequence of the fame he had acquired as a dramatic poet, a proposal that he should enter into the service of the emperor as colleague of Apostolo Zeno, who, having arrived at the age of sixty, desired assistance in the performance of his duties, and had recommended Metastasio as being pre-eminently qualified for the situation. It cost him a painful effort to make up his mind to leave his country, family, and friends; but, moved by the generous and disinterested counsels of Signora Bulgarini, and aware of the hazard of losing the tide,

" Which, taken at the full, leads on to fortune,"

he resolved to accept the offer.

A bitter feeling of disappointment, too, seems to have contributed to this act of voluntary expatriation. He had received plenty of vain and empty applause, and had enjoyed the smiles and favour of the great; but all his hopes of advancement, founded on their friendship and promises, had proved utterly delusive. After some correspondence, therefore, with the Prince of Savoy, an engagement was concluded, at a salary of three thousand florins (about 300l. sterling) per annum; and Metastasio quitted his native country for ever.

On leaving Rome, Metastasio left the management of all his affairs to the care of his zealous
friend, Signora Bulgarini; and an uninterrupted
and affectionate correspondence was kept up between them as long as she lived. In the ample
collection of his letters, those addressed to La
Romanina are among the most pleasing and interesting.

He arrived at Vienna in July 1730, and was received by the emperor and the court with the utmost
distinction. He appears at first to have produced
some little *pièces de circonstance*; but his first regular opera for the imperial theatre was *Adriano
in Siria*, which was performed, for the first time,
on the 4th of November 1731, with the music of
Caldara. His next opera, *Demetrio*, was performed
a few days afterwards. In a letter to La Romanina, dated November 10, 1731, he gives her the
following account of its reception:—" I did not
think I should have such good tidings to send you
to-day ; indeed I was quite prepared for the contrary. Last Sunday my opera of *Demetrio* was
performed for the first time, with such applause
that the oldest people in the country assure me
they do not remember approbation so universal.
The audience wept at the parting scene; and my
most august patron was not insensible to it. Notwithstanding the great respect for the sovereign,
his presence did not restrain the applause during
many of the recitatives. Those who previously
were my enemies are now become my advocates.

I am unable to express to you my surprise at this
success, as the opera is a gentle and delicate piece,
without any of those bold strokes which produce
great effects; nor did I believe it adapted to the
national taste. But I was mistaken. Everything
showed that it was well understood by the audience,
and they repeat parts of it in conversation, as if it
were written in German. My master began to
show his satisfaction from the end of the first act,
and afterwards expressed it openly to all around
him. The music is of the most modern kind that
Caldara has composed; but all the discontented
world is not to be satisfied." After speaking of the
scenery and the performers, he concludes: " And
here is my whole history, which I would not have
written to any one but you, as others would pronounce me to be a vain coxcomb." In the beginning of the following year this opera was brought
out at Rome under the direction of Signora Bulgarini, who acted as the poet's representative during
the rehearsals. In one of his letters to her, he
gives her some directions as to the representation,
and adds: " These were the arrangements here,
and I have seen the inhabitants of these northern
regions weep. Do you produce the same effects."

From the following passage in a letter to La
Romanina, dated 23rd February 1732, it would
seem that he had not entirely lost sight of his ec-
clesiastical views. " There is an abbey vacant in
Sicily, called *Santo Lucia*, by the death of a certain
Abate Barbara; but my misfortune is, that I do

not know in what diocese it is situated, or whether it is requisite that the incumbent should be a regular ecclesiastic." The matter, however, is not further alluded to in his correspondence.

On the 28th of July, 1733, he writes to La Romanina, telling her that he had received from the emperor the office of treasurer to the province of Cosenza in the kingdom of Naples; " a post for life," he says, " of honour and authority; and if I were to perform the duties of it in person, of considerable profit; but even after paying a deputy, the clear salary will amount to 1500 florins (about 150*l.* sterling) a year. You see," he adds, "that the appointment is not inconsiderable in point of pecuniary advantage ; but be assured that the honour done me by the solicitude, affection, and condescension with which the emperor has deigned to confer this benefit upon me, infinitely surpasses all considerations of lucre. It was publicly announced, at the emperor's table, to one of the members of the council, as a reward for my past and present labours; and his majesty was pleased to add that he had, unsolicited, mentioned this appointment as my just due. This public declaration of his majesty in my favour made such an impression, that yesterday, when the decree was mentioned, contrary to custom, there was not one of the counsellors who ventured to utter a syllable against it; but some of them said coldly that the order should be executed, while the rest applauded the justice and propriety of the appointment. I shall probably be put to some difficulty in paying the fees of office, which, I believe, will be considerable ; but I shall soon be reimbursed."

In February, 1734, Metastasio lost his friend Signora Bulgarini, who manifested the sincerity of her affection for him, by bequeathing to him, after the decease of her husband, all her property, to the amount of twenty-five thousand crowns.   But Metastasio instantly declined to accept this intended kindness, and made over to her husband his whole interest in the bequest.   There can be no doubt that Signora Bulgarini possessed this property independently of her husband, and that her bequest to Metastasio was perfectly legal; as all his biographers concur in speaking of his renunciation of it in terms of the highest eulogy.

What was the nature of Metastasio's connexion with this lady can only be subject of conjecture. There is certainly room for suspicion, in so close an intimacy of the young poet and a beautiful and highly accomplished woman, who, moreover, was much attached to him.   But yet there are circumstances not easily reconcilable to the supposition of anything criminal in their intercourse.   While they lived together, both at Naples and Rome, the husband, as well as the wife, was a member of the united family.   Metastasio was on the most friendly footing with him, and, in his letters, speaks of him with respect as well as affection.   For example, in a letter to Signora Bulgarini, written from Vienna in 1731, Metastasio says, " I now discover the

worth of my dear Marianna, who, in her letters and
her prudent conduct, not only pleases me at present,
but gives a different face to past times. You have
surpassed all my expectations. It is the fear of
trebling the expense of postage that prevents my
writing to Leopold [his brother] and my dear Bulgarini. Thank the latter heartily in my name,
and take that care of him which he merits. Tell
Leopold that I shall always love him, if he acts in
such a manner as to deserve your esteem." Immediately on hearing of Signora Bulgarini's death,
Metastasio wrote the following letter to her husband.

"TO SIGNOR DOMENICO BULGARINI.

"Oppressed by the afflicting news of the death
of our poor Marianna, I know not how to begin
this letter. The tidings are intolerable to me on so
many accounts, that I can devise no means to dimi-
nish the acuteness of my sufferings; and therefore
I trust you will not accuse me of want of feeling,
if I am unable to suggest to you any consolation
for your loss, as I have hitherto been utterly unable
to find any for myself.

"The last disposition of the poor deceased in
my favour augments the cause of my sorrow, and
obliges me to give a public and incontestable proof
of the disinterestedness of that friendship which I
professed to her while living, and which I shall preserve for her honoured memory to the last moment
of my life. Knowing, therefore, how much affec-

tion, kindness, and zeal for the welfare of the poor
Marianna you have always manifested, I shall best
show my gratitude to her by entirely renouncing in
your favour all claim to her property: not through
pride—God preserve me from such ingratitude!—
but because it appears to be my duty as an honest
man and a Christian.   The advantage which I shall
still derive from this inheritance, even after renouncing it, will not be inconsiderable; as the
knowing what was intended for me by the generous
testatrix will be a lasting proof of her friendship;
and the relinquishing it in your favour will be a
proof of my disinterestedness in respect to her, and
of my justice towards you.   I am at present, thank
God, in no need of such assistance, as I am recom-
pensed beyond my merit; so that I shall not suffer
by the sacrifice I make to you.   Though I entangle
you with no conditions in the renunciation which I
enclose, yet I have some requests to make, and
counsels to suggest to you.

" My first request is, that the relinquishment of
this claim may in nowise dissolve our friendship:
but that, according to the wish of the poor Marianna, our correspondence may continue as entire
as if she were still living; substituting you at all
times and in all places as her representative.

" My second request is, that you will undertake
the trouble of receiving the salaries of my three
offices at Rome, and the transacting of my Neapolitan concerns, in the same manner as was done
by our incomparable Marianna; for which purpose

I send you proper powers. I write likewise to Signor Tenerelli at Naples, who will communicate with you in the same manner as he did with Signora Marianna herself; remitting to you, from time to time, whatever sums may be due to me from that quarter, continuing to my poor family the usual assignments and provision, if you shall choose it, jointly with my brother.

"The advice which I would wish to give you is, that you would assist the poor family of Signor Francisco Lombardi by every means in your power, and try, by acts of charity, to do everything for them, which in a similar situation you would expect them to do to you. I have specified in my renunciation some particulars in which you should assist them; but besides my unwillingness to involve you in trouble and difficulty, I am so' certain of the goodness of your heart that I have left all the merit of your benevolence towards them to the liberality of your own determination.

"In all things else, you are at liberty to act as circumstances and your own prudence shall suggest.

"At present my mind is too much disturbed for me to attempt giving you a plan for the regulation of your conduct. I shall only say, that it appears to me that you should dispose of all the effects you can spare in order to raise a capital, and that you should live in a smaller house.

"I can think of no other testimony to offer you at present of my friendship and confidence. Be equally open in your correspondence with me, and consider your interests as my own, and me as your brother. I am unable now to write a longer letter; when my mind is more tranquil, I shall communicate to you such thoughts as may occur to me.

" In the mean time, love me, and endeavour to be comforted. Be assured, if it were in my power, that I would try to give you that consolation which I am unable to receive myself."

He wrote, at the same time, the following letter to his brother, the advocate, Leopold Trapassi.

" In the present agitation of my mind, in consequence of the unexpected death of the poor generous Marianna, my utmost efforts will enable me to write but little. I can only tell you, that both my honour and conscience have obliged me to relinquish in favour of her husband Domenico that bequest which she intended for me. I owe to the world an indisputable proof that my friendship for her was not founded on avarice or self-interest. I ought not to abuse the partiality of my poor friend at the expense of her husband; and God, I trust, will permit me, for my integrity, to prosper by some means. For myself, I am in need of no more than my present income; for my family, I have sufficient at Rome for their comfortable support. Indeed, if it shall please God to continue to me my present Neapolitan resources, I shall be able to give further proofs of my affection for my relations, and for yourself in particular. Communicate these resolutions to our father, to whom I am unable to write at present. Assure him of my fixed determination to assist him always as I have hitherto done, or rather to increase that assistance, if things are prosperous at Naples. In short, I beg you will use your utmost endeavours to make him enter into my reasons, that I may not be afflicted with his disapprobation of my honest and christian conduct.

"In the mean time, I beg you will unite interests with Signor Domenico, from whom I hope you will experience that friendship which may be expected in return for the confidence and consideration with which I have treated him. I have transmitted to him proper powers for transacting my money concerns, so that things will go on as usual. But poor Marianna will never return ! and I believe that the rest of my life will be tasteless and sorrowful. Do not condemn my resolution, I entreat you, and believe me ever yours."

We must add to these letters some passages from others, written at the same period, to a friend in Rome.

" Was it necessary for such a calamity to happen, to procure for me the long-wished-for pleasure of hearing from you? At least, since the price has been so great, I beg it may be continued, to soften, by the renewal of our intercourse, the remembrance of my misfortune ; a remembrance which seems to have placed me in the world as in a populous desert. In the midst of these imaginations, I have enough of reason left to tell me

who and what I am ; but that is not sufficient to
free me from affliction. May God, in whose hands
are all events, turn this affliction to my benefit,
and teach me, by such a manifestation, what a
vain hope it is to form plans of happiness without
his assistance ! "

He afterwards says to the same correspondent,
" If I should affect the philosopher, and tell you
that I was sorry to hear that my country had been
so lavish of applause for the renunciation I have
lately made, I should be very insincere. It pleases
me much, and will confirm my opinion of the justice of the act: indeed, I regard these praises as a
striking instance of affection from so great a mother
even to the meanest of her sons."

Though these letters do not absolutely prove the
innocence of Metastasio's connexion with Signora
Bulgarini, yet they furnish the strongest presumption of it. His tranquil and self-approving conscience, the solemn tenderness with which he speaks
of the departed, the tone in which he addresses her
husband, and, above all, the pious prayer, " May
God, in whose hands are all events, turn this affliction to my benefit ! "—are utterly inconsistent with
the state of mind in which a man of ordinary moral
feeling must have found himself, at the moment
when an adulterous intercourse was suddenly terminated by the stroke of death.

From this time, Metastasio passed the remainder
of his long and tranquil life at Vienna, in the uninterrupted enjoyment of the favour of the imperial

family. After the death of the emperor Charles VI., he was treated with still greater distinction by the empress-queen, the celebrated Maria Theresa, whose conduct towards him was uniformly marked by personal respect and even affection, as well as admiration of his genius. No circumstances occurred that were sufficient to disturb the even tenor of his life, or the natural equanimity of his mind: and it appears from his correspondence that in the latter years of his life his strongest emotions were those derived from the attachment of his august patroness. He was often deeply affected by her domestic afflictions, and by the misfortunes of her eventful life as a sovereign: and her death, which took place in November, 1780, about a year and a half before his own, was a blow from which he never recovered. His time was occupied in the composition of his numerous dramatic pieces, all of which were written for and originally produced at the court theatre of Vienna; and his " hours of ease " were spent in the society of a small number of friends, several of whom were of high rank and distinction. Among them was the accomplished Countess Althan, the sister of his early patroness the Princess di Belmonte.

Dr. Burney, who visited Metastasio at Vienna in 1772, gives some interesting particulars respecting him.* He had been described as difficult of access, and averse from society: but this Dr. Burney found to be by no means the case. On

* State of Music in Germany.

being introduced to the veteran poet by Lord
Stormont, the British ambassador, he was very
kindly received, and visited him frequently during
his stay in Vienna.

"The great poet," says Burney, "is lodged, as
many other great poets have been before him, in a
very exalted situation, up no less than four pair of
stairs. Whether modern bards prefer the sublimity
of this abode, on account of its being somewhat on
a level with Mount Parnassus, nearer their sire
Apollo, or in the neighbourhood of gods in general,
I shall not determine; but a more plain and humble reason can be assigned for Metastasio's habitation being 'twice two stories high,' if we consider the peculiar prerogative which the emperor
enjoys at Vienna, of appropriating to the use of the
officers of the court and the army the first floor of
every house and palace in the city, six or eight
privileged places only excepted. On this account,
princes, ambassadors, and nobles usually inhabit
the second stories; and the third, fourth, and even
fifth floors, the houses being very large and high,
are well fitted up for the reception of opulent and
noble families; and our poet, though he occupies
that part of a house which, in England, is thought
fit only for domestics to sleep in, has, nevertheless,
an exceeding good and elegant apartment, in which
an imperial laureate may, with all due dignity,
hold dalliance with the Muses. He received us
with the utmost cheerfulness and good breeding;
and I was no less astonished than pleased at find-

ing him look so well. He does not seem more than fifty years of age, though he is at least seventy-two; and, for that time of life, he is the handsomest man I ever beheld. There are painted on his countenance all the genius, goodness, benevolence, propriety, and rectitude, which constantly characterise his writings. I could not keep my eyes off his face, it was so pleasing and worthy of contemplation. His conversation was of a piece with his appearance — polite, easy, and lively. We prevailed on him to be much more communicative about music than we expected; for in general he avoids entering deeply into any particular subject."

Among other observations made by him in the course of conversation, "he did not think that there was now one singer left who could sustain the voice in the manner the old singers were used to do. I endeavoured to account for this, and he agreed with me that *theatrical music was become too instrumental,* and that the cantatas of the beginning of this century, which were sung with no other accompaniment than a harpsichord or violoncello, required better singing than the present songs, in which the noisy accompaniments can hide defects as well as beauties, and give relief to a singer." This is very much the way in which we contrast the music of our own time with that of " sixty years since:" will our successors, sixty years hence, draw a similar contrast between their music and that of our day !

Another of his opinions, according to Burney, was, "that the music of the last age was in general too full of fugues, of parts and contrivances, to be felt or understood, except by artists. All the different movements of the several parts, their inversions and divisions, he said, were unnatural, and, by covering and deforming the melody, only occasioned confusion." If this opinion is limited to the music of the theatre, it is sound and important. If taken in the general sense in which it is expressed, and especially if it is applied to the music of the church, it is entirely erroneous, and its adoption has caused the decay of ecclesiastical music in Italy.

"Metastasio," continues Burney, "like most other persons in years, has an aversion to talking about his own age, about the infirmities of his friends, or the calamities or death even of persons that are indifferent to him. He is extremely candid in his judgment of men of genius, and even of poets with whom he has had a difference, who, indeed, are very few. For, when he has been attacked by them, it has often happened, that, after writing an epigram or couplet, to show his particular friends how he could defend himself, he has thrown it into the fire; and he has never been known either to print or publish a line, by way of retaliation, against the bitterest enemy to his person or poems. He has a natural cheerfulness and pleasantry in his manner and conversation, which give a gaiety to all around him, and is possessed of as easy an eloquence in speaking as in writing. He is, indeed, one of the few extraordinary geniuses who lose nothing by approximation or acquaintance; for it is a melancholy reflection that very few, like him, are equally entitled to the epithets *good* and *great*." In these pleasing features there is a striking likeness between the character of Metastasio and that of our illustrious Scott: and Burney adds another point of resemblance; " Metastasio laughs at all poetic inspiration, and makes a poem as mechanically as another would make a watch, at what time he pleases, and without any other occasion than the want of it."

The whole circumstances of the life of this great poet indicate the purity of mind, piety, benevolence, and sweetness of disposition, which breathe throughout his writings.

Metastasio died on the 12th of April, 1782, at the age of eighty-four. Notwithstanding this advanced age, yet his faculties were so entire, his countenance was so florid, and figure so erect, his appearance so hale and active, and his constitutional cheerfulness so little impaired, that he seemed still to have many years of life before him. On the 1st of April he was in his usual health and spirits, and spent the evening, as usual, in the society of a few friends. On returning home he complained of a slight indisposition, and, at his usual hour, went to bed, from whence he never rose. In the morning he was seized with fever, and remained in a state of almost constant lethargy

till he expired.   By his will he had prohibited all
pomp and ostentation at his funeral; but his heir
obeyed his own feelings of respect and gratitude in
preference to this injunction; and the poet was
interred with great magnificence, in the church of
St. Michael.   Metastasio's property, at his death,
consisted of 130,000 florins (above 12,000*l.* sterling), with a well furnished house and a valuable
library.   He bequeathed it (having survived his
own relatives) to M. Joseph Martinetz, and Mlle.
Marianna Martinetz, the son and daughter of M.
Nicolo Martinetz, a gentleman of Vienna, in whose
house he had taken up his abode on his first arrival
in Vienna, half a century before, and with whose
family he continued, ever after, on a footing of the
most intimate friendship.   Mademoiselle Martinetz
had been carefully educated under his own eye,
and was a lady of extraordinary talents and accomplishments, especially in music.   She was not
only an exquisite singer and an excellent performer on the harpsichord, but, as a composer, was
worthy to be compared to the first musicians of the
age.   Metastasio, in his letters, spoke of her genius
with admiration, and communicated her compositions to his friends.   He mentions, in particular,
her music to a number of the psalms of the celebrated Saverio Mattei, in a letter, accompanying a
copy of it, written to that poet himself.   She received the distinguished honour of being chosen a
member of the Philharmonic Academy of Bologna.
She had received the instructions of Haydn, who,

when a young man, resided for a considerable time under her father's roof. Dr. Burney, who met her at Metastasio's house, describes her as a young lady of a very elegant appearance, and speaks in the highest terms of her manners and conversation, as well as her attainments as a composer and a performer.

CHAPTER XIV.

THE operas of Metastasio hold so high a place in the classical literature, not of Italy only, but of the modern world, that they have often been considered and judged of as tragedies; a test which cannot be properly applied to them. The French critics have drawn elaborate comparisons between the manner in which the same or similar subjects have been treated by Metastasio and by Corneille or Racine, forgetting the difference between an opera and a tragedy, in their objects, in the laws which must regulate their composition, and in the manner of their performance. Metastasio's operas are tragedies; but they are lyrical tragedies. Their object is, to rouse the feelings and sympathies of the audience; to touch the soul by "tender strokes of art;" to exalt the mind by noble sentiments and pictures of heroic virtue. But, while this is done, the ear must at the same time be gratified, and the taste delighted, by the sweetness of sounds and all the charms of music. A simplicity of structure, therefore, a brevity of language, and an absence of minute details, which would be bare and meagre in a drama merely spoken, are absolutely necessary to prevent confusion and tediousness in musical recitation and song. In Voltaire's tragedy of *Merope*, the heroine delivers a long and eloquent address to the tyrant Polifontes, adjuring him to restore her son. A mother introduced in similar circumstances by Metastasio, expresses the same feelings in these few words:—

> " Rendimi il figlio mio ;
> Ahi ! mi si sprezza il cor :
> Non son più madre, O Dio !
> Non ho più figlio."

These short and simple exclamations are the cry of nature ; but the greatest actress could not dwell upon them long enough to produce the requisite impression. The tragic poet must give her a great deal more to say to a similar purpose. But let them be reiterated in all the varieties of tone and expression with which the genius of a Jomelli is able to clothe them, and they move the feelings of the audience more strongly than all the elaborate eloquence of Voltaire.

The lyric poet, too, labours under this further restriction, that he must construct his piece not merely with a view to its dramatic, but its musical effect. His characters must be not only kings, princesses, lovers, and villains, but they must also be sopranos, contraltos, tenors, and basses ; and the scenes must be arranged so as to produce a pleasing variety and succession of airs, duets, concerted pieces, and choruses, as well as striking situations and affecting incidents. He is generally obliged, moreover, to accommodate himself to the peculiar talents, or even defects, of the performers who may constitute the company of the theatre for which he writes. This was, in a remarkable degree, the case with Metastasio, who not only wrote almost all his pieces for the single theatre of Vienna, but found it necessary to adapt some of them to the capacities of the amateur performers of the court. His pretty opera, *Il Re Pastore*, was written to be acted by four young arch-duchesses. The emperor disliked to have his feelings *too* painfully acted upon; and Metastasio, therefore, was often obliged to sacrifice historic truth, probability, and consistency of character, for the sake of a happy termination.

Metastasio is entitled to the benefit of all these considerations, and others of a similar nature; and yet it is wonderful how little he stands in need of them. He moves in his fetters with so much grace and freedom that they rarely seem heavy, and are often altogether imperceptible. Though written expressly for the musical stage, and under all the restraints which it imposes, his operas give a pleasure in the closet hardly inferior to that which they produce in representation: and though they have been superseded by an unceasing change of fashionable novelties in the theatre, they are and will continue to be familiar to every one who loves the classical literature of Italy.

It is remarkable that, in the perusal of these operas, the reader is delighted even with those things which belong entirely to their representation. He has given dignity and importance to the art of theatrical decoration; and, even in the closet, it is impossible to overlook his felicity in imagining the most convenient scenes for his incidents, his skill in giving variety to local situations, his taste in choosing such as are most delightful to the imagination, and his learning exhibited in his descriptions of the aspect and productions of various countries, and of the costumes, buildings, rites and ceremonies, of different ages and nations. His language, too, though written with a view to its fitness for musical recitation and song, is beautiful, independently of adventitious aid, and charms the reader, as well as the listener, by its purity, its elegance, the harmony of its numbers, its simplicity and clearness, and its variety and force of expression. His subjects are generally well chosen; being founded, for the most part, on some striking historical incident. He rejected the mythological and fabulous extravagances of his predecessors, as well as their incongruous buffoonery, and brought the lyrical drama close to the confines of tragedy. Some of his operas, indeed, are taken from the master-pieces of the French stage; as his *Clemenza di Tito* (though with a change of characters) from the *Cinna* of Corneille, and his sacred drama of *Gioas* from the *Athalie* of Racine.

His works, like those of every other voluminous writer, are very unequal in merit. His best dramas were produced during the earlier part of his residence at Vienna. In his later works a decay of vigour is perceptible: and *Ruggiero*, his last opera, is his feeblest. Among all his productions his *Attilio Regolo* was always his own favourite; and he said, that were all his works to be destroyed but one, this was the piece which he would wish to save. Some of his other operas have been more frequently set to music, and more popular on the stage ; but none of them is calculated, in the perusal, to give a higher idea of his powers as a tragic poet. It is full of moral grandeur mingled with the deepest pathos.

The music of Hasse to *Attilio Regolo*, in the composition of which he had the benefit of the author's admirable counsels, is among the finest of his works. It had the greatest success at Dresden, and continued to be performed in Italy and Germany for several years, till it was superseded by the still more powerful music of Jomelli.

In *La Clemenza di Tito*, with what beautiful colours has the poet painted the godlike " quality of mercy ; " and with what exquisite skill has he represented the mind of *Titus* as filled with tenderness even to overflowing, and yet preserving all the dignity and firmness becoming his lofty station ! How finely is his character contrasted with that of the violent and impetuous Vitellia, and the guilty yet ingenuous Sextus. That heart must be cold

which does not glow with emotion, even in perus-
ing the scene in which the repentant criminal is
brought before his sovereign—a scene which, says
Voltaire, is worthy of Corneille when he is not declamatory, and of Racine when he is not feeble.

In the " Osservazioni sopra i Drammi dell'
Abate Metastasio," published at Nice in 1785,
there is the following passage in relation to this
opera; " In the *Clemenza di Tito*, as in some of
his other works, Metastasio has dared to beat down
the idol to which modern music has offered so much
incense, namely, the *Duet*. We applaud his boldness. The fierce and furious Vitellia was not
permitted to warble along with the foolish Sextus
or the gentle Titus. But if this opera is again
brought on the stage in our time, who knows what
nonsense may be introduced into it by the tribe of
stage-poets, here to supply a duet, there to introduce a *rondeau*, now in compliance with the dic-
tates of caprice, and now to satisfy the demands of
ignorance!" All this has actually taken place.
The *Clemenza di Tito*, as set by Mozart, contains
many interpolations such as above described. The
first scene, for example, in which Vitellia instigates
Sextus to join the conspiracy against the emperor,
concludes with the following words, intended to be
delivered in recitative:

> " *Sesto*. Tutto, tutto farò. Prescrivi, imponi,
> Regola i moti miei:
> Tu la mia sorte, il mio destin tu sei.
> *Vitellia*. Prima che il sol tramonti
> Voglio Tito svenato, e voglio—."

But, in Mozart's opera, this brief and hasty conclusion of the colloquy, thus suddenly broken off, is amplified into the long and elaborate duet beginning, "Come ti piace, imponi;" in utter violation of dramatic propriety. The love scene between Annio and Servilia concludes with the beautiful lines beginning

<blockquote>"Ah, perdona al primo affetto,"</blockquote>

tenderly addressed by the lover to his mistress. But, instead of this, in Mozart's opera, there is a long duet, in which the lovers first express the same sentiments alternately, and then speak them both together. The exquisite beauty of Mozart's music in this duet, is universally acknowledged; but yet everybody must have felt, while it was singing, that Annio and Servilia vanished from their presence, and that they thought of nothing but the sweet warbling of Signor A. and Signora B. In the noble scene which has been already mentioned, between Titus and Sextus, the latter, on retiring from the emperor's presence, makes an appeal to his old friendship, in the most simple and affecting language,—

<blockquote>"Per questo istante solo
Ricordati, Signor, l' amor primiero," &c.</blockquote>

The music here ought to be as short and simple as the words; for Sextus is in no condition to *expatiate* before his sovereign and his judge. But we have a long *aria* in two movements, the last of which is a florid *rondeau.* There are a number of

other alterations and interpolations; and the concerted piece which forms the finale, beginning
" Tu, é ver, m'assolvi, Augusto," is not to be found
in Metastasio.

It is not to be understood, however, from the
above-quoted remark of the Italian critic, that Metastasio entirely rejected the use of the duet.   He
only avoided its abuse.   There are many duets in
his operas; but they are introduced sparingly, and
always with strict attention to dramatic propriety;
being constructed in the colloquial form, and having
those passages, in which the voices join, made very
brief.   As to trios, quartets, and *concerted pieces,*
they were utterly unknown in the musical tragedy
of his day.   Choruses are used by him only in
scenes where a multitude of people can be introduced with propriety; and their rarity adds to the
greatness of their effect.

Perhaps the most deeply interesting of all these
dramas is *L' Olimpiade.*   It is not only beautiful as
a whole, but contains some of the purest gems of
Metastasio's poetry.   The character of Megacles is
a divine picture of heroic friendship.   Loving and
beloved, he determines to sacrifice his mistress to
his friend; and yet feels less for his own wretchedness than for his Arìstea's sorrow when she shall
hear that he is gone.   What sadness in his parting
words to the friend for whom he abandons all that
is dear to him !—

> " Se cerca, se dice,
> L' amico dov' è ?

L' amico infelice,
Rispondi, mori.
Ah no ! sì gran duolo
Non darle per me :
Rispondi, ma solo,
Piangendo partì.
Che abisso di pene !
Lasciare il suo bene,
Lasciarlo per sempre,
Lasciarlo così."

A perfect example of a duet is to be found in this opera. Megacles, who has undertaken to enter the lists for his friend, in the games in which the fair Aristea is to be the reward of the victor, discovers that this Aristea is the mistress whom he himself adores. She, believing that it is for love of her that he has enrolled himself among the competitors, expresses the tender feelings inspired by his devotion, to which he responds with equal tenderness ; but his countenance, manner, and incoherent expressions, betray the grief and disturbance of his mind. Aristea, alarmed at his appearance, expresses her uneasiness, and tenderly inquires the cause of his agitation : and Megacles, unable to bear his own distracted thoughts and the sight of his mistress's distress, leaves her, overcome with anxious forebodings. The conclusion of this scene is contained in the following duet, which shows how this form of musical dialogue can be rendered natural and dramatic, as well as beautiful.

Megacle. Ne' giorni tuoi felici
Ricordati di me.

Aristea.	Perchè così mi dici,
	Anima mia, perchè ?
Megacle.	Taci, bel idol mio.
Aristea.	Parla, mio dolce amor.
Megacle.	Ah ! che parlando ⎱ Oh Dio!
Aristea.	Ah ! che tacendo ⎰
	Tu mi traffigi il cor !
Aristea (aparte).	Veggio languir chi adoro
	Ne intendo il suo languir !
Megacle (aparte).	Di gelosia mi moro
	E non lo posso dir !
Megacle.	Chi mai provò di questo
Aristea.	Affanno piu funesto
	Più barbaro dolor ?"

Metastasio's poetry exhibits innumerable traces of his familiarity with the beauties of ancient literature. The following air, in this opera, sung by Megacles, is an instance :

> " Lo seguitai felice
> Quand' era il ciel sereno,
> Alle tempeste in seno
> Voglio seguirlo ancor.
> Come del' oro il fuoco
> Scopre le masse impure,
> Scoprono le sventure
> De' falsi amici il cor."

We have here the sentiment in the following verses of Ovid, expressed with more elegance than in the original.

> " Dum juvat, et vultu ridet fortuna sereno
>   Indelibatas cuncta sequuntur opes ;
> Scilicet, ut fulvum spectatur in ignibus aurum,
>   Tempore sic duro est inspicienda fides."*

---

* Trist. lib. i. eleg. 5.

The morality of this great poet is always lofty and beautiful. He does not love the darkest shades of human character. Even his vicious personages are rescued from unmitigated hatred or scorn by traits of feeling, or nobleness of mind, contending with the influence of evil passions. But no one has painted virtue in more glowing and captivating colours. What can be more sublime than the heroism of his Regulus and Cato? What more noble than the magnanimity of Titus, or more pathetic than the tender and devoted friendship of Megacles? His dramas are full of these exalted views of man's nature. When Themistocles, banished by his ungrateful countrymen, takes refuge at the court of the Persian king, Xerxes offers him the means of revenge by placing him at the head of the immense army assembled for the invasion of Greece. The Athenian refuses to be the foe of his country. " E che tant' ami in lei?"—" What can *you* love in your country?"—is the question of the angry monarch;—and how exquisite is the answer !—

> " Tutto, O Signor : le ceneri degli avi,
>   Le sacre leggi, i tutelari Numi ;
>   La favella, i costumi ;
>   Il sudor che mi costa ;
>   Lo splendor che ne trassi ;
>   L' aria, i tronchi, i terren, le mura, i sassi."

One of Metastasio's beauties lies in the reflections and in the felicity with which they generally flow from the circumstances of the scene. Timantes,

about to die, naturally meditates on the vanity of
human life. How full of matter are his thoughts,
and yet how simple his expressions!—" Why," he
asks, " why wish for life?"—

> " Perchè bramar la vita ? e qual piacere
>   In lei si trova ? Ogni fortuna è pena ;
>   E miseria ogni età ; Tremiam fanciulli
>   D' un guardo al minacciar : Siam gioci, adulti,
>   Di fortuna e d' amor. Or ne trafigge
>   La brama d' ottenere : or ne tormenta
>   Di perdere il timore. Eterna guerra
>   Hanno i rei con se stessi : i giusti l' hanno
>   Coll' invidia e la frode : ombre, deliri,
>   Sogni, follie son nostre cure, e quando
>   Il vergognoso errore
>   A scoprir s' incomincia, allor si muore.'"

With all their beauties, however, the dramas of
Metastasio are chargeable with many faults. He
has introduced *Love* to an immoderate and absurd
extent. In every one of his pieces love is a principal feature—even in those, such as *Catone, Temistocle*, and *Attilio Regolo*, where it seems most
out of place. Sometimes there are three or four
love affairs in one piece; and in *Semiramide* all
the characters are in love. Love is frequently introduced by him, not as the primary passion on
which the subject of the piece hangs, but in a sort
of subordinate and episodical way, as if in mere
compliance with theatrical usage: and in these cases
it is necessarily cold, languid, and insipid. What
interest can anybody take in the affected sighs
and languishments of Amenossi, Barsene, Cleofile,

Megabise, Selene, Tamiri, and others, who are in love purely for form's sake; " in the same way," says Arteaga,* " as Don Quixote was in love with Dulcinea del Toboso, whom he had never seen and knew nothing of, solely that he might conform to the laws of chivalry, which required that every knight should have a lady of his love." Who cares for the languid passion of Barce, in conjunction with the sublime self-devotion of Regulus—the imbecile gallantry of Xerxes, besides the incomparable nobleness of Themistocles—or the frigid jealousy of Arbaces, alongside of the "indomitable will" of Cato? Such personages as these, with their puling and mincing sentimentalities, provoke only impatience or ridicule.

This constant introduction of love gives an effeminate and affected air even to characters in themselves noble and striking. It is preposterous to make Amilcar, the Carthaginian envoy to Rome, in the midst of the momentous affairs of his mission, employ himself in " sighing like furnace " for the charms of a slave, under the very eyes of the stern and austere Romans; to make Fulvius, sent to decide the dispute between Cæsar and Cato, which involved the destinies of the world, fall in love with Pompey's widow, and assail her with a profusion of gallantries and soft speeches; and to make Cæsar himself address a fair one in the language of an Arcadian shepherd. And, to make the matter still worse, all the personages, however different in

* Rivoluzioni del Teatro Italiano.

country, age, station, or character, make use in
their love-dialogues of one unvarying phraseology,
filled with a sickly repetition of amorous common-
place and hackneyed terms of endearment. Even
Polyphemus himself exhales his sighs for the fair
Galatea in the following *arietta;*

> " Mio cor, tu prendi a scherno
>   E folgori, e procelle,
>   E poi due luci belle
>   Ti fanno palpitar.
>   Qual nuovo moto interno
>   Prendi da quei sembianti ?
>   Quai non usati incanti
>   T' insegnano tremar ? "

Had Metastasio, like the English poet, formed to
himself the image of the giant Cyclop roaring out,
before he began his love-ditty,

> " Bring me a hundred reeds, of proper growth,
>   To make a pipe for my capacious mouth,"

he would not have put into that " capacious mouth "
a delicate sentimental effusion, in the style of
Tibullus or Petrarch,

This conventional love, which enters so largely
into Metastasio's operas, has the necessary effect of
making his language forced and artificial—full of
the cold suggestions of the fancy instead of the
warm impulses of the heart. Hence we find his
heroes and heroines, when supposed to be under
the influence of the most agitating feelings, amusing themselves with making strings of ingenious
similes— comparing themselves to ships beat by

the waves, streams dashed against the rocks, flowers, or turtle-doves; and tracing the points of resemblance through a dozen labouring lines. What can be more intolerable than the following frozen conceit, uttered, too, by a passionate lover? When Fulvius, in *Catone*, makes an untimely declaration of his love to Emilia, she answers him,

> " Qual mai può darti
>   Speranza una infelice
>   Cinta di bruno ammanto,
>   Coll' odio in petto, e sulle ciglie il pianto ?' "

And he replies,

> " Piangendo ancora
>   Rinascer suole
>   La bella aurora
>   Nunzia del sole ;
>   E pur conduce
>   Sereno il dì."

Could it be believed that the poet should have made the lover reply to so simple and affecting an appeal by such a piece of double-refined nonsense?

This appears to be Metastasio's greatest fault, and that for which he is most liable to censure; for it was voluntary and might have been avoided. His other defects, the want of individuality and historic truth in his characters, the frequent improbability of his incidents, and the deficiency of variety in his denouements, arose from the nature of the musical drama, and the restraints under which he laboured ; and, after all, he is in need of

less indulgence for them than might reasonably be
allowed him.

In his own department of the drama, Metastasio
stands alone and unrivalled. He is the Shakspeare of the Italian opera, and has surpassed all
who have followed him, as well as all who have
gone before him. " Sans modèle, dans sa carrière,"
says Sismondi, " il s'est trouvé aussi sans imita-
teurs. Tous les jours de nouveaux opéras serieux
sont fournis aux compositeurs et présentés au
public, et pas un seul ne peut soutenir la lecture ;
pas un seul auteur ne s'est fait seulement la ré-
putation d'esprit et de goût dans un genre qui
a donné à Metastase une place parmi les plus
grands poètes."

───────────

Though Metastasio is the only poet who has
achieved greatness by devoting himself exclusively
or chiefly to the musical drama, yet several eminent
Italian writers may be mentioned as having occasionally turned their attention to this branch of
literature, in the earlier part of the last century.
Marcello, the celebrated composer of the Psalms,
wrote two operas, *La fede Riconosciuta* and *Arata
in Sparta*, about the year 1710. Count Scipio
Maffei, the author of the tragedy of *Merope*,
wrote an elegant pastoral opera, *La Ninfa fida*.
Signora Gozzi, a Venetian lady of distinguished
literary attainments, who published a collection of
the poetry of the most celebrated women in Italy,

270 GOLDONI.

is the author of two operas, *Agide Rè di Sparta* and *L'Elenia*, performed at Venice in 1725 and 1730. Count Durazzo wrote *L'Innocenza giustificata* for the *début* of the famous singer Gabrielli. It was performed a hundred times successively. Of Calsabigi, the fellow-labourer of Gluck, we shall have occasion to speak in conjunction with that composer. Goldoni, the celebrated comic poet, was also the author of many operas all of which are now forgotten, except *La Buona Figliuola*, which, in conjunction with the beautiful music of Piccini, was long popular throughout Europe, and is still well known to the lovers of the older Italian stage.

CHAPTER XV.

STATE OF THE ITALIAN OPERA IN THE EARLIER PART OF THE 18TH CENTURY—GREAT COMPOSERS—LEO—VINCI—SARRO—PORPORA—RINALDO DI CAPUA—PERGOLESI—HASSE—DOMENICO SCARLATTI—FEO—GALUPPI—TERRADELLAS—PEREZ—LOGROSCINO.

AT the same time that the poetry of the Italian opera was refined and exalted by the writings of Apostolo Zeno and Metastasio, its music was undergoing a similar process by the labours of Alessandro Scarlatti, Caldara, and the other composers who have been already mentioned as having flourished at the beginning of the eighteenth century. These composers set the example of freeing dramatic music from the complication of fugues, canons, and harmonical contrivances, with which every description of music had previously been encumbered. They discovered that the essence of dramatic music consisted in melody and expression. They established the distinctions between recitative and air; gave to each of these species of musical language its peculiar features, and assigned to it its proper functions.

Their successors proceeded in the same course. Leonardo Leo added grace and melody to the airs, and richness and brilliancy to their accompaniments. Vinci increased the energy of dramatic language by means of the *recitativo obbligato*, or accompanied recitative : and further improvements were made in this department by Porpora and Rinaldo di Capua ;—the one having given greater variety to the phrases and greater facility to the cantilena, while the other heightened its effect by the instrumental accompaniments. Pergolesi carried melody to as great a degree of perfection as it perhaps has yet reached. From his grand and simple style, strong and natural expression, unity of design, beauty, and grace, this composer has very happily been called the Raphael of music. About this time a host of great musicians flourished almost contemporaneously, among whom may be enumerated Domenico Scarlatti, Hasse, Perez, Terradellas, Galuppi, Sarro, and Mancini ; and the period to which they belong has been called by Arteaga, and other critics, the golden age of the Italian musical drama.

Nothing contributed more to the elevation of music at that period than the number of excellent singers. In the general improvement of taste, the art of singing had arrived at a high degree of purity. The singers had acquired a simple and natural style, exquisite skill in the management of the voice, and perfect intonation. Expression was the great object of their study : and they had not yet learned to consider the execution of bravura passages as the perfection of the vocal art. Embellishments were valued only as being the means of expression : and the singer studied to accommodate the musical accents to the prosody of the language in such a manner, that the poetry was recited with proper emphasis and distinct pronunciation. Dramatic action, too, was carefully studied ; and many performers of that day appear to have deserved eulogies as glowing as that bestowed by the *Spectator* upon Nicolini.

There were, at that period, excellent vocal schools in several of the principal cities of Italy. At Rome, from that city being the chief seat of the performance of sacred music, the utmost purity of execution, and nicety in the management of the voice, were particularly studied. The celebrated masters, Fedi and Amadori, were accustomed to carry their pupils to a place without the walls of Rome, where there was a remarkable echo, which repeated the same sound a number of times : and there, in imitation of Demosthenes, they were exercised in singing to the echo, which, by its repetition of their tones, admonished them of their defects. The schools of Bologna, Naples, Venice, Milan, and Florence, were also celebrated, and produced many great disciples.

The principal female singers of that period were Signora Tesi, who was esteemed the first actress of the age, Marianna Bulgarini, the friend of Metastasio, Faustina, Cuzzoni, Mingotti, and Gabrielli. Among the men were Farinelli (probably the greatest singer that has ever existed), Caffarelli,

Gizziello, Guarducci, Mancini, Carestini, and Senesino.

Besides the above, many other eminent composers and performers flourished during this "golden age" of the Italian opera; but the names which have been enumerated appear to be the most worthy of commemoration.

LEONARDO LEO was born at Naples in 1694, and became principal organist in the Chapel Royal of that city. According to Burney, his first opera, *Sofonisba*, was performed at Naples in 1718, and his last, *Siface*, at Bologna in 1737. He was possessed of great versatility of talent; being not only a great composer for the church, but equally successful in the serious and the comic opera. His first opera in the comic style is called *Cioè*; its subject being the absurdity of a man who has the habit of adding "Cioè," or, "That is to say," to everything he says, and puzzles everybody about him by his explanations. It is described as being very lively and humorous; and it was very popular, not only at Naples, where it was first represented, but all over Italy.

Leo was the founder of a school of singing at Naples, which produced many great performers. As a composer, his labours conduced greatly to the progress of the art. He is remarkable for the purity of his harmony and the elegant simplicity of his melody, which he contributed to clear from the stiff and formal divisions with which it had been previously encumbered. He composed the music

to several of Metastasio's operas; particularly the
Olimpiade and *Artaserse*. His biographers enumerate among his works sixteen serious operas, besides several comic operas and *intermezzi*. He
died at Naples in 1745, at the age of fifty-one.
His death was occasioned by an apparently trifling
circumstance. Having a small tumour, or wen,
upon his cheek, he was advised to have it taken
off; but, owing to the unskilfulness of the operator,
or a bad habit of body, a mortification ensued,
which caused his death.

LEONARDO VINCI was born at Naples in 1690.
When a boy, he is said to have run away from the
Conservatorio of *Gli Poveri in Giesu Cristo*, where
he was a scholar, in consequence of a quarrel with
Porpora, with whom his rivalry appears to have
continued in after life. When yet very young, he
was engaged, on the strength of his early reputation, to compose an opera for Rome, and succeeded, by his *Semiramide*, in satisfying the fasti-
dious audience of that city. In 1725 he produced
his *Siface* at Venice, and had the satisfaction of
seeing that opera preferred to the *Siroe* of his
rival Porpora. In 1726 he composed the music of
Metastasio's *Didone Abbandonata* for Rome, which
established his reputation. The public were
struck, not only with the beauty of the airs, but
with the extraordinary power and dramatic effect
of the accompanied recitatives. "Virgil himself,"
says Count Algarotti, "would have been pleased
to hear a composition so animated and so terrible,

in which the heart and soul were at once assailed by all the powers of music." This opera is considered as the masterpiece of the composer. His music to the *Artaserse* of Metastasio, also composed at Rome, was performed in England; where the air, "Vo solcando un mar crudele," originally composed for Carestini, was long popular.

Vinci's death was tragical. While he was in the height of his success at Rome, he became attached to a lady of distinguished rank and great beauty, who, it is said, returned his passion. Having been foolish and unmanly enough to boast of her favours, she took her revenge, in the true Italian spirit, by presenting him with a poisoned cup of chocolate. He was thus cut off in the year 1732, in his forty-second year.

NICOLO PORPORA was born at Naples in 1689. At an early age he was placed under the care of Alessandro Scarlatti, and is considered the most celebrated scholar of that great master. He devoted himself chiefly to dramatic music, and began his career at Vienna, where, however, his merit was not at first appreciated. Before he was able to distinguish himself, he lived for a considerable time in that city, poor and unemployed. The Emperor Charles VI., who was a musical connoisseur, was not pleased with his music, which, he said, was too full of shakes and other vocal ornaments. Through the friendship of Hasse, the imperial *dilettante*, notwithstanding his prepossession, was prevailed upon to hear an oratorio of Porpora's composition. Porpora, having received a hint from his friend, did not introduce a single shake in the course of the oratorio. The Emperor was quite surprised, and kept continually repeating, " Why, this is quite a different thing—there is not a single shake!" At last, however, the concluding fugue began, and the Emperor observed that its theme set out with four trilled notes. These, of course, were taken up in succession, in the answers, by the different parts, and worked upon according to the rules of that species of composition. " When the Emperor," says the author of the Life of Haydn, who tells the story with his usual liveliness, " who was privileged never to laugh, heard, in the full height of the fugue, this deluge of shakes which seemed like the music of a set of crazy paralytics, he could no longer preserve his gravity, but laughed outright, perhaps for the first time in his life. In France, the land of jokes, this pleasantry might have given offence, but at Vienna it was the beginning of Porpora's fortune."

His first opera, *Ariana e Teseo*, performed at Vienna, in 1717, laid the foundation of his fame, and he produced several other works in that city with great success. At Venice he was less fortunate at first; the preference, as has been already mentioned, having been given to Vinci; but the Venetians soon learned to appreciate his talents; and his *Ariana* obtained the applause which it merited. He afterwards went to Dresden, where he was engaged as *maestro di capella* and singing master to the Princess Maria Antonietta. He had there to contend with another formidable rival, in the person of Hasse, whom if he did not conquer, he was at least not conquered by him; for his operas, though performed in competition with those of Hasse, were received with great applause by the court and the public. It was here that he introduced to the public his pupil, the young and beautiful Mingotti, whom he opposed with success to the hitherto unrivalled wife of Hasse, the celebrated Faustina.

In 1733 Porpora came to England, in consequence of an invitation from the nobility and gentry who had set on foot an opera in opposition to Handel. Musical faction at that time ran high in England. The aristocratic subscribers to the opera had taken different sides in the quarrels which had arisen between Handel and his principal singers, Senesino and Cuzzoni; and were, moreover, offended at the advanced price for admission to the operas on oratorio nights. They therefore opened a subscription for a rival opera, engaging Porpora as composer and conductor, and a company of singers, containing Handel's mutinous troops, and strengthened by the addition of Farinelli. But Porpora, successful as he had been in his previous campaigns, was unable to withstand the "giant Handel." His *Ariana e Teseo*, indeed, was brought out, and sustained twenty representations during the season; and another opera by him, called *Ferdinando*, was performed three or four times. He conducted this establishment for three seasons; but most of the pieces performed were by other composers. His most successful production appears to have been *Polifemo*, which (as is said in the title-page) was composed by Porpora, "per la Nobilità Britannica," and performed during a considerable part of the season of 1735. "In examining," says Burney, "the favourite songs of this opera that were printed by Walsh, among which are five of Farinelli's, with one of Senesino's, and one of Montagnana's, there appears to be considerable merit in the melody. Indeed, so much of the new taste and new passages of this period seem to have been derived from Porpora's songs, that the difference of style and fancy in the airs of Farinelli, from those that were sung by Nicolini two or three and twenty years before, is wonderful. Yet the songs of Nicolini, being the best of the time, were equally admired by the public, who reason from what they hear, and improve in criticism by excellence in composition and performance, so much as never to tolerate inferiority while memory enables them to form a comparison. The King, Queen, Prince of Wales, and Princesses (Burney adds), honoured the first representation of *Polifemo* with their presence, and there was the fullest house of the season."

Porpora, who exhibited no lack of courage in this warfare, ventured also to dispute the palm with Handel in the composition of an oratorio. But his *David*, brought out at the King's Theatre, in 1735, was performed only three times, while Handel continued the performance of different oratorios, including *Deborah*, *Esther*, and *Athalia*, without operas, for nearly two months. Notwithstanding his undoubted merit, and the support of a powerful party, Porpora at length found himself unable to carry on the struggle, and left England in 1737. His operas continued to be occasionally performed in London. In 1743, in particular, Apostolo Zeno's *Temistocle*, with Porpora's music, was performed at the opera-house, and had a run of eight nights. "The air in this opera," says Burney, "beginning *Di che a sua voglia eleggere*, is in a grand and original style: the shakes, however, on the first note of a phrase or passage, seem strange from so great a singing-master. *L' ire tue* has some new effects and embellishments, and was pillaged by Weideman* in his minuet. I never saw music in which shakes were so lavished; Porpora seems to have composed the air, *Contrasto assai*, in a shivering fit." This remark, by the way, reminds us of the anecdote of the composer and the Emperor Charles VI., the truth of which it confirms. Porpora seems to have retained his propensity towards shakes.

After Porpora's departure from England, he was for some time master of the Conservatorio of the *Incurabili* at Venice. In 1759, we find him residing

---

* A celebrated composer for and performer on the German flute, whose music was long very popular among the amateurs of that instrument.

at Vienna, in a state of indigence. At this time, Haydn, then an obscure young man, derived the benefit of his musical instructions. "Haydn," says the author of that composer's life, "did not learn recitative of Porpora: the inferiority of his recitatives to those of the inventor* of this kind of music is a sufficient proof of this: but he learned from him the true Italian style of singing, and the art of accompanying on the pianoforte, which is not so easy a thing as is commonly supposed. He succeeded in obtaining these lessons in the following way. A noble Venetian, named Cornaro, at that time resided at Vienna, as ambassador from the Republic. He had a mistress passionately fond of music, who had harboured old Porpora in the hotel of the embassy. Haydn found means to get introduced into the family on account of his musical attainments ; and his excellency carried him, along with his mistress and Porpora, to the baths of Mariensdorff, which were at that time a place of fashionable resort. The young man, who cared for nobody but the old Neapolitan, employed all sorts of devices to get into his good graces, and to obtain his harmonic favours. Every day he rose early, brushed the old man's coat, cleaned his shoes, and combed out his old-fashioned periwig, though he was as sour as can well be imagined. Haydn obtained at first nothing but the courteous salutation of 'fool,' or 'blockhead,' when he entered

---

* Not the *inventor*, but certainly one of the greatest improvers of recitative.

his room in a morning. But the bear, finding that he was served gratuitously, and observing at the same time the rare qualities of his self-devoted servant, allowed himself to soften now and then, and gave him good advice. Haydn was favoured with it more especially, whenever he had to accompany the fair Wilhelmina in singing Porpora's airs, which were filled with basses by no means easy to understand. Joseph thus learned in this house to sing in the best Italian taste."

Porpora's situation, at this time, is affectingly described by Metastasio, in a letter written by him, in March 1759, to his friend Farinelli, then at Madrid, and in high favour at the Spanish court. " I am unable," says the benevolent poet, " to resist the compassion which our poor friend Porpora excited in me yesterday, when he entreated me to second the letter, which I now enclose, with one from myself. It is sufficient to draw tears from every one possessed of humanity, to see a man of such merit in his profession reduced to absolute want of bread by the well-known misfortunes of Saxony, whence he derived a certain pension sufficient at least for his subsistence. He understands that your compassionate sovereigns, in their munificence and charity, are in the custom of granting small pensions, under the title of Eleemosynaries, to persons in distress; and he entreats me to recommend him to your intercession, that he might obtain one, which would just enable him to subsist; and this is not saying much." The death of

Ferdinand VI., which took place soon after the date of this letter, and which deprived Farinelli of his influence at Madrid, prevented him from doing anything in behalf of the veteran composer.

Porpora spent his latter years at Naples, the place of his nativity, where he appears to have lived in great poverty. He died in 1767, at the age of eighty-two.

The name of GIOVANNI BATTISTA PERGOLESI is one of the most illustrious in the history of music. He was born at Caforia, a little town in the neighbourhood of Naples, in the year 1704. Having discovered in his childhood a disposition for music, he was placed in the *Conservatorio dei poveri in Giesu Cristo*, a celebrated musical seminary at Naples, where he produced specimens of genius which would have done honour to the first masters of the time, at an age when others could scarcely have acquired the rudiments of the art. When only fourteen, he discovered that, according to the prevailing system of education, melody and expression were sacrificed to laborious counterpoint, and the art of solving harmonical problems; and, after making himself master of the principles of harmony and the rules of orchestral writing, he entreated his family to release him from the trammels of a school from which he felt that he could derive no further benefit. As soon as he quitted the conservatory, he commenced a course of study more suitable to the bent of his own genius. He sought the instructions of Vinci and Hasse, as being the purest and simplest melodists of the time, and soon not only equalled, but surpassed them in their own style. He attained their simplicity and clearness, while he excelled them in the grace, variety, and expression of his melody.

For a time, however, his countrymen did not discover his merits; and his first opera was brought out at Naples with little success. He obtained the patronage of the Prince of Stigliano, who was able to appreciate his genius, and procured for him employment in composing for the *Teatro Nuovo*. The works by which he first distinguished himself were *intermezzi*, which were received by his countrymen with great favour, but being written in the Neapolitan dialect, their popularity was confined to that city. That this was the case is much to be regretted; for the only one of them that was written in generally intelligible Italian, *La Serva Padrona*, speedily became popular throughout Europe. Its introduction into France was almost sufficient, of itself, to effect a revolution in the national taste; and, though long laid aside in the theatres, it is to this day delightful to those who love the elegant gaiety and charming simplicity of the old Italian school.

This celebrated piece is called an " Intermezzo *a due voci*," and has only two characters, Uberto, an old bachelor, and Serpina, his servant-maid, an artful, witty damsel, who has completely subjugated her master, and finally, by the power of her charms and her coquetry, brings him to marry her. The

dialogue is carried on in lively recitative, mingled
with airs and duets of the utmost grace and beauty.
The instrumental score consists merely of two
violins, tenor, and bass, without any wind instruments. The two violin parts are frequently in
unison, and the tenor often doubles the bass. The
accompaniments, however, are spirited, ingenious,
and so effective that every note tells ; and the
harmony, thin as it is, is beautifully transparent.
The voices are perfectly well supported, without
being overpowered or placed under restraint; and
the effect would be delightful to ears not spoiled
by the excessive richness of the modern orchestra.
We are inclined, indeed, to think, that even as it
is, were the *Serva Padrona* revived, and performed with the archness, grace, and humour
which could be imparted to it by Grisi and
Lablache, it would be as attractive now as it was
a hundred years ago.

We have met with another of Pergolesi's Intermezzi, called *Tracollo*, also for a male and female
performer; but it is written in a dialect intelligible
only to a Neapolitan. It seems, however, to be
very lively and amusing; and the music is in a
similar style to that of the *Serva Padrona*. In
one movement only there are parts for two oboes
and two horns ; the rest of the score being merely
for the quartet of stringed instruments.

These intermezzi were composed from the year
1730 to 1734. In 1735, on the strength of his
reputation, he was engaged to compose an opera

for the Tordinona theatre at Rome. Animated by the hope of distinguishing himself by the production of a classical work, he chose the *Olimpiade* of Metastasio, and set to work with the ardour of hope and the enthusiasm inspired by so beautiful a subject. But his hopes were cruelly, indeed fatally disappointed. The Roman audience, under the influence of some strange caprice, received his opera with the utmost coldness, while they lavished their applause upon a very inferior work, called *Nerone*, by Duni, a young composer who afterwards acquired considerable reputation in France.

Duni, who was a man of a candid and liberal spirit, was ashamed and mortified at having gained a triumph at the expense of a man whom he knew to be far superior to himself. But he had foreseen Pergolesi's failure and his own success. Having been invited to Rome to compose the second opera of the season (Pergolesi being to compose the first), he felt so strongly the superiority of Pergolesi, that he had not courage to write a note till he had heard a rehearsal of the *Olimpiade*. He then saw that Pergolesi had not hit the prevailing taste of the time, and frankly told him that his own opera would not be so good as the *Olimpiade*, but would succeed better. When he witnessed the cold reception given to Pergolesi, he declared, with honest indignation, that he was "frenetico contro il publico Romano;" and, during the few days that the *Olimpiade* languished upon the stage, he united himself to the small body of enlightened artists and *dilet-*

tanti, who were charmed with the work, in their endeavours to support it. But their efforts were vain, and Pergolesi's opera was thrown aside.

He immediately returned to Naples, mortified, and, as the event showed, broken-hearted. From that time he wrote no more for the stage, and probably would never have resumed the pen, had not the Duke of Matalon, a Neapolitan nobleman, prevailed upon him to compose a Mass and Vespers for a religious festival which was about to take place at Rome. He accordingly composed the mass, *Dixit Dominus*, and *Laudate*, which are to this day reckoned among the finest specimens of ecclesiastical music. They were performed in the church of *San Lorenzo* at Rome, and listened to with rapture. The young composer was now extolled to the skies: but the Roman public had inflicted an injury which they were unable to remedy. Their applauses came too late to counteract the effects of their cruel and unmerited coldness and neglect. His wounded spirit had preyed upon a frame naturally delicate, and he fell into a rapid consumption. His friend and patron, the Prince Stigliano, advised him to retire to a small house at Torre del Greco, a situation supposed to be beneficial in cases of pulmonary complaints. But his disease was past cure ; and, after remaining a short time in this secluded retreat, he expired at the age of thirty-three.

During his last sickness he composed his cantata of *Orfeo ed Euridice*, his *Stabat Mater*, and his

Salva Regina, which was the last of his works.
The *Stabat Mater*, a divine emanation of genius
and feeling, is still the delight of every lover of
the pure and beautiful ecclesiastical music of the
old Italian masters.   His dramatic works consist of
a single opera, the *Olimpiade*, and the *intermezzi*
which have been already mentioned.

No sooner was it known that Pergolesi was dead,
than all Italy joined in doing honour to his memory.   The *Olimpiade* was revived at Rome, and
performed with the utmost splendour ; and the
same people, who, a short time before, had received
it with indifference and neglect, now flocked in
crowds to hear it, and applauded it with enthusiasm : a memorable instance of the fickleness and
caprice of popular taste.

A story was at one time current that Pergolesi's
death was caused by poison ; but Dr. Burney, from
all the information he could acquire both at Rome
and Naples, is of opinion that it is without foundation.   There can be no doubt that Pergolesi laboured under consumption for a considerable time
before his death ; and besides, the success of his
works was not such as to make him an object of
jealousy or envy.

The *Olimpiade* was first performed in England
in 1742, when the character of Megacle was acted
by the celebrated Monticelli.   " The whole exquisite scene," says Burney, "where ' Se cerca, se
dice' occurs, was rendered so interesting by the
manner in which it was acted as well as sung by

Monticelli, that I have been assured by attentive hearers and good judges, that the union of poetry and music, expression and gesture, seldom have had a more powerful effect on an English audience." The first air in Monticelli's part, " Tremendi oscure atroci " (the words of which are not by Metastasio), was sung at concerts by Frasi for ten years at least after the run of the opera was over.

Pergolesi's music is remarkable for the exquisite grace and beauty of its melody, and its true and natural expression. The *Olimpiade* is as tender and affecting as the *Serva Padrona* is gay and comic. An absence of labour and effort seems to characterise all his productions, even those for the church. But this facility was more apparent than real; for we are informed that he composed slowly and carefully. Ease in writing is the result of consummate art: and Pergolesi might have said with Carissimi, who, like him, was celebrated for the grace and ease of his melodies, " Ah, questo facile, quanto è difficile ! " This ease and simplicity of Pergolesi's style, however, produced effects for which he certainly was not responsible. He was followed by imitators, who, by copying the thinness, and seemingly inartificial structure of his scores, without possessing the genius which could give to a few simple notes an effect beyond what could be produced by the most elaborate contrivance, rendered the music of the opera trifling and insipid.

ADOLFO HASSE is generally mentioned by Italian writers under the name of *Il Sassone.* Though a

German, he belongs entirely to the Italian school; and Count Algarotti calls his music " d'Italia l'armonia divina." He was born at Bergedorf, near Hamburg, in 1699. He learned the rudiments of music at Hamburg, and became a tenor singer at the opera of that city. The celebrated Keiser was then composer for that theatre, and Hasse took his works as the models on which he formed his own style. He afterwards obtained the situation of singer to the court and theatre of Brunswick, where he brought out his first opera, *Antigono*, when he was only eighteen years of age. He now determined to enter upon the study of his art in one of the great schools of Italy; and in 1724 went to Naples, where he at first received instructions from Porpora. He earnestly desired to profit by the lessons of Alessandro Scarlatti, but was prevented from applying for them by the want of means of remuneration. Fortunately, however, he met Scarlatti in society, and made such an impression on the venerable master by his talents, modesty, and respectful behaviour towards himself that he gave him lessons gratuitously, and treated him with the affection of a parent.

Soon afterwards he obtained the notice of a great Neapolitan banker, who employed him to compose a serenata for two voices. It was performed by Farinelli and Tesi, the greatest singers of the time; and Hasse gained so much reputation by it, that he was engaged to compose a piece for the great opera-house. This was *Sesostrate*, performed in 1726 : and it so completely established his fame, that all the great theatres of Italy disputed the advantage of having him at the head of their orchestras.   In 1727 he went to Venice, where he was appointed chapel-master to one of the conservatories; and his success in this city was increased by the interest of the celebrated Faustina, whom he afterwards married.   He remained at Venice till 1730, when he was offered the situations of chapel-master and composer to the king of Poland and elector of Saxony, with a salary of twelve thousand dollars for himself and Faustina, who was now his wife.

He remained many years in the service of the court of Dresden.   The king of Poland gave him unlimited power and ample resources, of which he availed himself to place the Dresden opera on the most complete and splendid footing.   He new-modelled the orchestra, the admirable disposition of which is minutely described by Rousseau, in his *Dictionnaire de Musique.*

He resided at Dresden till the year 1763, when the reverses experienced by the king of Poland compelled him to dismiss many persons from his employment, among whom were Hasse and his wife, who were obliged to retire upon a small pension.   He had previously suffered severely by the bombardment of Berlin by the Prussians in 1760. Among other property, all his manuscripts were destroyed ; a heavy loss, as he was about to publish a complete collection of his works, the expense of which the king had undertaken to defray. He then resided at Vienna till about the year 1775, when he retired to Venice, the birth-place of his wife. There they both ended their days in the year 1783 ; Faustina, at the age of ninety, and her husband soon afterwards at the age of eighty-four.

Dr. Burney, in his musical tour through Germany, visited Hasse and Faustina (of whose musical career we shall afterwards have occasion to speak) at Vienna in 1773, and gives some interesting particulars respecting them.

BALDASSARE GALUPPI, one of the greatest musicians of the last century, was born in 1701, in the little island of Burano near Venice, whence he received the name of Buranello. He was a pupil of Lotti. His two first operas, *La Fede nell' Inconstanza* and *Gli Amici Rivali,* were produced in 1722. He soon acquired great celebrity, and composed an immense number of operas for the principal cities of Italy.

In 1741, after Handel had ruined himself by carrying on operas in opposition to the nobility, and had abandoned the attempt, the management of the opera was undertaken by the Earl of Middlesex, who engaged Galuppi as a composer. In this capacity he remained for two or three seasons, and produced several operas, among which were *Penelope, Scipione,* and *Enrico.* He then returned to Italy; but some of his most celebrated operas were afterwards performed in London at different periods, and always with success. His *Ricimero* was performed in 1755. His comic opera, *Il Mondo della Luna*, was performed in 1760, and delighted the public, not only by the lightness and gaiety of the music, but by the admirable acting and singing of Signora Paganini. In the following year a still greater effect was produced by his *Filosofo di Campagna*. " This burletta," says Burney, " surpassed in musical merit all the comic operas that were performed in England till the *Buona Figliuola ;* and its success was proportioned to its merit."

The popularity of Galuppi's compositions in England had a perceptible influence on our own dramatic music. His airs were introduced into the English operas of the day ; and English composers imitated the Italian melody in their own productions ; a practice which, though it contributed to polish and refine their style, yet, as generally happens in the case of imitations, was carried to an extravagant excess, and English songs frequently became caricatures of Italian bravuras.

Galuppi was for many years maestro di capella of the church of St. Mark, and president of the conservatory of the *Incurabili* at Venice. In 1766 he went to Petersburgh, where he was received with great distinction ; and had just returned from thence when Dr. Burney saw him at Venice in 1770, " at which time, though near seventy years of age, he was as full of genius and fire as ever." He died at Venice in 1785, at the age of eighty-four.

Among the minor composers of this period were Feo, Terradellas, Perez, and Logroscino. Their works are now forgotten; but the last named master deserves honourable mention as inventor of the *finale*, or that species of concerted music, terminating each act of an opera, in which a portion of the business of the piece is carried on. The extent to which this species of dramatic music is now carried is one of the principal features which distinguish the opera of the present day, and has mainly contributed to throw the works of the older masters out of use.

The composers of whom some account has been given in this chapter, were the principal stars of the most numerous and brilliant constellation that ever has appeared in the musical hemisphere. They may be called a constellation, because, though they rose, reached their zenith, and set at different times, yet there was a period when the whole of them were together above the horizon. Differing, too, as they did, in individual genius, they all belonged to one great school, possessed of common qualities and characteristics.

The same period was illumined by an equally numerous, splendid, and unequalled constellation of great singers, several of whom have already been incidentally mentioned, but some of them demand more ample and regular notice.

CHAPTER XVI.

GREAT ITALIAN SINGERS DURING THE ABOVE PERIOD—TESI—
FAUSTINA—CUZZONI—FARINELLI—SENESINO.

VITTORIA TESI was born at Florence about the
year 1690.   She was a pupil of the celebrated
school of Bernacchi at Bologna.   In 1719 she was
at the opera of Dresden, where she used to sing,
all' ottava, airs for bass voices; but the compass of
her voice was so extraordinary, that no difficulty in
regard to pitch ever gave her any trouble.   She
was not remarkable for her performance of rapid
passages; but she had a grand and majestic style,
and great powers of declamation.   Though not
beautiful, she captivated everybody by the graces
of her deportment and action.   She spent the latter
part of her life at Vienna, having for many years
retired from the stage.   She died about the year
1775.   Burney gives the following particulars respecting her, which he learned at Vienna in 1770.
" The great singer, Signora Tesi, who was a celebrated performer upwards of fifty years ago, lives
here: she is now more than eighty, but has long
quitted the stage.   She has been very sprightly in
her day, and yet is at present in high favour with

the empress-queen. Her story is somewhat singular. She was connected with a certain count,
a man of great quality and distinction, whose fondness increased by possession to such a degree as to
determine him to marry her; a much more uncommon resolution in a person of high birth on the
continent than in England. She tried to dissuade
him, enumerating all the bad consequences of such
an alliance; but he would listen to no reasoning,
nor take any denial. Finding all remonstrances
vain, she left him one morning, went to a neighbouring street, and addressing herself to a poor
labouring man, a journeyman baker, said she would
give him fifty ducats if he would marry her, not
with a view to their cohabiting together, but to
serve a present purpose. The poor man readily
consented to become her nominal husband. Accordingly they were formally married; and when
the count renewed his solicitations, she told him it
was now utterly impossible to grant his request, for
she was already the wife of another,—a sacrifice
she had made to his fame and family."

FAUSTINA BORDONI, the wife of Hasse, was born
in 1693. She first appeared as a theatrical singer
at Venice in 1716. In 1725 she was at Vienna,
where she received great honours and rewards.
Apostolo Zeno, in one of his letters, describes her
brilliant success, and adds, " But whatever good
fortune or encouragement she meets with, she
deserves it all by her courteous and agreeable
manners; as well as by her talents, with which she

has enchanted and gained the esteem and affection of the whole court." He afterwards speaks of the regret expressed at Vienna, on her quitting that city to go to London. She arrived here in 1725, when Cuzzoni was in the height of her favour; and the rivalry of these sirens produced violent feuds among the patrons of the opera. After remaining in England for two seasons, she returned to Italy, and, in 1732, was married to Hasse.*

FRANCESCA CUZZONI was a native of Parma. Her first public appearance on the stage seems to have been with her rival Faustina, in 1719, at Venice. After having sung in most of the great theatres of Italy, she arrived in England in 1723, where she continued in undiminished favour till 1729, when she returned to Italy.

While Cuzzoni and Faustina were in England together, the spirit of rivalry between themselves, and of party among their patrons, was carried to an extravagant pitch. It is told by Horace Walpole, that his mother, Lady Walpole, had them at her house to sing in a concert at which an assemblage of the first people in the kingdom were present. She was under the greatest difficulty how to settle the precedence, or prevail on either to relinquish the *pas.* The knot could not be untied, but it was cut by the following expedient. Finding it impossible to prevail on the one to sing while the other was present, she took Faustina to a remote part of the house, under the pretext of

* See *antè*, page 291.

showing her some curious china, during which time the company obtained a song from Cuzzoni, who supposed that her rival had quitted the field. A similar device was practised in order to get Cuzzoni out of the room while Faustina performed.

In a short time each of the rivals found partisans among the ladies of quality, and violent animosities broke out among them. The party on each side became numerous and formidable, and the fashionable world was convulsed by their feuds. At first the heroines themselves behaved civilly to each other. Sir Robert Walpole having taken the part of Faustina, his lady, in order that Cuzzoni might not be borne down by his influence, countenanced her; and when Sir Robert was from home used to invite them both to dinner. She was at first puzzled how to adjust the precedence between them at her table; but they behaved politely, and relieved their hostess by mutual concessions. But this did not last; their mutual jealousy and hatred rose to such a height, that on one occasion, when they happened to meet in public, they actually came to blows in the presence of the company.

The Cuzzoni party was headed by the Countess of Pembroke, whose followers used to hoot whenever Faustina appeared. The *London Journal* of June 10th, 1727, says, " A great disturbance happened at the opera, occasioned by the partisans of the two celebrated rival ladies, Cuzzoni and Faustina. The contention at first was only carried on by hissing on one side and clapping on the other;

but proceeded at length to the melodious use of catcals and other accompaniments, which manifested the zeal and politeness of that illustrious assembly. The Princess Caroline was there, but neither her royal highness's presence, nor the laws of decorum, could restrain the glorious ardour of the combatants." This affair produced the following epigram:

> " Old poets sing that beasts did dance
> Whenever Orpheus play'd;
> So, to Faustina's charming voice
> Wise Pembroke's asses bray'd."

Faustina's chief friends among the ladies were the Countess of Burlington and Lady Delawar. The men were generally on her side; as she was handsomer and more agreeable than her rival.

These contentions were the more absurd, as the styles of the two singers were essentially different, and the utmost admiration of the one could be no disparagement to the other. Their qualities are thus contrasted by Tosi, their contemporary, in his *Osservazzioni sopra il Canto Figurato.* " Their merit," he says, " is superior to all praise; for with equal strength, though in different styles, they help to keep up the tottering profession from immediately falling into ruin. The one is inimitable for a privileged gift of singing, and enchanting the world with an astonishing felicity in executing difficulties with a brilliancy, I know not whether derived from nature or art, which pleases to excess. The delightful, soothing, cantabile of the other, joined to the sweetness of a fine voice, a perfect intonation, strictness of time, and the rarest productions of genius in her embellishments, are qualifications as peculiar and uncommon as they are difficult to be imitated. The pathos of the one and the rapidity of the other are distinctly characteristic. What a beautiful mixture it would be, if the excellencies of these two angelic beings could be united in a single individual ! "

The interest of the opera was greatly injured by these disputes ; and the directors fell upon a device to put an end to them by getting one of the rivals out of the way. The time for a new contract with each of them was at hand ; and, as it was known that Lady Pembroke and Cuzzoni's other patronesses had made her swear never to take a smaller salary than Faustina, the directors resolved to offer her a guinea less. To this resolution they steadily adhered : and Cuzzoni found herself ensnared by her oath into the necessity of leaving England. The following lines were written by Ambrose Philips on her departure.

> " Little syren of the stage,
> Charmer of an idle age,
> Empty warbler, breathing lyre,
> Wanton gale of fond desire ;
> Bane of every manly art,
> Sweet enfeebler of the heart ;
> O, too pleasing is thy strain,
> Hence to southern climes again !
> Tuneful mischief, vocal spell,
> To this island bid farewell ;

> Leave us as we ought to be,
> Leave the Britons rough and free."

After her return to Italy she frequently met her rival Faustina, particularly at Venice in the carnivals of 1729 and 1730 ; but they do not appear ever to have sung upon the same stage. In 1734 she came to England a second time, being engaged to sing in the opera established by the nobility in opposition to Handel; and appears to have remained for two seasons. She came to London a third time in 1750, and had a benefit concert at the Haymarket theatre ; but being now old, poor, and almost deprived of voice by infirmities, she failed to attract an audience. After this she went to Holland, where she was thrown into prison on account of her debts. Being, however, allowed to go out and sing at the theatres, though in custody, she was at length enabled to pay her debts and obtain her release. In her latter days she subsisted, it is said, by button-making, and at last died in great indigence at Bologna in 1770.

Her misfortunes were caused by her folly, caprice, and extravagance. She squandered her earnings with the most reckless profusion, and quarrelled with her best friends from the ungovernable petulance of her temper. On one occasion, when, at a rehearsal, she pertinaciously refused to sing an air, belonging to her part, in one of Handel's operas, the composer brought her to reason by threatening to throw her out of the window.

CARLO BROSCHI, surnamed FARINELLI,* was born at Andria, a small town in the territory of Naples, in 1705. He received instructions in singing from Porpora, who, discovering his extraordinary vocal powers, bestowed the utmost care upon his education. When he was seventeen, he accompanied his instructor to Rome, Porpora being engaged to compose an opera for one of the theatres of that city; and here he performed the celebrated vocal feat which at once placed him above all his competitors. In an opera which was then performed, there was a song with an *obligato* accompaniment for the trumpet, sung by Farinelli, and accompanied by a great performer on that instrument. Every night there was a contest between the singer and the trumpet-player, which gradually became more and more earnest, as the audience began to take an interest in it, and to take different sides. At length both parties seemed resolved to bring it to an issue. After each of them had swelled out a note, and tried to rival the other in brilliancy and force, they both had a swell and a shake together, in the interval of a third, which was continued so long that both seemed to be exhausted; and the trumpeter at length gave it up, imagining, probably, that his antagonist was as much spent as himself. But Farinelli, with the greatest apparent ease, and with a smile on his face, as if to show that

* It is said that he derived this *cognomen* from the circumstance of his father having been a miller, or a dealer in flour.

he had been all the while only sporting with his adversary, broke out all at once in the same breath with fresh vigour, and not only continued the swell and shake upon the note, but started off into a series of rapid and difficult divisions, till his voice was drowned by the acclamations of the audience. From that time he maintained an undisputed supremacy over all his contemporaries.

He afterwards sang in all the principal theatres in Italy, and then went to Vienna, which city he visited three times in the course of his life. He was received there with the same distinction as at other places; but he used to mention an admonition he received from the Emperor Charles VI., which he said, was of more use to him than all the precepts of his masters, or the examples of his rivals. The emperor, after listening to him one day with great admiration, told him, that in his singing he neither moved nor stood still like any other mortal;—all was supernatural : " But," he added, " these gigantic strides, these never-ending notes, are merely surprising, and it is now time that you should think of pleasing : you are too lavish of the gifts with which nature has endowed you; if you wish to reach the heart, you must take a plainer and simpler road." These few words, Farinelli said, wrought an entire change in his style. From that time he studied to be simple and pathetic, as well as grand and powerful; and thus charmed his hearers as much as he astonished them.

In the year 1734 he came to England, being
engaged to perform at the theatre in Lincoln's
Inn Fields, where the nobility's opera was carried
on, under the direction of Porpora, in opposition to
Handel.

The terms of Farinelli's engagement are not recorded; but the amount of his profits, arising from
his salary, his benefit, and presents from people of
distinction, was estimated at about 5,000*l.* a year.
To admire Farinelli became a rage, which led the
votaries of fashion, not the lovers of music, into
extravagant folly and absurdity.   Hogarth, in one
of the numbers of his *Rake's Progress*, has ridiculed
the infatuation of the hour.   He represents his hero
at his levee, surrounded by toad-eaters and hangers-
on—a bravo, a jockey, a dancing-master, a fencing-
master, and others.   A musical composer is seated
at a harpsichord, and from the back of his chair
hangs a long scroll, on which is written, "A list
of the rich presents Signor Farinelli, the Italian
singer, condescended to accept of the English nobility and gentry, for one night's performance in the
opera of Artaxerxes.   A pair of diamond knee-
buckles, presented by ————, a diamond ring,
by ————, a bank-note enclosed in a rich gold
case, by ————, a gold snuff-box, chased with
the story of Orpheus charming the brutes, by T.
Rakewell, esq., 100*l.*, 200*l.*, 100*l.*"   These were
presents mentioned in the newspapers of the day
as having been actually made.   On the floor lies
a picture representing Farinelli on a pedestal, with

an altar before him, on which are several flaming hearts. Near him stand a number of people with extended arms, offering him presents; and at the foot of the altar is a lady kneeling, with a label issuing from her mouth, on which are the words, "One God, one Farinelli,"—an impious expression really used by a lady of fashion in her affected ecstasies during his performance of one of his songs. During his engagement at the Haymarket, Sir John Hawkins says, " All the world flocked thither, even aldermen and other citizens, with their wives and daughters, to so great a degree, that in the city it became a proverbial expression, that those who had not heard Farinelli sing, and Foster * preach, were not qualified to appear in genteel company."

At the first private rehearsal after his arrival here, in Signora Cuzzoni's apartments, Lord Cooper, who acted as manager of the opera, observing that the band did not follow him, but were all gaping with wonder as if thunderstruck, desired them to be attentive; when they all confessed that they had been so overpowered with admiration and astonishment as to be unable to accompany him.†

* A celebrated Anabaptist preacher, who lectured on Sunday evenings in the Old Jewry. Pope, who knew him, and frequently went to hear him preach, thus mentions him in the *Epilogue to the Satires*:
> " Let modest Foster, if he will, excel
> Ten metropolitans in preaching well."

† This remarkable circumstance was related to Dr. Burney by one of the band.

With the exception of a short excursion to Paris in the summer of 1736, Farinelli remained in London till May 1737. During the time of his stay, he was employed in supporting the party by whom he was engaged, in their struggle against Handel; a struggle, which though unsuccessful on their part, was ruinous to the object of their hostility, and injurious to the interests of music, from the dissensions and factions to which it gave rise among the patrons of the art. Although the admiration of Farinelli's powers, among the real dilettanti, continued unabated, yet the foolish and ignorant rage caused by his arrival gave way to the excitement produced by greater novelties. " There is always such a rage for novelty at the opera," says Cibber in his *Apology*, published in 1739, " that within these two years we have seen even Farinelli sing to an audience of five-and-thirty pounds." When he left England, however, it was with the intention of returning the following year, as he had entered into an engagement to that effect with the noble managers of the opera. But this was prevented by an invitation which he received to visit the court of Spain. In his way to Madrid he sang at Paris, where, according to Riccoboni, he enchanted the French themselves, though the prejudice against Italian music and Italian singing was then at its height.

Farinelli's journey to Madrid was in consequence of an invitation from the Queen of Spain. Her husband, Philip V., laboured under a mental disease which exhibited itself in a dejection of spirits, rendering him incapable of attending to business, or of taking the ordinary care of his person. He would not even allow himself to be shaved, and remained in a state of total apathy. He had always shown great love of music, and sensibility to its effects; it was therefore determined to try its power, as a remedy for his disease; and it was with this view that the greatest singer of the age was called in as his physician.

On Farinelli's arrival, the queen contrived that there should be a concert in a room adjoining the king's apartment; and the singer performed one of his most pathetic airs. Philip appeared at first surprised, and then moved. At the end of the second air he called the singer into his chamber, loaded him with compliments and kind expressions, asked him how he could sufficiently recompense such talents, and assured him that he could deny him nothing. Farinelli, who had been previously instructed, only begged that his majesty would allow his attendants to shave and dress him, and that he would endeavour to appear in council as usual. From this time the king's disease gave way to medical treatment; and the singer had the honour (to which he was undoubtedly entitled) of the cure.

Farinelli was taken into the service of the court. A pension of about 3,000*l.* per annum was settled upon him, and he was not permitted to sing any longer in public. During the first ten years of his

residence at the court of Spain, he sang every
night to the king the same four airs, one of which
was the famous " Pallido il sole " of Hasse.   By
singing to his majesty every evening, his favour
increased to such a degree, that he was honoured
with the order of St. Jago, and acquired so much
influence that he was regarded as the king's first
minister.   Raised to such a height, most men
would have been giddy with their elevation; but
Farinelli never forgot his true position.   He remembered that he was a musician, and conducted
himself to the Spanish nobility with that proper
humility which became his situation; so that, instead of becoming an object of their jealousy and
hatred, he gained their confidence and esteem.
These sentiments were confirmed when it was observed that he kept himself entirely aloof from
every species of intrigue, and never made use of
his influence for any selfish or unworthy motive.

Several pleasing anecdotes are related of him
at this period.   One day as he was going to the
king's closet, to which he had access at all times,
he overheard an old officer of the guard curse
him, and say to another, " Honours can be heaped
on such scoundrels as this, while a poor soldier,
like myself, after thirty years' service, remains
unnoticed."   Farinelli, without seeming to hear
this reproach, took occasion to remind the king
that he had neglected an old servant, and procured
a regiment for the man who had spoken of him so
harshly.   In passing out, after leaving the king,

he gave the officer his commission, telling him that
he had heard him complain of having served thirty
years without promotion; " but," he added, " you
did wrong to accuse the king of neglecting to reward your zeal."

A circumstance, which happened to Farinelli
during the first year of his residence at Madrid,
has been made the subject of a favourite little
German opera. The singer ordered a superb suit
of clothes for a court gala, and when the tailor
brought it home, asked him for his bill. " I have
made no bill, sir," said the tailor, " nor do I intend to make one. Instead of money, I have a
favour to beg of you. I know that what I desire is
inestimable, and fit only for monarchs; but since I
have had the honour to work for a person of whom
everybody speaks with rapture, all the payment I
shall ever require is a song." Farinelli tried in
vain to prevail on the tailor to take his money.
At length, giving way to the tradesman's humble
entreaties, and probably more flattered by this tribute to his talents than by the applauses he had
received in the saloons of princes, he sat down to
the harpsichord, and sang some of his finest airs,
enjoying the pleasure and astonishment of his enchanted hearer: and the more the poor tailor
seemed charmed and affected, the more Farinelli
exerted himself in displaying every species of excellence. When he had done, the tailor thanked
him in the most rapturous and grateful manner,
and took his leave. " No, my friend," said Fari-

nelli, "I am a little proud, and it is perhaps from that circumstance that I have acquired some small superiority over other singers. I have given way to your weakness; and it is but fair that you, in your turn, should indulge me in mine." And, taking out his purse, he insisted on the tailor receiving nearly double the amount of his bill.

After the death of Philip V., Farinelli continued to enjoy the favour of his successor, Ferdinand VI., by whom he was dignified with the order of Calatrava. He persuaded that prince to establish an opera, of which he was director. He brought from Italy the best composers and singers of the time, and got his friend Metastasio to write for this theatre.

On the death of Ferdinand, Farinelli was dismissed from his employment and obliged to leave Spain; but his pension was still continued. Charles III., the brother and successor of Ferdinand, was not only without taste for music, but had a positive dislike to it, and would not suffer a voice or an instrument to be heard in his palace. He ordered Farinelli to return to Italy; but, by a strange caprice, stipulated, in consideration of Farinelli's retaining his pension, that he should not return to Naples, but should spend the remainder of his days at Bologna. It was with much sorrow that he left the country in which he had lived four-and-twenty years, and in which he had formed many friendships and connexions. There cannot be a stronger proof of the prudence

and moderation of his character than the circumstance of his having been so many years the chief
favourite of the sovereign, a situation in itself
sufficiently obnoxious, without having incurred
odium or made himself enemies.

Dr. Burney, who visited Farinelli at Bologna in
1770, and was hospitably entertained by him,
describes him as tall and thin, but by no means
infirm, and younger in appearance than Dr. Burney expected. He had long left off singing, but
amused himself still on the harpsichord and *viol
d'amour*. He had a number of harpsichords made
in different countries, which he had named, according to the place they held in his favour, after the
greatest of the Italian painters. His first favourite
was a pianoforte, made at Florence so early as the
year 1730, on which was inscribed in gold letters,
Raffaelle d'Urbino; then he had a Correggio, a
Guido, a Titian, and others. He played a considerable time upon his Raphael with great judgment and delicacy. He had a sister living in his
house with her two children, one of whom was an
infant, and he was dotingly fond of it, though it
was cross, sickly, homely, and unamiable: " a con-
vincing proof," says Burney, " among others, to
me, that he was designed by nature for family
attentions and domestic comforts."

He was always most polite and attentive to the
English who visited him in his retirement, and
seemed to remember the kindness and favour of
individuals, more than the neglect of the public

during the last year of his residence in London. When the Marquis of Carmarthen paid him a visit, on being told that he was the son of his patron and friend the Duke of Leeds, Farinelli threw his arms round his neck and embraced him with tears of joy. He died at Bologna in 1782, in the seventy-seventh year of his age.

It is evident from the whole tenor of Farinelli's life, that he was a man of a powerful and well-regulated mind, and of a very amiable disposition. During the whole of Metastasio's life, he was that great poet's principal correspondent; and the topics discussed in their letters, frequently involving nice and profound speculations on the principles of poetry and music, show that the one, as well as the other, was possessed of an enlarged and cultivated understanding. As a singer, there is every reason to believe, from all that can be gathered from contemporary accounts, that he has never yet been surpassed. In respect to the execution of musical passages, though he transcended any notion that had previously been formed of the powers of the human voice, and though it would seem that the composers of those times were unable to invent passages sufficiently difficult to display his force and rapidity, yet the utmost difficulties of this kind which he achieved, (as may be seen by the passages of execution in his *bravura* songs), are within the reach of any ordinary singer of the present day. But none of his successors, it may be confidently said, has excelled him, or even equalled him, in beauty of voice and skill in its management, in truth of intonation, in purity of style, and, above all, in the power of moving the feelings of his hearers. Of this power a most striking illustration is afforded by an incident which would have appeared incredible had he not confirmed its truth to Dr. Burney. When Senesino and he were in England at the same time, they had not for some time an opportunity of hearing each other, in consequence of their engagements at different theatres. At last, however, they were both engaged to sing on the same stage. Senesino had the part of a furious tyrant, and Farinelli that of an unfortunate hero in chains; but, in the course of the first air, the captive so softened the heart of the tyrant, that Senesino, forgetting his stage-character, ran to Farinelli and embraced him in his own.

FRANCESCO BERNARDI, commonly called SENESINO, was born at Sienna, about the year 1680. We first hear of him as a celebrated singer when he was at Dresden, in the year 1719. The Italian opera of that city was then on a splendid footing, and the company consisted of the greatest singers of the time. According to Quantz,* who heard Senesino at that time, he had a powerful, clear, equal, and sweet *contralto* voice, with a perfect intonation and an excellent shake. His manner of singing was masterly and his elocution unrivalled. Though he never loaded *adagios* with too many ornaments, yet he delivered the original and essen-

* Burney's State of Music in Germany, vol. ii.

tial notes with the utmost refinement. He sang *allegros* with great fire, and marked rapid divisions, from the chest, in an articulate and pleasing manner. His countenance was well adapted to the stage, and his action was natural and noble. To these qualities he joined a majestic figure; but his aspect and deportment were more suited to the part of a hero than of a lover.

When the establishment for the performance of operas in London, under the title of the Royal Academy of Music, was set on foot by a body of the nobility and gentry in 1720, Handel, who was commissioned to form a company, hearing of the splendour of the Dresden opera, took a journey to that city, and engaged Senesino and several other members of the company. He was the principal singer in Handel's operas till the year 1726, when he found it necessary, from the state of his health, to go to Italy. In 1730 he returned to England, and resumed his situation at the Haymarket. When the musical quarrels broke out, which ended in the establishment of an opera, in 1733, in opposition to Handel, Senesino became a member of the hostile company: but Farinelli being engaged by the same party in 1734, Senesino soon afterwards left England. He retired to his native country of Tuscany, and died about the year 1750.

CHAPTER XVII.

CAFFARELLI—GIZZIELLO—CARESTINI—GUARDUCCI—DURASTANTI —GUADAGNI—MINGOTTI—GABRIELLI—WANT OF TENOR AND BASS SINGERS.

CAFFARELLI, or CAFFARIELLO, was born in 1703. He was the son of a Neapolitan peasant, and his name was Gaetano Majorano, though he is commonly known by the above surname. His natural gifts attracted the notice of Porpora, who gave instructions at the same time to him and to Farinelli, whose origin was equally obscure. Porpora, it is said, taught him in a very extraordinary manner. For a period of five years he permitted him to sing nothing but a series of scales and exercises, all of which he wrote down successively on a single sheet of paper. In the sixth year he proceeded to give his scholar instructions in articulation, pronunciation, and declamation. Caffarelli submitted without a murmur to this unexampled discipline; though, even at the end of six years, he imagined he had got a very little way beyond the mere rudiments of the art: but, to his astonishment, his master one day thus addressed him:— " Young man, you may now leave me. You have nothing more to learn from me, and are the greatest singer in the world." This story has been repeated by the best informed writers, and, no doubt, is founded in truth, though with much exaggeration. A slow and progressive method of tuition is certainly the only way to produce excellence; but this seems to be carrying the principle to a most extravagant length. None but a plodding drudge, without a spark of genius, could have submitted to a process which would have been too much for the patient endurance even of a Russian serf; or if a single spark had existed at first, it must have been extinguished by so barbarous a treatment.

Be this, however, as it may, Caffarelli did become one of the greatest singers of his time, though he did not arrive rapidly at the height of his fame. His first appearance in public was at Rome, in 1726; and he gained such reputation in Italy, that he was engaged, in 1738, to supply the place of Farinelli at the London opera-house. He was not very successful here. He had to contend with the disadvantage arising from the remembrance, yet recent, of Farinelli's wonderful powers; and he was never well, or in good voice, during the time he remained in London, which was only a single season.

At a subsequent period Caffarelli was looked upon as Farinelli's rival, and many critics considered him the greater singer of the two. Among these was Porpora, who had been master to both. Though he could not bear the insolence of Caffarelli's disposition, he used to say that he was the greatest singer that Italy had ever produced. At the marriage of the king of Sardinia, then prince of Savoy, with the infanta of Spain, who had long been Farinelli's scholar, it was with great difficulty that Caffarelli was prevailed upon to go to Turin to sing at the royal nuptials. Being obliged to go by an order of the king of Naples, he was sullen and not disposed to exert himself, saying, that he had lost his book of closes on the road, and should be able to do nothing. This was told to his Sardinian majesty, who did not well know how to treat such impertinence, Caffarelli not being his subject. But, on the first night of performance, the prince of Savoy went behind the scenes, as the opera was going to begin, and said to Caffarelli that he was very happy to see him, though his princess thought it hardly possible that any singer could give him pleasure after Farinelli. " Now, Caffarelli," added the prince, clapping him on the shoulder, "do exert yourself a little, and cure the princess of this prejudice in her master's favour." Caffarelli's vanity was piqued; " Sir," he exclaimed, " her highness shall to-night hear two Farinellis in one!" and, exerting all his faculties, he sang in a manner which produced acclamations of delight and astonishment.

He went to Vienna in 1749. Metastasio, in one of his letters to Farinelli, gives an account of his reception in the Austrian capital.

" You will be curious," says the poet, " to know how Caffarelli has been received. The wonders related of him by his adherents had excited expectations of something above humanity; but the first night he absolutely displeased everybody. He said he was so oppressed and disconcerted by the presence of their imperial majesties that he could not recover himself; and, indeed, in the subsequent representations he regained his credit so much, that some of the nobility and gentry now exalt him to the firmament, and even go so far as to make heretical comparisons. There are, however, innumerable critics, who find his voice strong, but false, screaming and disobedient; so that he can do nothing considerable without forcing it, and when forced it becomes harsh and disagreeable. They say he has no judgment, and that by frequently attempting what he is unable to execute he leaves it unfinished; that he has an old-fashioned and bad taste; and that they can discover in his graces the antique and stale flourishes of Nicolini and Matuccio. They maintain that he treads the stage abominably; that in the recitatives he is an old nun; and that in all he sings there is a whimsical tone of lamentation sufficient to sour the gayest allegro. They allow that he can sometimes please excessively, but say that these happy moments are uncertain, and depend on the caprice of his voice and temper, and do not make amends for the suffering produced by his imperfections. You will be pleased to observe that I only quote, but do not decide; on the contrary, I protest to you that I have all the esteem for the performer which he merits. The failure of the first night, the diversity of opinions, and the little appearance there is of his having acquired the favour of your august patroness, a princess whom you know to be an exquisite judge of music, have humbled him so extremely, that from his present modesty and resignation you would not know him. If he continues in this disposition, I hope he will acquire many of those suffrages which were at first refused him."

His arrogance and turbulent spirit, however, speedily revived, and produced a *fracas* of which Metastasio gives the following lively account in one of his letters to the Princess di Belmonte.

" In exchange for the musical news with which your excellency has honoured me concerning our amiable friend Monticelli, I shall give you some military tidings of our valiant Caffarelli, who a few days ago gave public proofs of his being no less a votary of Mars than of Apollo. For my misfortune I was not present at these warlike feats, but the following is a most faithful narrative.

" The poet of this theatre is a Milanese young man, descended from very worthy parents ; but inconsiderate, a great admirer of the fair sex, despising money, and as deficient in judgment as he is rich in talent. To this young author the managers of the theatre have entrusted the whole arrangements of the stage. I know not whether it proceeded from rivalry in abilities or in personal beauty, but the poet and the singer have all along been on the *qui vive,* and have treated each other

with sneers and sarcasms.   At length Migliavacca
(the poet) issued orders for a rehearsal of the opera
in preparation.   All the performers obeyed the
summons except Caffarelli ; he appeared, however,
at the end of the rehearsal, and asked the company, with a very disdainful air, what was the use
of these rehearsals ?   The conductor answered, in
a voice of authority, that no one was accountable
to him for what was done ; that he ought to be glad
that his failure in attendance had been suffered ;
that his presence or absence was of little consequence to the success of the opera, but that whatever he chose to do himself, he ought at least to
let others do their duty.   Caffarelli, in a great rage,
exclaimed that he who had ordered such a rehearsal
was a solemn coxcomb.   At this all the patience
and dignity of the poet forsook him ; and getting
into a towering passion, he honoured the singer
with all those glorious titles which Caffarelli had
earned in various parts of Europe, and slightly
touched, but in lively colours, some of the most
memorable particulars of his life : nor was he likely
soon to come to a close ; but the hero of the pane-
gyric, cutting the thread of his own praise, boldly
called out to his eulogist, ' Follow me, if thou
hast courage, to a place where there is none
to assist thee !' and, moving towards the door,
beckoned to him to come out.   The poet hesitated
a moment, and then saying with a smile, ' Truly
such an adversary makes me blush ; but come
along, since it is a Christian act to chastise a fool

or a madman,'— advanced to take the field. But Caffarelli, who had flattered himself, perhaps, that the muses would not be so valiant, or imagined that, according to the rules of the criminal law, a delinquent ought to be punished *in loco patrati delicti,* changed his first resolution of seeking another field of battle, and intrenching himself behind the door, drew his bright blade, and presented its point to the enemy. Nor did the other refuse the combat—

> ' Ma fiero anch' egli il rilucente acciaro
> Liberò dalla placida guarina.'

The by-standers tremble; each calls on his tutelar saint, expecting every moment to see poetical and vocal blood besprinkle the harpsichords and double basses. But at length, the Signora Tesi, rising from under her canopy, where till now she had remained a most tranquil spectator, walked with a slow and stately step towards the combatants; when—O sovereign power of beauty !—the frantic Caffarelli, even in the fiercest paroxysm of his wrath, captivated and appeased by this unexpected tenderness, runs with rapture to meet her, lays his sword at her feet, begs pardon for his error, and generously sacrificing to her his vengeance, seals, with a thousand kisses upon her hand, his protestations of obedience, respect, and humility. The nymph signifies her forgiveness by a nod; the poet sheathes his sword; the spectators begin to breathe again; and the tumultuous assembly breaks up amid the joyous sounds of laughter.

In collecting the numbers of the wounded and the slain, none was found but the poor copyist, who, in trying to part the combatants, had received a small contusion in the clavicula of the foot, from an involuntary kick of the poet's Pegasus. Next day the battle was commemorated in an anonymous sonnet; and soon after an answer was produced by the belligerent poet. I hope to procure a copy of both to enclose in this epistle. To-day the German comedians are to represent this extraordinary event on the stage. They say that already not a place is to be had for love or money, and it is not yet twelve o'clock. I should like to be one of the audience, if I had an invisible ring."

Caffarelli's success at Vienna does not appear to have been equal to his deserts as an artist. His conceit and self-sufficiency must have created an unfavourable impression; and Metastasio's opinion, we may suppose, was in some degree influenced by the circumstance that Caffarelli looked upon himself, and was looked upon by others, as the rival of Farinelli, to whom the poet was so greatly attached.

Mr. Garrick, who heard Caffarelli at Naples in 1764, when he was turned of sixty, thus speaks of him in a letter to Dr. Burney: " Yesterday we attended the ceremony of making a nun; she was the daughter of a duke, and the whole was conducted with great splendour and magnificence. The church was richly ornamented, and there were two large bands of music of all kinds. The consecration was performed with great solemnity, and I was very much affected; and to crown the whole, the principal part was sung by the famous Caffarelli, who, though old, has pleased me more than all the singers I ever heard. He *touched* me; and it is the first time I have been touched since I came into Italy."

Caffarelli spent his latter days at Naples, in the enjoyment of a large fortune which he had made by his profession. He resided in a magnificent house which he had built for himself, and over the door of which he had placed this inscription: "*Amphion Thebas, ego domum.*" He bought a dukedom, to be possessed after his own decease by his nephew, who accordingly became Duca di Santi Dorato. Caffarelli died in 1783, in his eightieth year.

GIZZIELLO (whose name was CONTI) was engaged by Handel, and came to England in 1736. Though then a young man, he had gained great reputation in Italy; but such were his modesty and diffidence, that when he first heard Farinelli at a private rehearsal, he burst into tears, and fainted away from despondency. He was in London for two seasons, and received with much favour. His voice was then a very high soprano, and his style remarkable for pathos, delicacy, and refinement. His manner of singing is said to have had a considerable effect in modernising the character of Handel's opera airs.

When Gizziello first sang at Rome, before he came to England, his performance was considered so admirable that it became the subject of conversation throughout Italy. Caffarelli, who was then at Naples, and at the height of his fame, was so struck by what he heard of the young singer, that he seized the first opportunity, when he could be spared from the opera, of going to Rome to hear him. He travelled post all night, and arriving at Rome the following evening, entered the pit wrapped up in a cloak, and unknown to anybody. Gizziello sang; and, when he had done, Caffarelli cried out with a loud voice, " Bravo, bravissimo, Gizziello ! e Caffarelli che ti lo dice !' and, immediately quitting the theatre, set out the same night on his return to Naples.

After leaving England, Gizziello pursued his studies so diligently and successfully, that he even contested the palm with Farinelli at Madrid. He was at Lisbon during the earthquake in 1775: and his mind was so deeply impressed by the horror of that tremendous visitation, that he retired into a monastery, where he ended his days.

CARESTINI first appeared at Rome in 1721. In 1723 he was at Prague, during the great musical performances there, on the occasion of the coronation of the emperor Charles VI., as king of Bohemia ; on which occasion an opera was performed in the open air, in which the chorus consisted of a hundred voices, and the orchestra of two hundred instruments. He came to England in 1733, being engaged by Handel to supply the place of Senesino, who, with almost the whole of

Handel's company, had deserted him and joined the rival establishment set on foot by the nobility. Carestini remained about seven years in England ; a proof of the estimation in which he was held. After leaving England he sang for many years in Italy, Germany, and Russia, with the highest reputation. He died about the year 1758. " Carestini's person," says Burney, " was tall, beautiful, and majestic. He was a very animated and intelligent actor; and having a considerable portion of enthusiasm in his composition, with a lively and inventive imagination, he rendered everything he sung interesting by good taste, energy, and judicious embellishments. He manifested great agility in the execution of difficult divisions from the chest in a most articulate and admirable manner."

Among the principal singers of this period was GUARDUCCI, a pupil of the famous Bolognese school of singing conducted by Bernacchi. Guarducci came to England in 1767, and remained for several seasons. He was then somewhat in years, tall and awkward in his figure and an inanimate actor; circumstances which at first created a prepossession against him ; but his merit at length was recognised. " He soon discovered," says Burney, " that a singer could not captivate the English by tricks or instrumental execution, and told me some years after that the gravity of our taste had been of great use to him." The English are as liable to be caught by tricks of execution as their neighbours ; but it would rather appear that

Guarducci's powers of execution were insufficient
to produce this effect. " He was," continues Burney, " the plainest and most simple singer, of the
first class, I ever heard. All his effects were produced by expression and high finishing, nor did he
ever aim at execution." Such qualities will be
appreciated by all hearers, however much they
may be dazzled by the performance of brilliant
difficulties.

MARGHERITA DURASTANTI was engaged by
Handel at the same time with Senesino, and came
with him to England. She sang in the operas
composed by Handel, Buononcini, and Attilio
Ariosti, till the year 1723, when she quitted England, finding herself unable to contend with the
superior powers of Cuzzoni. She took a formal
leave of the English nation, by singing on the stage
the following song, written for her by Pope, at
the desire of her patron the Earl of Peterborough.

> " Generous, gay, and gallant nation,
>   Bold in arms and bright in arts ;
> Land secure from all invasion,
>   All but Cupid's gentle darts !
> From your charms, oh who would run ?
> Who would leave you for the sun ?
>
>   Happy soil, adieu, adieu !
>   Let old charmers yield to new ;
>   In arms, in arts, be still more shining ;
>   All your joys be still increasing,
>   All your tastes be still refining,
>   All your jars for ever ceasing :
>   But let old charmers yield to new ;
>   Happy soil, adieu, adieu ! "

This effusion was thus burlesqued by Arbuthnot:—

> " Puppies, whom I now am leaving,
>   Merry sometimes, always mad,
> Who lavish most when debts are craving,
>   On fool, on farce, and masquerade !
> Who would not from such bubbles run,
> And leave such blessings for the sun ?
>
>   Happy soil, and simple crew !
>   Let old sharpers yield to new.
> All your tastes be still refining ;
> All your nonsense still more shining :
>   Blest in some Berenstadt or Boschi,*
>   He more awkward, he more husky ;
> And never want, when these are lost t' us,
> Another Heidegger and Faustus.
>   Happy soil, and simple crew !
>   Let old sharpers yield to new !
>   Bubbles all, adieu, adieu ! "

In the *Evening Post* of 7th March, 1721, there
is the following paragraph: " Last Thursday his
majesty was pleased to stand godfather, and the
princess and the Lady Bruce godmothers, to a
daughter of Mrs. Durastanti, chief singer in the
opera-house. The Marquis Visconti for the king,
and the Lady Lichfield for the princess." This
circumstance deserves mention, as a remarkable
indication of the respect which was paid in the
highest quarters to this lady's private character.

CATERINA MINGOTTI was born at Naples about
the year 1726. Her father, an officer in the Austrian service, carried her, in her infancy, into Ger-

* Two favourite singers of the day.

many; and, being soon afterwards left an orphan, she was placed by an uncle in a convent at Gratz in Silesia, where her fine voice and ardent love of music induced the abbess to give her a musical education. When she was fourteen, she was left, by the death of her uncle, in a destitute situation, and was soon afterwards induced to marry Signor Mingotti, manager of the opera at Dresden, a man advanced in years. At Dresden she attracted the notice of Porpora, who procured an engagement for her at the theatre, where, it is said, her performance made so great an impression, that the celebrated Faustina was impelled by jealousy to leave Dresden. The fame she acquired in that city procured for her an invitation to Naples, where she first appeared in Aristea, in the *Olimpiade*, composed by Galuppi, and gained prodigious applause, not only by her singing, but the new reading which, as an actress, she gave the character.

From Naples she returned to Dresden, and afterwards went to Madrid, where she sang, with Gizziello, in the operas, under the direction of Farinelli, who was so rigid in his restrictions, that he would not allow her to sing anywhere but in the opera at court, or even to practise in a room next the street. She was requested to sing at private concerts by many of the Spanish nobility, but could not obtain permission from the opera-director, who carried his rigour so far as to deny a pregnant lady of high rank the pleasure of hearing her, though she was unable to go to the theatre, and declared that she *longed* for a song from Mingotti. In Spain this species of mental malady is treated with the utmost attention. The lady's husband complained to the king of Farinelli's obduracy, which, he said, might be fatal to his wife and his child; and the consequence was a royal mandate, ordering Mingotti to receive the lady at her house and gratify her longing.

After remaining two years in Spain, Signora Mingotti came to England in 1754, and excited unbounded admiration. She soon engaged in disputes with Vaneschi, the manager of the opera, which occasioned violent feuds and animosities in the musical world, almost every person of fashion thinking it necessary, in supporting that character, to side with one or other of the parties.

Many amusing anecdotes are told of the absurdities committed, under the influence of this musical mania, by the votaries of *ton*. Mrs. Fox Lane, afterwards Lady Bingley, a warm patroness of Mingotti, desirous to enlist in her cause the Hon. General Crewe, gave him one day a long history of the disputes between the singer and the manager, appealing to him for his judgment on so momentous a subject. The general listened with much seeming attention; but when she thought him sufficiently impressed with the wrongs of Signora Mingotti, he asked her very quietly, " And pray, madam, who is Signora Mingotti ?"—" Get out of my house ?" cried the lady in a passion, "you shall never hear her sing another note at my

concerts, as long as you live." — Admission to
Mrs. Lane's concerts, at which Mingotti and the
famous violinist Giardini used exclusively to perform, was considered, like the *entrée* to Almack's
at present, as the conclusive stamp to the character of a person of fashion.   There was no
sacrifice or mortification to which fashionable
people would not submit in order to obtain it;
" And," says Burney, " *la Padrona della casa* lost
but few opportunities of letting them know the
value she set on her invitations, by using them like
dogs when they were there.   Whenever a benefit
was in contemplation for one of her *protégés*, taking
care of the honour of her guests, she obliged them
to behave with due gratitude and munificence on the
occasion.   ' Come !' she would say to her friends,
' give me five guineas,'—a demand as implicitly
obeyed as if made on the road.   Nor had any one,
who wished ever to be admitted into such good
company again, the courage to ask the occasion of
the demand; but patiently waited to know the
lady's pleasure to tell them whether they should be
honoured with a ticket to Giardini's or Mingotti's
benefit."

Vaneschi having become bankrupt and left the
country, Giardini and Mingotti were foolish enough
to undertake the management of the opera, which
brought them both, as it has done many others, to
the brink of ruin.   Mingotti left England in 1758,
and afterwards sang at the principal cities in Italy.
In 1763 she established herself at Munich, where

she was residing when Dr. Burney visited that city in 1772. Her ruinous speculation in London had swallowed up the fortune she had previously made by her exertions; and her income was barely sufficient, with economy, to support her respectably. "She seemed," Burney says, "to live very comfortably, was well received at court, and esteemed by all who were able to judge of her understanding and enjoy her conversation. It gave me great pleasure," he adds, "to hear her speak concerning practical music, which she does with as much intelligence as any maestro di capella with whom I ever conversed. Her knowledge in singing, and powers of expression, in different styles, are still amazing, and must delight all such as can receive pleasure from song, unconnected with the blandishments of youth and beauty. She speaks three languages, German, French, and Italian, so well that it is difficult to say which of them is her own. English she likewise speaks, and Spanish, well enough to converse in them, and understands Latin; but in the three languages first mentioned she is truly eloquent."

As a singer and actress, Dr. Burney thus describes her: "Her style of singing was always grand, and such as discovered her to be a perfect mistress of her art. She was a most judicious and complete actress, extending her intelligence to the poetry and every part of the drama; yet her greatest admirers acknowledged that her voice and manner would have been still more irresistible, if

she had possessed a little more feminine grace and
softness."

The last star which we shall enumerate in this
vocal constellation, is the celebrated CATERINA
GABRIELLI—celebrated not less for the singularity
of her character than for her powers as a singer.
She was the daughter of a cardinal's cook, and
thence acquired the appellation (after the Italian
fashion) of *La Cuochetina.* She was a pupil of
Porpora's; and at an early age made herself remarkable throughout Italy for her extraordinary
talents, and her capricious and untractable disposition. She was engaged to go to Madrid in 1758,
on which occasion Metastasio gave his friend Farinelli the following account of her. " The amusing
stories which you hear from Italy concerning our
Signora Gabrielli are but too true: she is young,
an Italian, favoured by nature, and of transcendent
abilities in music; so that it is not surprising that,
like other sirens, she should be capricious. But in
your hands I hope she will be more prudent. She
is perfectly aware of her own merit, and yet extremely timid. In order to moderate her impetu-
osity, it will be necessary, perhaps, to impress her
mind with great respect for, or rather positive fear
of, the sovereign and the court; but that this may
not depress her spirits too much in performance,
you should likewise encourage her by your approbation and the applause of your friends; and I assure you she will deserve it. Indeed you are a
more expert pilot than I, and I have no doubt will

turn your skill to good account. At Vienna, Milan, and Lucca, where this young singer was dexterously managed, she enchanted everybody who heard her; but at Padua, where they tried to use the whip more than the spur, they threw away their money." We do not learn how far, or how successfully, Farinelli availed himself of these hints of the good-natured poet.

Brydone, in his Tour through Sicily and Malta, gives an ample and entertaining account of this singular person. " The first woman," says this agreeable writer, " is Gabrielli, who is certainly the greatest singer in the world, and those who sing in the same theatre must be capital, otherwise they never can be attended to. This, indeed, has been the fate of all the performers, except Pacchierotti, and he too gave himself up for lost on hearing her performance. It happened to be an air of execution, exactly adapted to her voice, in which she exerted herself in so astonishing a manner, that, before it was half done, poor Pacchierotti burst out a crying, and ran in behind the scenes, lamenting that he had dared to appear on the same stage with so wonderful a singer, where his small talents must not only be lost, but where he must ever be accused of presumption, which he hoped was foreign to his character. It was with some difficulty they could prevail upon him to appear again; but from an applause well merited, both from his talents and modesty, he soon began to pluck up a little courage; and in the singing of a tender air, even she herself, as well as the audience, is said to have been moved.

"The performance of Gabrielli is so generally known and admired, that it is needless to say anything to you on that subject. Her wonderful execution and volubility of voice has long been the admiration of Italy, and has even obliged them to invent a new term to express it; and would she exert herself as much to please as to astonish, she might almost perform the wonders that have been ascribed to Orpheus and Timotheus; but it happens, luckily perhaps for the repose of mankind, that her caprice is, if possible, even greater than her talents, and has made her still more contemptible than these have made her celebrated. By this means, her character has often proved a sufficient antidote both to the charms of her voice and those of her person, which are, indeed, almost equally powerful; but if these had been united to the qualities of a modest and an amiable mind, she would have made dreadful havoc in the world. However, with all her faults, she is certainly the most dangerous syren of modern times, and has made more conquests, I suppose, than any one woman breathing. It is but justice to add, that, contrary to the generality of her profession, she is by no means selfish or mercenary, but, on the contrary, has given many singular proofs of generosity and disinterestedness. She is very rich, from the bounty, as is supposed, of the last emperor, who was fond of having her at Vienna: but she was at

last banished that city, as she has likewise been
most of those in Italy, from the broils and squab-
bles that her intriguing spirit, perhaps, still more
than her beauty, had excited.

" There are a great many anecdotes concerning
her that would not make an unentertaining volume,
and, I am told, are, or will soon be, published.
Although she is considerably upwards of thirty, on
the stage she scarcely appears to be eighteen; and
this art of appearing young is none of the most
contemptible she possesses.   When she is in good
humour, and really chooses to exert herself, there
is nothing in music I have ever heard, to be
compared to her performance; for she sings to the
heart as well as to the fancy, when she pleases,
and she then commands every passion with unbounded sway.   But she is seldom capable of
exercising these wonderful powers; and her caprice
and her talents, exerting themselves by turns, have
given her all her life the singular fate of becoming
alternately an object of admiration and contempt.
Her powers in acting and reciting are scarcely
inferior to those of her singing: sometimes a few
words in the recitative, with a simple accompaniment, produce an effect that I have never been
sensible of from any other performer, and incline
me to believe what Rousseau advances on this
branch of music, which with us is so much
despised.   She owes much of her merit to the
instruction she received from Metastasio, particularly in acting and reciting; and he allows that

she does more justice to his operas than any other actress that ever attempted them.

" Her caprice is so fixed and stubborn, that neither interest, nor flattery, nor threats, nor punishments have the least power over it; and it appears that treating her with respect and contempt have an equal tendency to increase it. It is seldom that she condescends to exert these wonderful talents; but most particularly if she imagines that such an exertion is expected. And instead of singing her airs as other actresses do, for the most part she only hums them over, *a mezza voce:* and no art whatever is capable of making her sing when she does not choose it. The most successful expedient has ever been found, to prevail on her favourite lover (for she always has one) to place himself in the centre of the pit or the front box; and if they are on good terms, which is seldom the case, she will address her tender airs to him, and exert herself to the utmost. Her present inamorato promised to give us this specimen of his power over her. He took his seat accordingly; but Gabrielli, probably suspecting the connivance, would take no notice of him; so that even this expedient does not always succeed. The viceroy, who is fond of music, has tried every method with her to no purpose. Some time ago he gave a great dinner to the principal nobility of Palermo, and sent an invitation to Gabrielli to be of the party. Every other person arrived at the hour of invitation. The viceroy ordered dinner to be put back, and sent to let her know that the company waited her. The messenger found her reading in bed. She said she was sorry for having made the company wait, and begged he would make her apology, but that really she had entirely forgot her engagement. The viceroy would have forgiven this piece of insolence, but when the company came to the opera, Gabrielli repeated her part with the utmost negligence and indifference, and sang all her airs in what they call *sotto voce*, that is, so low that they can scarcely be heard. The viceroy was offended; but as he is a good-tempered man, he was loth to make use of authority; but at last, by a perseverance in this insolent stubbornness, she obliged him to threaten her with punishment in case she any longer refused to sing. On this she grew more obstinate than ever, declaring that force and authority should never succeed with her; that he might make her cry, but never could make her sing. The viceroy then sent her to prison, where she remained twelve days; during which time she gave magnificent entertainments every day, paid the debts of all the poor prisoners, and distributed large sums in charity. The viceroy was obliged to give up struggling with her, and she was at last set at liberty amidst the acclamations of the poor.

" Luckily for us, she is at present in good humour, and sometimes exerts herself to the utmost of her power. She says she has several times been on terms with the manager of our opera, but thinks she shall never be able to pluck up resolution enough to go to England. What do you think is her reason? It is by no means a bad one. She says she cannot command her caprice, but for the most part it commands her; and that there she could have no opportunity of indulging it. For, says she, were I to take it into my head not to sing, I am told the people there would certainly mob me, and perhaps break my bones; now I like to sleep in a whole skin, although it should even be in a prison. She alleges, too, that it is not always caprice that prevents her from singing, but that it often depends upon physical causes. And this, indeed, I can readily believe: for that wonderful flexibility of voice, that runs with such rapidity and neatness through the most minute divisions, and produces almost instantaneously so great a variety of modulation, must surely depend on the very nicest tone of the fibres. And if these are in the smallest degree relaxed, or their elasticity diminished, how is it possible that their contractions and expansions can so readily obey the will as to produce these effects? The opening of the glottis which forms the voice is extremely small, and in every variety of tone its diameter must suffer a sensible change; for the same diameter must ever produce the same tone. So wonderfully minute are its contractions and dilatations, that Dr. Keil, I think, computes that in some voices its opening, not more than the tenth of an inch, is divided into upwards of twelve

hundred parts, the different sound of every one of
which is perceptible to an exact ear. Now, what a
nice tension of fibres must this require ! I should
imagine even the most minute change in the air
must cause a sensible difference, and that in our
foggy climate the fibres would be in danger of
losing this wonderful sensibility, or at least that
they would very often be put out of tune. It is
the same case with an ordinary voice, where the
variety of divisions run through, and the volubility
with which they are executed, bear no proportion
to those of Gabrielli." *

* The public do not make sufficient allowance for the extreme delicacy of the vocal organs of great singers. Signora
Mingotti told Burney, that " she was frequently hissed by the
English for having the toothache, a cold, or a fever, to which
the good people of England will readily allow every human
being to be liable, except an actor or a singer." Our vocal
performers are constantly twitted with *theatrical* ailments, as
if they, of all people in the world, can never have an illness
unless there is a design in it ; and are thus inconsiderately
treated with great injustice. Look at the life of an Italian
prima donna—Madame Grisi, for instance—during the London season ; her continual and seemingly indefatigable exertion, night after night, and morning after morning, at operas,
concerts, rehearsals, and musical parties at the houses of the
great, exposed to the effects of heated rooms and chilling
draughts, and suffering, moreover, under those influences of
our climate which are so strongly felt by the " children of
the south." Observe, at the same time, with what steadiness
she goes through her various labours, and how very seldom
the public have to complain of disappointment ; and we shall
be convinced that no class of persons are less apt than great
singers to allow even real indisposition to interfere with the
fulfilment of their duties.

Notwithstanding her dread of the English public, however, Gabrielli came to London in 1775. She, did not make so great an impression as she ought to have done; for, though no longer young, she had neither lost her beauty nor her vocal powers. " She had no indications," says Burney, " of low birth in her countenance or deportment, which had all the grace and dignity of a Roman matron. Her reputation was so great before her arrival in England, for singing and caprice, that the public, expecting perhaps too much of both, was unwilling to allow her due praise in her performance, and too liberal in ascribing everything she said and did to pride and insolence. It having been reported that she often feigned sickness, and sang ill when she was able to sing well, few were willing to allow she could be sick, or that she ever sang her best when she was here; and those who were inclined to believe that sometimes she might perhaps have exerted herself in pure caprice, thought her voice on the decline, or that fame, as usual, had deviated from the truth in speaking of her talents. Her voice, though of an exquisite quality, was not very powerful. As an actress, though of low stature, there were such grace and dignity in her gestures and deportment as caught every unprejudiced eye; indeed she filled the stage and occupied the attention of the spectators so much, that they could look at nothing else while she was in view. Her freaks and *espiègleries*, which had fixed her reputation, seemed to have been very much subdued before her arrival in England. In conversation she seemed the most intelligent and best-bred *virtuosa* with whom I had ever conversed; not only on the subject of music, but on every subject concerning which a well-educated female, who had seen the world, might reasonably be expected to have obtained information. She had been three years in Russia previous to her arrival in England, during which time no peculiarities of individual character, national manners, or court etiquette, had escaped her observation. In youth, her beauty and caprice had occasioned a universal delirium among her young countrymen, and there were still remains of both sufficiently powerful, while she was in England, to render credible their former influence." Soon after leaving England she retired to Bologna, where she spent the remainder of her life in tranquillity.

Besides the singers of whom some account has now been given, many others (some of them of hardly inferior pretensions) might be enumerated as being the immediate disciples of the great Italian schools in the beginning of the last century. Among these may be mentioned the names of Valentini, Guadagni, Amorevoli, Monticelli, Manzoli, Raaf, Signora Strada, and Signora Frasi.

It is to be remarked, that, during the period when the Italian school of singing was in its most flourishing state, the principal male performers were possessed of *soprano* or *contralto* voices. In the operas of that time, subordinate parts only were written for tenor or base voices, and given to performers of inferior note. In several of Handel's Italian operas, written for our stage, there are parts for a bass, which were performed by Roschi, a singer of ability, though it does not seem that he had any reputation on the continent. When Handel, in 1729, formed a company for the performance of Italian operas, and announced their names in the newspapers, he said that there was "a bass voice from Hamburgh, there being none worth engaging in Italy." This bass voice belonged to a singer of the name of Reimschneider, and there were two other German singers, Reinhold and Waltz, whose names are attached to the bass parts in the published music of several Italian operas performed in London. Parts for a tenor voice are of very rare occurrence : and the only tenor singer belonging to the Italian school of the period in question, who acquired any great degree of celebrity, was Raaf, a native of Germany. At a time when the hero or the lover was a *soprano* or a *contralto*, the tenor must necessarily have been excluded, except in the very rare instances where parts for these different voices could be introduced without interfering with each other, and producing an incongruous effect. In tyrants, old men, or rough and harsh characters, the bass voice could be appropriately introduced: but it would seem that nothing more was required from the performance than force and energy, without any of the polish and cultivation which have been attained by the bass-singers of more recent times.

CHAPTER XVIII.

THE ITALIAN OPERA ESTABLISHED IN ENGLAND — HANDEL'S
RINALDO—CALYPSO AND TELEMACHUS—GALLIARD—ANASTASIA
ROBINSON—AMADIGI—THE CONTRIVANCES—THE ROYAL ACA-
DEMY OF MUSIC — ITS FIRST COMPOSERS AND SINGERS—
RADAMISTO—ASTARTO — MUZIO SCEVOLA — OPERA SUBSCRIP-
TIONS—GRISELDA—BONONCINI—ARIOSTI—NEGLECT OF THE
ITALIAN OPERA — TOLOMEO RÉ D'EGITTO — CLOSE OF THE
ROYAL ACADEMY OF MUSIC—OPERA CONDUCTED BY HEIDEG-
GER AND HANDEL—NEW SINGERS ENGAGED—PARTHENOPE—
THE NOBILITY'S OPERA — OPPOSITION TO HANDEL —RUINOUS
CONSEQUENCES TO HIM — HE ABANDONS DRAMATIC COMPOSI-
TION — CHRONOLOGICAL LIST OF HIS ITALIAN OPERAS—HIS
PUBLISHED OPERAS — OBSERVATIONS ON HANDEL'S ITALIAN
MUSIC—OPERAS OF CONTEMPORARY COMPOSERS — DECLINE OF
THE ITALIAN OPERA ABOUT THE MIDDLE OF THE EIGHTEENTH
CENTURY.

THE establishment of the Italian opera in England may be dated from the arrival of Handel, and the appearance of his first opera, *Rinaldo*, which (as has been mentioned in a previous chapter) took place in 1711. From that time, Italian operas, by him and the most distinguished composers of the day, were regularly performed by complete Italian companies ; and such were their attractions, that the English opera, for a time, was almost entirely abandoned.

Rinaldo, though inferior to many of Handel's subsequent operas, was beyond comparison the most masterly work of this description that had been heard in England. The airs are generally antiquated in their form ; and the phrases of melody have been so often repeated by subsequent composers, that they now appear hackneyed and common. To imagine their effect when originally produced, it is necessary to keep in view the state of music at that time : and this remark is generally applicable to music of an old date, especially if it is of a melodious and popular kind. One air, however, in this opera, furnishes a remarkable exception ;—the air " Furie terribile," sung by Armida. It is a wild burst of passion, full of the force and energy of Gluck, whose style, too, it resembles in its brevity, and the want of the eternal *da capo* of Handel's days. There is an impassioned air in this opera, " Il tricerbero humiliato," which became so popular from Nicolini's singing, that it was adapted to a bacchanalian song beginning " Let the waiter bring clean glasses," and long sung at convivial meetings throughout the kingdom. In the published music of the opera, the words of this jovial ditty are joined to the air, in addition to the original Italian words ! The music (besides the dialogue in recitative) consists entirely of airs, with one duet, and a chorus by way of *finale*, a trivial and flimsy production.

This opera, with repetitions of *Hydaspes* and *Almahide*, and two operas, *Antiochus* and *Hamlet*,

both of them written by Apostolo Zeno, and composed by Gasparini, supplied the stage for a couple
of seasons. In 1712, another attempt was made to
produce an English opera. This was *Calypso and
Telemachus*, written by Mr. Hughes, and composed
by Mr. Galliard. Mr. Hughes assigned as a reason
for this attempt, that "it could never have been
the intention of those who first promoted the Italian
opera, that it should take entire possession of our
stage, to the exclusion of everything of the like
kind that could be produced here."—" Though the
English language," he further says in his preface,
"is not so soft and full of vowels as the Italian, it
does not follow that it is therefore incapable of
harmony. It is certainly of great importance in
dramatic entertainments that they should be performed in a language understood by the audience;
and though the airs of an opera may be heard with
delight, as instrumental pieces, without words, yet
it is impossible that the recitative should give
pleasure when the words are either taken away or
unintelligible."

In pursuance of these views, Mr. Hughes constructed his opera in the Italian form, with the
dialogue in recitative. The piece was well written,
and the songs possessed of poetical merit. Mr.
Galliard, too, was an able composer, and competent
to do justice to the music: but, whether from the
piece being wanting in interest and dramatic effect,
or from the inferiority of the singers, or from the
unfitness of the English language for dialogue in

recitative, the opera supported but five representations, and these only at intervals. After the third
performance, Nicolini appeared in *Antiochus* for
the last time previous to his departure for Italy, as
was then imagined, for ever. Mr. Addison, in the
Spectator for June 14th, 1712, says, "I am sorry
to find by the opera-bills for this day, that we are
likely to lose the greatest performer in dramatic
music that is now living, or that perhaps ever
appeared upon a stage. I need not acquaint my
readers that I am speaking of Signor Nicolini.
The town is highly obliged to this excellent artist
for having shown us the Italian music in its perfection, as well as for that generous approbation he
lately gave to an opera of our own country, in
which the composer endeavoured to do justice to
the beauty of the words, by following that noble
example which has been set him by the greatest
foreign masters in that art."—This little bit of
puff seems to have done *Calypso* little good : for,
after two performances more, it was finally laid
aside.

This opera deserved a better fate, if we may
judge from the printed music, which contains a
number of beautiful things. Some of the airs are
loaded with long divisions, which could have been
no objection to them at that time : but others are
so graceful and expressive, and in so pure a taste,
that they cannot fail to give pleasure at any time.
The opening air, "For thee the rilling waters
flow," sung by Calypso, is full of tender melan-

choly, and has some fine descriptive passages in the accompaniments. There is a great deal of passion throughout this part. The opera concludes with an air by Calypso, expressive of her despair at being forsaken, and ending with a burst of grief, " O that Calypso too could die ! " The high note sustained for two bars is the very cry of agony, and given by such a singer as Margherita de l'Epine, who performed the part, ought to have produced a powerful effect. The air in the part of Minerva, " See these golden beams," is a noble composition, and would still make an excellent concert song. There are, indeed, many things in this opera which are worthy the attention of our best singers even at this day.

John Ernest Galliard, the composer of this opera, was a native of Zell, and came to England, in the suite of Prince George of Denmark, in the capacity of a performer on the oboe. He spent the remainder of his life in this country; and, notwithstanding his want of success in the above instance, became a popular composer for the theatres in Lincoln's Inn Fields and Covent-garden. His hunting song, " With early horn," was long in great vogue at the theatres and concerts, and is still well known to the lovers of old English melody. At his last benefit, in 1746, among other compositions of his that were performed, was a piece for twenty-four bassoons and four double-basses. He died in 1749.

In 1714, the celebrated ANASTASIA ROBINSON

made her first appearance as a dramatic singer. This lady was the daughter of a portrait painter, of a good family in Leicestershire. She at first learned music as an accomplishment: but her father, being afflicted with a disease in his eyes which terminated in blindness, and, being thus rendered unable to support his family by the exercise of his art, thought of availing himself of his daughter's extraordinary disposition for music, by educating her for it as a profession. She accordingly received instructions in Italian, and in the different branches of music, from the first teachers of the time. Her general improvement was not neglected, and she acquired those accomplishments which add grace and elegance to the female character. To these advantages she added a considerable share of beauty, and a cheerful and engaging disposition; so that she had become a general favourite in a respectable circle of society, even before her entrance into public life. Her first appearances as a vocalist were at concerts, where she used to accompany herself on the harpsichord. She soon gained the favour of the public, and the countenance and patronage of some persons of high rank; and her father, encouraged by her success, took a house in Golden-square, where he established a weekly concert, or musical *conversazione*, which was much frequented by people of taste and fashion.

Her first appearance at the Italian opera was in an opera called *Creso*, the music of which seems to

have been a *pasticcio*, or compilation from the
works of various composers of the time. She next
appeared, the same season, in *Arminio*, an opera by
an anonymous composer. From this period, till
the year 1724, she continued to occupy a principal
situation at the opera, with increasing reputation
and applause. Her salary, Dr. Burney says, was
1000*l.*, and her emoluments by benefits and presents were estimated at nearly as much more.
She quitted the stage, and the exercise of her profession, in consequence of a private marriage with
the Earl of Peterborough, who made himself so
celebrated by his brilliant exploits at the head of
the British troops in Spain during the war of the
Succession.

Dr. Burney has inserted in his History an account of this lady, and of the circumstances connected with her marriage, communicated to him by
Mrs. Delany, Lady Peterborough's contemporary
and intimate friend. It is very pleasing, and must
necessarily be authentic.

" Mrs. Anastasia Robinson," says Mrs. Delany,
" was of a middling stature, not handsome, but of
a pleasing, modest countenance, with large blue
eyes. Her deportment was easy, unaffected, and
graceful. Her manner and address very engaging,
and her behaviour, on all occasions, that of a gentlewoman, with perfect propriety. She was not only
liked by all her acquaintance, but loved and
caressed by persons of the highest rank, with
whom she appeared always equal, without assum-

ing. Her father's house, in Golden-square, was frequented by all the men of genius and refined taste of the times. Among the number of persons of distinction who frequented Mr. Robinson's house, and seemed to distinguish his daughter in a particular manner, were the Earl of Peterborough and General H————. The latter had shown a long attachment to her, and his attentions were so remarkable, that they seemed more than the effects of common politeness; and as he was a very agreeable man and in good circumstances, he was favourably received, not doubting but that his intentions were honourable. A declaration of a very contrary nature was treated with the contempt it deserved, though Mrs. A. Robinson was very much prepossessed in his favour.

" Soon after this, Lord Peterborough endeavoured to convince her of his partial regard for her; but, agreeable and artful as he was, she remained very much upon her guard, which rather increased than diminished his admiration and passion for her. Yet still his pride struggled with his inclination; for all this time she was engaged to sing in public, a circumstance very grievous to her; but, urged by the best of motives, she submitted to it, in order to assist her parents, whose fortune was much reduced by Mr. Robinson's loss of sight, which deprived him of the benefit of his profession as a painter.

" At length Lord Peterborough made his declaration to her on honourable terms. He found it would be vain to make proposals on any other, and as he omitted no circumstance that could engage her esteem and gratitude, she accepted them, as she was sincerely attached to him. He earnestly requested her keeping it a secret till a more convenient time for him to make it known, to which she readily consented, having a perfect confidence in his honour.

" Mrs. A. Robinson had a sister, a very pretty accomplished woman, who married Dr. Arbuthnot's brother. After the death of Mr. Robinson, Lord Peterborough took a house near Fulham, in the neighbourhood of his own villa at Parson's-green, where he settled Mrs. Robinson and her mother. They never lived under the same roof, till the earl, being seized with a violent fit of illness, solicited her to attend him at Mount Bevis, near Southampton, which she refused with firmness, but upon condition that, though still denied to take his name, she might be permitted to wear her wedding ring; to which, finding her inexorable, he at length consented.

" His haughty spirit was still reluctant to the making a declaration that would have done justice to so worthy a character as the person to whom he was now united; and indeed his uncontrollable temper and high opinion of his own actions made him a very awful husband, ill suited to Lady Peterborough's good sense, amiable temper, and delicate sentiments. She was a Roman Catholic, but never gave offence to those of a contrary opinion, though very strict in what she thought her duty. Her excellent principles and fortitude of mind supported her through many severe trials in her conjugal state. But at last he prevailed on himself to do her justice, instigated, it is supposed, by his bad state of health, which obliged him to seek another climate, and she absolutely refused to go with him unless he declared his marriage. Her attendance on him in this illness nearly cost her her life.

"He appointed a day for all his nearest relations to meet him at the apartment over the gateway of St. James's palace, belonging to Mr. Poyntz, who was married to Lord Peterborough's niece, and at that time preceptor of Prince William, afterwards Duke of Cumberland. He also appointed Lady Peterborough to be there at the same time. When they were all assembled, he began a most eloquent oration, enumerating all the virtues and perfections of Mrs. A. Robinson, and the rectitude of her conduct during his long acquaintance with her, for which he acknowledged his great obligation and sincere attachment, declaring he was determined to do her that justice which he ought to have done long ago, which was, presenting her to all his family as his wife. He spoke this harangue with so much energy, and in parts so pathetically, that Lady Peterborough, not being apprised of his intentions, was so affected that she fainted away in the midst of the company.

"After Lord Peterborough's death, she lived a

very retired life, chiefly at Mount Bevis, and was seldom prevailed on to leave that habitation but by the Duchess of Portland, who was always happy to have her company at Bulstrode, when she could obtain it, and often visited her at her own house.

" Among Lord Peterborough's papers, she found his memoirs, written by himself, in which he declared he had been guilty of such actions as would have reflected very much upon his character, for which reason she burnt them. This, however, contributed to complete the excellency of her principles, though it did not fail giving offence to the curious inquirers after anecdotes of so remarkable a character as that of the Earl of Peterborough."

Lord Peterborough's declaration of his marriage took place in 1735, and he died at Lisbon the same year. Lady Peterborough died in 1750.

Anastasia Robinson's voice was a *contralto*. From the airs written for her by Handel and other composers, it appears that it was of small compass, and that her powers of execution were not great. Her success must be ascribed to an expressive simplicity in her style of singing, and her agreeable qualities as an actress.

Handel's next opera, *Amadiga*, or *Amadis of Gaul*, was first performed on 25th May, 1715. The music of this piece was never published, but Dr. Burney, who examined the MS. score, describes it as containing many beauties. The principal characters were performed by Nicolini (who had returned to England) and Anastasia Robinson. For several seasons this was the only new production of any importance.

During this period no English operas were attempted, but some little musical entertainments, or afterpieces, appear to have been brought forward. One of these was *The Contrivances,* a musical farce, the words and music of which were by HENRY CAREY. It was first performed in 1715, and was very successful. " Arethusa," says the *Biographia Dramatica,* " used to be the probationary part for female singers before they were bold enough to venture upon characters of more consequence: a mode of conduct which would be more serviceable to the stage than beginning, as is usual now, with stepping on the top round of the ladder at once, a circumstance which precludes ascension and includes the danger of a fall." Nothing, indeed, can be more absurd or more disadvantageous to themselves, than the course which has been generally followed by aspirants to theatrical fame. Every unfledged actor must take his first flight in Hamlet, Othello, or Macbeth ; and Mandane, as being the greatest and most difficult part in our musical drama, has been especially chosen for the *début* of young female vocalists. How many promising commencements of this sort have been followed by total disappointment !

In 1717, an attempt was made to call the attention of the public to English operas, by the performance of *Camilla* and *Thomyris,* at the little theatre in Lincoln's Inn Fields, entirely by English singers, except Margherita de L'Epine ; but the experiment was unsuccessful. From this time there was an intermission for some years in the performance of Italian operas, so that London appears to have been without any musical dramatic entertainments till the establishment of the Italian theatre, called the Royal Academy of Music, in 1720.

This establishment was the result of a plan formed by a number of distinguished members of the aristocracy, for patronising and carrying on the Italian opera. A fund of 50,000*l.* was raised by subscription, among the first personages of the kingdom, his majesty, George I., contributing 1,000*l.* The subscribers were incorporated into a society or company, whose affairs were conducted by a governor, deputy governor, and twenty directors. The first year the Duke of Newcastle was governor ; Lord Bingley, deputy governor ; and the directors were the Dukes of Portland and Queensberry, the Earls of Burlington, Stair, and Waldegrave, Lords Chetwynd and Stanhope, Generals Dormer, Wade, and Hunter, Sir John Vanburgh, Colonels Blathwayt and O'Hara, and James Bruce, Thomas Coke of Norfolk, Conyers D'Arcy, Brian Fairfax, George Harrison, William Pulteney, and Francis Whitworth, Esquires.

These gentlemen proceeded in their enterprise with great spirit. Handel, who at that time was residing with the Duke of Chandos at Cannons, was engaged as composer, and commissioned to procure singers; and Bononcini and Attilio Ariosti, composers of reputation on the continent, were also engaged to write operas. Handel immediately proceeded to Dresden, where Italian operas were then performed with great splendour at the court of Augustus, king of Poland and elector of Saxony; and there he engaged Senesino, Berenstadt, Boschi, and Signora Durastanti.

The first opera composed by Handel for the Royal Academy of Music was *Rhadamisto*, written by Haym, a work superior to any which the composer had yet produced in this country. " It seems," says Burney, " as if he was not insensible of its worth; as he dedicated the book of the words to the king, George I., subscribing himself his majesty's ' most faithful subject;' which, as he was neither a Hanoverian by birth, nor a native of England, seems to imply his having been naturalised here by a bill in parliament." Whether Handel was, or was not, naturalised in England, *de jure*, he certainly was so *de facto*, by an uninterrupted residence of half a century in this country, where he arrived a youth of five-and-twenty, and where, at the age of seventy-five, he closed his life full of years and honour.

Bononcini, Handel's celebrated rival in dramatic composition, produced his first opera, *Astarto*, in the same year. It had great success, and was frequently performed for several seasons; though, on an examination of the music, it does not seem to have deserved the favour with which it was received.

The next novelty was the opera of *Muzio Scevola*, remarkable from the circumstance of being the joint production of the three composers, Handel, Bononcini, and Ariosti. It has been said that the division was made by the directors of the Royal Academy, for the purpose of trying the abilities of the different composers, and of deciding which of them was deserving of preference. But there seems no ground for any other supposition than that the expedient was adopted for the sake of despatch. No step was consequently taken by the directors, implying a preference of any of the supposed competitors; and all three continued, for several years afterwards, to compose operas for this theatre.

Notwithstanding the efforts of three great composers, aided by the strongest company of performers that had ever been assembled in England, the Royal Academy of Music did not prosper. About 15,000*l.* of the capital subscribed was spent in the course of little more than a year from the establishment of the academy; and the subscribers appear to have become very reluctant to answer the calls made upon them, as appears from the advertisements published by the directors in the newspapers, urging the payment of the instalments in arrear, and threatening the defaulters with " the utmost rigour of the law." A new mode of subscription was therefore adopted. Intimation was made to the public, that tickets for the ensuing season should be issued on these terms; that each subscriber, on the delivery of his ticket, should pay ten guineas; that, on the 1st of February ensuing, each subscriber should pay a further sum of five guineas, and five guineas more on the 1st of May. The Academy promised fifty performances, and obliged themselves to allow a deduction proportionably, in case they did not give that number. This announcement, which was made on the 25th of November 1721, was the origin of the plan of an annual subscription, free from all risks or demands beyond its amount, which has been followed ever since.

The comparative merit of Handel and Bononcini became the subject of violent disputes in the fashionable circles. The Italian composer, though far inferior to his illustrious rival, was a man of great merit, and had a large body of warm partisans. Swift, who bestows a passing lash on many of the follies of his day, ridiculed the dissensions on this subject.

> " Some say that Signor Bononcini
> Compared to Handel 's a mere ninny;
> While others say that, to him, Handel
> Is hardly fit to hold a candle.
> Strange, that such difference should be
> 'Twixt tweedle-dum and tweedle-dee !"

Bononcini's *Griselda*, the best opera he produced in this country, was brought out in 1722, and had a very great run. The character of the patient heroine was represented by Anastasia Robinson, whose performance of this part is said to have completed her conquest of the heart of Lord Peterborough. The drama, written by Rolli, and founded on the well-known legend, is pleasing and interesting; and the airs, though frequently disfigured by the flounces and furbelows of the day, have a great deal of sweetness, elegance, and expression. His accompaniments have not the depth and solidity of those of Handel; but they are free and brilliant, and contain pretty effects by means of wind instruments, particularly the oboes. An examination, in short, of the score of *Griselda* (the only one we have seen of this author's) convinces us that Bononcini was by no means undeserving of the favour he enjoyed in his lifetime; though his reputation has suffered with posterity from his name being always associated, much to its disadvantage, with that of Handel.

GIOVANNI BATTISTA BONONCINI (or BUONONCINI) was a native of Modena. Long before his arrival in England he had distinguished himself as a composer both in Italy and Germany; and was also known in this country by the music of *Camilla*, adapted to English words by Haym. In 1720 he was in high reputation as a dramatic composer at Rome, when he was invited to London by the directors of the Royal Academy of Music. He continued in London, maintaining a respectable footing as composer for the opera-house, even while Handel was producing his finest dramatic works, till 1727, when his last opera, *Astyanax*, was produced. After this time a pension of 500*l.* a-year was settled on him by the Duchess of Marlborough, by whom he had been always warmly patronised; and he was received by her into her house, where he lived in ease and affluence, presiding at the duchess's concerts, and gaining large sums by the publication of his compositions. He fell into discredit, however, by publishing, as his own, a madrigal which was discovered to have been composed by Lotti, of Venice. The work was claimed by its true author : and a correspondence took place between him and the secretary of the Royal Academy, in the course of which Lotti produced such evidence of the madrigal being his, that Bononcini stood convicted of the theft. After this discovery his reputation suffered so much, that soon afterwards, in 1733, he left England. It is said that he quitted this country along with a notorious impostor who, under the title of Count Ughi, had obtained a footing in the fashionable circles, and pretended to possess the art of making gold. Bononcini became his dupe, and was persuaded to share his fortunes ; but the connexion does not appear to have subsisted long; for, a few years after leaving England, Bononcini was at Paris, subsisting by the exercise of his profession. At the conclusion of the peace of Aix-la-Chapelle in 1748, he was invited to Vienna by the emperor to compose the music for the rejoicings on that occasion ; and afterwards went to Venice, in company with Monticelli, where they were both engaged for the ensuing carnival. This is the last account we have of him; neither the dates of his birth nor of his death being recorded. His *eighth* work, a book of chamber duets, was published (according to Burney) at Bologna, in 1691. If we suppose that he was then no more than thirty, he must, in 1748, have been eighty-seven. When in England, he was in the habit of calling himself a very old man ; an assertion which, being seemingly contradicted by his appearance and activity, was ascribed to an unaccountable affectation. But the date of the above publication corroborates it, and gives countenance to what Dr. Burney says was the general opinion, that Bononcini's life was extended to nearly a century.

ATTILIO ARIOSTI, the third member of this musical triumvirate, maintained a respectable position in England, though his music was not so much in vogue as that of Bononcini. Like that composer, Ariosti was a veteran when he arrived in this country. We find his name among the Italian composers as early as 1696. He composed several operas for the Royal Academy of Music, the last of which, *Vespasiano*, which appeared in 1724, was the best and most successful. Burney describes this opera as having considerable merit ; and says that " Attilio seems to have been a perfectly good harmonist, who had treasured up much good music in his head, but had little invention." The *bravura* air, composed for Senesino, given by Burney as a specimen, though full of what he properly calls " the vocal fopperies of the times," is well constructed, and contains some remarkably pretty and ingenious imitations in the accompaniment. We have no account of Ariosti's life after his departure from England.

The Royal Academy of Music closed its existence in 1728. Notwithstanding the zeal with which its musical management was conducted by Handel, the series of beautiful works which he himself furnished, and the efforts of the first performers of the age, the affairs of this establishment never prospered. The annual receipts were always below the expenditure; so that constant demands were made upon the subscribers of the original capital of 50,000*l.*, the whole of which was thus called up and expended in less than seven years. The decline of the Italian opera, during this period, may be ascribed to various causes; one of them certainly was, the rivalries which existed among Handel's principal singers, especially Faustina and Cuzzoni, and the foolish violence with which the leaders of fashion took part in their quarrels, in place of joining (as they ought to have done) in supporting an entertainment to which both these rivals contributed their talents, without paying any regard to petty jealousies, which never would have been indulged in, had they not been so absurdly instigated and abetted. The public, too, had begun to grow weary of an entertainment, the character and beauties of which were, as yet, but little understood in England, and which had been supported exclusively by the aristocracy, more for the sake of fashion than from any real taste for the Italian musical drama. The appearance of the *Beggar's Opera*, which at once became the rage among all classes, was an additional cause of the neglect of the Italian theatre.

A letter by the celebrated Dr. Arbuthnot, in the *London Journal* of March 23, 1728, gives a good view of the state of musical taste at that time. " As there is nothing," he says, " which surprises all true lovers of music more than the neglect into which the Italian operas are at present fallen, so I cannot but think it a very extraordinary instance of the fickle and inconstant temper of the English nation; a failing which they have been always endeavouring to cast upon their neighbours in France, but to which they themselves have just as good a title, as will appear to any one who will take the trouble to consult our historians." He goes on to notice the childish eagerness with which we had at first discarded our own language and music for the Italian, which, the instant we had acquired it in perfection, served only to raise disputes among us and divide the nation into parties, proving that our excessive fondness for Italian operas proceeded, not from a true taste for good music, but from a mere affectation of it; and he concludes thus: "The *Beggar's Opera* I take to be a touchstone to try British taste on, and it has accordingly proved effectual in discovering our true inclinations, which, however artfully they

may have been disguised for a while, will one
time or another start up and disclose themselves.
Æsop's story of the cat, who at the petition of her
lover was changed into a fine woman, is pretty
well known; notwithstanding which alteration, we
find that, upon the appearance of a mouse, she
could not resist the temptation of springing out of
her husband's arms to pursue it, though it was on
the very wedding-night.   Our English audience
have been for some time returning to their cattish
nature, of which some particular sounds from the
gallery have given us sufficient warning.   And
since they have so openly declared themselves, I
must only desire that they will not think they
can put on the fine woman again just when they
please, but content themselves with their skill in
caterwauling.—For my own part, I cannot think it
would be any loss to real lovers of music, if all
those false friends who have made pretensions
to it only in compliance with the fashion, would
separate themselves from them; provided our
Italian opera could be brought under such regula-
tions as to go on without them.   We might then
be able to sit and enjoy an entertainment of this
sort, free from those disturbances which are frequent in English theatres, without any regard, not
only to performers, but even to the presence of
majesty itself.*   In short, my comfort is, that

* This evidently alludes to the disgraceful *row* in the opera-
house a few months before, when the fashionable partisans of
Faustina and Cuzzoni converted the theatre into a bear-garden,

though so great a desertion may force us so to contract the expenses of our operas, as would put an end to our having them in as great perfection as at present, yet we shall be able at least to hear them without interruption."

In 1728 Handel brought out his *Tolomeo Rè d'Egitto*, the last opera he composed for the Royal Academy of Music. In his dedication to the Earl of Albemarle, he implores that nobleman's protection for operas in general, as being "on the decline." Notwithstanding its merit, it was performed only seven times. The parties who had embarked in the establishment now refused to come under any new engagements for carrying it on: and, at the end of the season, when the theatre closed, the company broke up, and the performers went abroad in search of other engagements.

In the same year, Handel, finding the Italian opera no longer supported by its former patrons, entered into an engagement with Heidegger, who was then in possession of the opera-house, to carry it on at their own risk. He set out for Italy in autumn 1728, where he engaged a new company of singers, who, however, did not arrive in London till the autumn of the following year. Their arrival was thus announced to the public in the *Daily Courant :*—"Mr. Handel, who is just returned from Italy, has contracted with the following persons to perform in the Italian operas: Signor Bernacchi,

unrestrained by the presence of the princess Caroline. See *antè*, p. 299.

who is esteemed the best singer in Italy. Signora Merighi, a woman of a very fine presence, an excellent actress, and a very good singer, with a counter-tenor voice. Signora Strada, who hath a very fine treble voice, a person of singular merit. Signor Annibale Pio Fabri, a most excellent tenor, and a fine voice. His wife, who performs a man's part well. Signora Bertoldi, who has a very fine treble voice; she is also a very genteel actress, both in men and women's parts. A bass voice from Hamburgh, there being none worth engaging in Italy." This bass singer, whose name was not mentioned, was John Gottfreid Reimschneider.

These performers, announced in this pompous and ridiculous style (no doubt by Mr. Heidegger), formed a very inferior company to that of the Royal Academy of Music, which comprised Senesino, Faustina, Cuzzoni, and Anastasia Robinson. None of them were of first-rate talents. Bernacchi owes his posthumous fame, not to his own vocal powers, but to the celebrated school of singing which he founded at Bologna. Strada, though a good singer, was unable to make any impression after Faustina and Cuzzoni; and her figure was so much the reverse of handsome, that she was usually called *the pig*. None of the others had acquired, or deserved, any celebrity; and Handel was singularly injudicious, or unfortunate, in the execution of his mission.

Whether from this cause, or a continued indifference on the part of the public towards the Italian opera, the new undertaking did not flourish, although Handel exerted all the powers of his genius in its support. *Parthenope*, one of the finest of his operas, which was first performed in February 1730, had only seven representations in the course of the season. In order to strengthen the company, Senesino was again engaged, though Handel and he had previously been on bad terms. The re-engagement of this singer was unfortunate for Handel; for their former differences were renewed, and went on increasing till they terminated in a total breach in 1733. The people of fashion, as was usual in those days, took part in these disputes; and the result was an association of a body of the nobility and gentry to carry on Italian operas in opposition to Handel. This party opened a subscription for performing operas at the theatre in Lincoln's Inn Fields; invited Porpora as composer and conductor; and engaged a powerful company, comprising Senesino and Cuzzoni.

In order to make head against this opposition, Handel again repaired to Italy to engage performers, a task in which he appears to have been by no means skilful. At Bologna he heard Farinelli and Carestini, the latter of whom he unaccountably preferred; and his opponents, availing themselves of his error, immediately engaged Farinelli. The two rival establishments continued to be carried on, the one in the Haymarket and the other in Lincoln's Inn Fields, till 1735; when Handel's contract with Heidegger having expired, he left the Haymarket, and removed to Covent-garden, while " the nobility" took possession of the Haymarket theatre.

Handel made the most strenuous efforts to contend against the weight of aristocratic influence; and though a large portion of the nobility were opposed to him, he had the support of the king and the royal family. The king subscribed a thousand pounds towards carrying on the operas at Coventgarden the first season; and their majesties and their family several times visited the theatre. By their struggle, the two hostile establishments only ruined themselves and each other; and at the end of the season of 1737, both of them were broken up. The appetite for Italian music, never very great or general, had now become palled by satiety; and the English ballad operas, now frequently performed, were more congenial to the general taste of the public.

By this contest Handel for the time was ruined, having spent, in the course of it, the whole fortune, to the extent of ten thousand pounds, which he had previously accumulated. Both his body and mind sank under his distresses. In the spring of 1737, apologies were made in the newspapers for his absence from the theatre, on the score of indisposition, which was ascribed to rheumatism. But he laboured under deep depression of spirits, and had a stroke of palsy. In this condition he was removed to Tunbridge, and afterwards to Aix-la-Chapelle, where he derived so much benefit from the waters, or rather from a life of tranquillity, that he was able to return to London in November with renovated health and spirits.

Heidegger had now resumed the management of the theatre in the Haymarket, which had been abandoned by the nobility; and Handel again joined him. The affairs of the opera went on as calamitously as before; and Handel, after another vigorous but unavailing struggle, brought out, on the 10th of January, 1740, the opera of *Deidamia*, the last work he ever composed for the stage. Though one of the best of his dramatic productions, it was performed only three times; but the public were less inexcusable on this occasion than they had been on some previous ones; for the company did not contain a single first-rate performer, and were quite incapable of doing it justice.

Here, at the age of fifty-six, Handel terminated his labours as a dramatic composer; but it was to follow the much more glorious career which has raised him to unrivalled and unapproachable greatness.

From 1711 to 1740 inclusive, Handel composed thirty-five Italian operas for the English stage: a greater number than those of all the other composers put together, which were performed in London during that period. The following is a chronological list of them:

Rinaldo, first performed in 1711	Amadigi (Amadis of	
Il Pastor Fido . . 1712	Gaul) . . . 1715	
Teseo (Theseus) . 1713	Radamisto . . 1720	

Muzio Scevola	.	. 1721	Poro (Porus)	.	. 1731
Floridante	.	. ——	Ezio (Ætius)	.	1732
Ottone (Otho)	.	. 1723	Sosarme	.	. ——
Flavio .	.	. ——	Orlando	.	. 1733
Giulio Cesare	.	. 1724	Ariadne	.	. 1734
Tamerlano	.	. ——	Ariodante	.	. 1735
Rodelinda .	.	. 1725	Alcina	.	. ——
Scipione	.	. 1726	Atalanta	.	. 1736
Alessandro	.	——	Arminio	.	. 1737
Admeto	.	. 1727	Giustino	.	——
Riccardo Primo .	.	——	Berenice .	.	. ——
Siroe	.	. 1728	Faramondo .	.	1738
Tolomeo (Ptolemy)	.	——	Serse (Xerxes) .	.	——
Lotario .	.	. 1729	Imeneo (Operetta)		1740
Partenope .	.	. 1730	Deidamia	.	——

Of these operas, the following, as far as we have
been able to discover, are those which were published: — *Rinaldo, Radamisto, Floridante, Otho,
Flavio, Giulio Cesare, Tamerlano, Rodelinda, Scipione, Alessandro, Admeto, Riccardo Primo, Siroe,
Lotario, Partenope, Poro, Ezio, Sosarme, Orlando,
Atalanta,* and *Deidamia.* They were all printed
by Walsh, the well-known publisher of that day;
and many copies of them are still in existence.
Of the others which, from their not having been
printed entire, may be supposed to have been less
successful, many of the most favourite pieces were
published in various collections. One of these is
" Apollo's Feast," in four volumes, containing "the
favourite songs out of all Mr. Handel's operas;"
and another is " Twelve Duets, collected out of
all the late operas composed by Mr. Handel;"
both printed by Walsh: and the favourite songs

in Ptolemy, Amadis, and Theseus, were also published. The manuscript scores of the whole, we
believe, are preserved in the king's library.

It is much to be lamented that Handel's Italian
operas, the rich fruits of his genius during thirty
years of his life, are now, and must in a great
measure ever be, lost to the world. They never
were known out of England; and even in England, in consequence of the changes which took
place in the structure and style of dramatic music,
they were soon laid aside and forgotten. That
they should cease to be performed on the stage
was a necessary result of these changes: but it by
no means follows that an immense body of vocal
music, of the highest class, and full of imperish-
able beauties, should be consigned to oblivion.

It would profit nothing to enter into any detailed review of forgotten dramatic pieces which
no supposable revolution in public taste can ever
have the effect of reviving. As might be expected
from Handel's sense and judgment, the poems on
which he employed his genius were generally (if
not uniformly) possessed of merit. They are
generally upon striking heroic or romantic subjects, affording ample scope for dramatic effect and
musical expression; and, represented as they were
by the greatest performers of the time, they must
have given as much delight as ever has been
afforded by the musical drama.

But whatever pleasure they must have given to
the audiences of that age, they would fail to do so

now; and, indeed, their performance would be
impracticable. The music of the principal parts
was written for a class of voices which no longer
exists; and for these parts no performers could
now be found. A series of recitatives and airs,
with only an occasional duet, and a concluding
chorus of the slightest kind,* would appear meagre
and dull to ears accustomed to the brilliant concerted pieces and finales of the modern stage; and
Handel's accompaniments would appear thin and
poor amidst the richness and variety of the modern
orchestra. The vocal parts, too, are to a great
extent in an obsolete taste. Many of the airs are
mere strings of dry, formal divisions and unmeaning passages of execution, calculated to show off
the powers of the fashionable singers; and many
others, admirable in their design, and containing
the finest traits of melody and expression, are spun
out to a wearisome length, and deformed by the
cu brous trappings with which they are loaded.
Musical phrases, too, which, when Handel used
them, had the charm of novelty, have become
familiar and common through repetition by his
successors.

Handel's Italian operas must now be looked

---

* There is a *trio* in *Alcina* for a soprano and two contralto
voices, beautifully constructed, impassioned, dramatic, and so
free from any tinge of antiquity, that it might have appeared
in an opera of yesterday. It is surprising that Handel, who
thus showed himself aware of the use that might be made of
concerted pieces, has harldly ever employed them.

upon as affording materials for concert or chamber performance; and, in this point of view, they contain rich and ample treasures. Though Handel to a certain extent, conformed to the fashion of his time, yet his genius and taste prevented him from being enslaved by it; and his operas contain multitudes of airs which are models of simplicity, symmetry, and grace—airs which, in every age, must charm the ear and reach the heart, not of one, perhaps, who looks upon music as a matter of fashion, and thinks nothing worth listening to but the newest importation from Italy, but of every one who has ears to hear, and a heart to feel, the everlasting beauties of pure melody and true expression. A disposition to recur to the works of the old masters has begun to characterise the musical taste of England, and is becoming more and more prevalent. The madrigals of the age of Elizabeth, the songs of Purcell, the fugues of Sebastian Bach, the sonatas of Scarlatti, are applauded by audiences who a few years ago were ignorant of their existence. The same thing would be the case with the opera airs of Handel, were our chief vocalists to explore them, study them, and bring them before the public. And were a skilful musician to raise some of these " gems of purest ray serene " from the " dark unfathomed caves " of oblivion in which they now lie buried, by publishing an elegant selection of them with the accompaniments written in the modern manner, he would render an essential service to his art, and his labours could not fail to be highly and extensively appreciated.

In thus using these songs as concert or chamber music, there would not be any difficulty on the score of the words, or any occasion for changing them. An opera air (especially in works of the old school) is a single thought or feeling, briefly and simply expressed; and, being generally quite intelligible without reference to any particular person or situation, may be sung by itself with perfect propriety and good effect. Take, for example, the beautiful air in *Sosarmes*, so well known under its English name of "Lord, remember David."

> " Rendi 'l sereno al ciglio :
> Madre, non pianger più.
> Temer d' alcun periglio
> Oggi come puoi tu ? "

This is the whole; and it is understood as a tender and soothing address by a daughter to a mother, which does not require, in order to comprehend its meaning and feel its expression, any reference to the opera in which it is sung. Any listener may imagine a situation in which a mother may be thus addressed by her child. By preserving the original words, full effect is given to the exquisite tenderness, as well as the graceful flow of the melody, both of which are much impaired by the English words. So much, indeed, is this the case, that " Rendi 'l sereno al ciglio," and " Lord remember David," hardly appear to be the same music. Several others of Handel's Italian airs have been united to sacred English words, with similar injury to their beauty and expression.

Another consequence of the English public knowing a very small number of these airs, only in connexion with sacred English words, is an impression that they are of too grave and solemn a cast for their original purpose, and better fitted to express the language of devotion than of earthly passion. This is an error, caused by a perverted association between the airs and the English words. There is a certain degree of vagueness in musical expression ; and an air, by the words applied to it, may be made to assume a new character, which, to those who know it under no other, may appear to be its real one. The music of " Holy, holy, Lord God almighty," may seem sufficiently devotional; but the same music, as the air in *Rodelinda*, " Dove sei, amato bene ?" addressed to a lover by his mistress, glows with ardent passion. We know this beautiful air, only in the cold, measured style in which we hear it sung at our sacred music-meetings : but imagine it breathed by a Grisi in her most passionate accents, and we shall conceive its true meaning and expression.

The fame of Handel is spreading from day to day, and the number of his admirers increasing. His chief title to immortality rests upon his sublime oratorios ; but a full knowledge of his genius, in all its variety and extent, cannot be gained without exploring the treasures which lie hid in the dusty scores of his Italian operas.

During the period in which Handel produced his Italian operas, many of the pieces of the most distinguished composers of the time were also performed on the London stage. Besides Bononcini and Ariosti, operas by Porpora, Vinci, Veracini, Domenico Scarlatti, Hasse, and other masters, who have been already mentioned, were represented. After this time the theatre was supplied for a while with pieces by Galuppi, Gluck (neither of whom had as yet given much promise of their future greatness), Pescetti, Lampugnani, and several other composers of very inferior rank to those who had preceded them. England felt the effects of the decay of the musical drama in Italy; and mediocrity was the characteristic of the singers as well as of the composers. Owing to this decline on the one hand, and probably, on the other, to the gradual rise of our national opera, and the attention paid to it, the Italian opera fell into such neglect, that for several years, about the middle of the last century, the performance of serious operas appears to have been given up.

END OF VOLUME I.